E. C. Welldon J., J. E. C. Welldon

The Rhetoric Of Aristotle

E. C. Welldon J., J. E. C. Welldon

The Rhetoric Of Aristotle

ISBN/EAN: 9783348010047

Printed in Europe, USA, Canada, Australia, Japan

Cover: Foto ©ninafisch / pixelio.de

More available books at **www.hansebooks.com**

THE RHETORIC OF ARISTOTLE

TRANSLATED

WITH AN ANALYSIS AND CRITICAL NOTES

BY

J. E. C. WELLDON, M.A.

FELLOW OF KING'S COLLEGE, CAMBRIDGE, AND
HEAD-MASTER OF HARROW SCHOOL.

London
MACMILLAN AND CO.
AND NEW YORK
1886

Cambridge:

PRINTED BY C. J. CLAY, M.A. AND SONS,
AT THE UNIVERSITY PRESS.

PREFACE.

THIS Translation of the *Rhetoric* of Aristotle is a companion volume to my Translation of the *Politics*. But it differs from it in the greater fulness of the notes; for, as I have no thought of publishing an edition of the *Rhetoric*, it seems to me necessary to explain as well as I can my interpretations of some difficult passages and my reasons for them. It is well known that Mr Cope published in his lifetime an *Introduction to Aristotle's Rhetoric* and at his death left an elaborate commentary, which has since been edited with scrupulous care by Dr Sandys. Nobody, who has not been led to a close study of the *Rhetoric*, can appreciate the extent and exactness of Mr Cope's labours. Next to his works, but below them in judgment, stands the critical commentary of Spengel. There are many other books bearing upon the *Rhetoric*, which a Translator is bound to consult, as the British Museum Catalogue (s. v.

Aristotle) so fully shews; but it is not worth
while to enumerate them.   Among personal
helps it is a pleasure to remember that I owe
an especial debt of gratitude to my friend,
Mr W. T. Lendrum, who was one of my col-
leagues at Dulwich, for his kindness in reading
my proof-sheets and in giving me the benefit
of his opinion, to which his accurate scholar-
ship lends peculiar value, upon several points
in the Translation.   The science or, as Aristotle
would call it, the art of Rhetoric has had a
curious history.   It was his creation; and whatever has been best in it from this time to the
present is due to him.   The definition of Rhetoric,
its relation to Psychology, the distinction of its
three kinds, the nature of its proofs, the use of
enthymeme and example, the special and common
topics, the style and arrangement of a speech,
all are his.   Where the Latin writers, such as
Cicero and Quintilian, amplified the field of
Rhetoric, it is not unfair to say that they
amplified it in a direction which he had deliberately left alone.   Nor is there any rhetorical
work of a later age which can be placed in
comparison with his.   Even so late a book as
Archbishop Whately's *Elements of Rhetoric*
is in its method essentially Aristotelian and
hardly goes beyond his statement of principles.

The study of Rhetoric as an educational instrument, although it formed a part of Roman as well as of later Greek culture, although in the middle ages it was one of the subjects of the *Trivium*, although from the era of the Revival of Learning it entered into the curriculum of the Universities, has at least in England been practically neglected since the beginning of the eighteenth century. There are several reasons for this neglect, and they are valid; but it is not a gain without a loss. It is possible that the time will come again when the world will recognize that "it is not enough to know what to say, but it is necessary also to know how to say it" (οὐ γὰρ ἀπόχρη τὸ ἔχειν ἃ δεῖ λέγειν, ἀλλ᾽ ἀνάγκη καὶ ταῦτα ὡς δεῖ εἰπεῖν). Then the *Rhetoric* of Aristotle will, I think, be widely read, as being perhaps a solitary instance of a book which not only begins a science but completes it.

It is one of my hopes in publishing this Translation that I may bring the *Rhetoric* within the reach, if I may so express it, of the modern world. The office of a translator, even if he is also in some sense an interpreter, may not unfairly be regarded as a humble one. But as knowledge broadens, and the mass of men have less leisure for studying Greek thought in the language of the Greeks, it would seem to become more and more desirable that the links which unite the new civilization with the old should be strengthened and multiplied; and of these links translation is the chief. For, as Goethe says in one of his letters to Carlyle, So ist jeder Uebersetzer anzusehen, dass er sich als Vermittler dieses allgemein geistigen Handels bemüht, und den Wechseltausch zu befördern sich zum Geschäft macht. Denn was man auch von der Unzulänglichkeit des Uebersetzens sagen mag, so ist und bleibt es doch eines der wichtigsten und würdigsten Geschäfte in dem allgemeinen Weltwesen.

HARROW SCHOOL,
   October 13, 1886.

N.B. The text adopted is that of Bekker's octavo edition. The marginal references are to the pages of the Translation, the references in the foot-notes to the pages and lines of Bekker's text.

As in the *Politics*, the words italicized, except in a few self-evident instances, are inserted in order to make the original fully intelligible.

ANALYSIS.

BOOK I.

CHAPTER I.

RHETORIC is a counterpart (ἀντίστροφος) of Dialectic. Both are general in their application; neither is limited to any definite science.

At present Rhetoric, like Dialectic, is unmethodical; or its method is purely empirical. Still it is possible to treat Rhetoric systematically.

The artistic part of Rhetoric consists in the proofs (πίστεις)—although this is a part of it which is neglected in rhetorical hand-books (τέχναι)—to excite the emotions of the audience is to warp their judgment.

(There are three reasons for preferring the authority of the laws to the decisions of particular judges:

(1) It is easier to find a few competent legislators or judges than a large number.

(2) Laws are the results of mature deliberation; judicial decisions are given on the spur of the moment.

(3) The legislator's decisions are general and prospective; the judge's decisions relate to the issues of the moment in which his personal feelings may be and often are involved.

Still there are certain questions, such as questions of fact, which are necessarily left to the decision of the judges.)

The reason why writers upon Rhetoric have generally confined themselves to forensic Rhetoric is that it affords the most opportunity of "travelling out of the record," i.e. of introducing other topics than strict proof.

The only proper subjects then of artistic treatment are the proofs.

But proof (πίστις) is a species of demonstration (ἀπόδειξίς τις), and the rhetorical form of demonstration is the enthymeme (ἐνθύμημα).

Also the enthymeme is a species of syllogism (συλλογισμός τις). It follows that to understand the construction of syllogisms is—with certain limitations—to understand the construction of enthymemes also.

The four uses of Rhetoric :

(1) It is the means by which truth and justice maintain and assert their natural superiority to falsehood and injustice.

(2) It is the only method of persuasion suitable to unscientific audiences.

(3) As it teaches us to see both sides of a case and to sustain either the one side or the other, so it enables us to see through our adversary's arguments, if they are unfair, and to refute them.

N.B. This capacity of drawing opposite logical conclusions (τἀναντία συλλογίζεσθαι) is peculiar to Rhetoric and Dialectic among the arts.

(4) It is a means of self-defence.

If it is urged that Rhetoric, when used unjustly, may do great harm, the answer is that this objection holds good equally of all good things, except virtue itself.

The function (ἔργον) of Rhetoric is not to persuade but to discover the available means of persuasion in any subject (τὸ ἰδεῖν τὰ ὑπάρχοντα πιθανὰ περὶ ἕκαστον).

N.B. There are apparent or fallacious, as well as real, means of persuasion ; but the discovery of both belongs to the same art.

CHAPTER II.

Rhetoric may be defined as a "faculty of discovering all the possible means of persuasion on any subject" (δύναμις περὶ ἕκαστον τοῦ θεωρῆσαι τὸ ἐνδεχόμενον πιθανόν).

Rhetorical proofs are of two kinds :

(1) inartistic (ἄτεχνοι), which the rhetorician finds ready to his hand, e. g. witnesses, tortures, contracts.

(2) artistic (ἔντεχνοι), which he invents.

The artistic proofs are threefold, consisting in

(1) the manifestation of moral character (ἦθος) in the speaker,

(2) the production of a certain disposition in the audience,

(3) the argument of the speech itself.

Accordingly the complete rhetorician should possess

(1) the power of argumentative reasoning,

(2) a knowledge of character,

(3) a knowledge of the nature and quality of the emotions (πάθη).

Hence it follows that Rhetoric is an offshoot of Dialectic on the one hand and of Ethics on the other.

The proofs conveyed by the argument are

(1) the example (παράδειγμα), corresponding to the induction (ἐπαγωγή) in Dialectic,

(2) the enthymeme, corresponding to the syllogism,

(3) the apparent enthymeme (φαινόμενον ἐνθύμημα) corresponding to the apparent syllogism (φαινόμενος συλλογισμός).

The enthymeme may be called a rhetorical syllogism,

The example a rhetorical induction.

Rhetoric then discovers the means of persuasion in any subject.

But no art takes particular cases into consideration. Hence Rhetoric will consider probability not in relation to an individual, but in relation to a class of persons similarly constituted.

Also the materials of Rhetoric are the ordinary subjects of human deliberation; and these are such subjects as admit of two possibilities, or in other words human actions.

And further, the audience to which Rhetoric addresses itself, is a popular one, without the power of following lengthy arguments.

The propositions of which enthymemes are constructed are probabilities (εἰκότα) and signs (σημεῖα);

and signs are either necessary and conclusive, being then called demonstrations (τεκμήρια),

or not necessary, but only generally true.

The example is an induction, where the example itself and the thing exemplified both fall under the same general law, but the example is the better known instance of it.

The materials of enthymemes are

(a) such as are common to many various arts and faculties; these are the "common topics" or "topics," as they are sometimes called *par excellence* (κοινοὶ τόποι or τόποι);

(b) such as are special to one art or faculty (ἴδια, ἴδιοι τόποι, εἴδη), e.g. physical propositions to Physics, ethical to Ethics, and so on.

An over-skilful use of the "special topics" is not appropriate to the rhetorician; it leads him into the province of the special art or faculty to which they belong.

CHAPTER III.

There are three kinds of audience, and corresponding to them three kinds of Rhetoric, viz.

deliberative (συμβουλευτικόν),

forensic (δικανικόν),

epideictic (ἐπιδεικτικόν), i.e. the Rhetoric of display.

They admit of the following classification:

Kind of Rhetoric.	Divisions.	Time.	End (τέλος).
Deliberative	Exhortation / Dissuasion	Future	Expediency and Inexpediency.
Forensic	Accusation / Defence	Past	Justice and Injustice.
Epideictic	Eulogy / Censure	Present	Honour and Disgrace, or Nobleness and Shamefulness (τὸ καλὸν καὶ τὸ αἰσχρόν).

Hence the deliberative orator employs propositions (προτάσεις) relating to expediency and inexpediency,

the forensic orator propositions relating to justice and injustice,

the epideictic orator propositions relating to honour and disgrace;

and these are the "special topics" of each kind of Rhetoric.

But they all employ propositions relating to possibility and impossibility, the occurrence or non-occurrence of events in the past and in the future, and magnitude both absolute and comparative;

these are the "common topics."

CHAPTERS IV—VIII.

Deliberative or political Rhetoric (τὸ συμβουλευτικὸν ἢ δημηγορικὸν γένος).

CHAPTER IV.

As the end (τέλος) which deliberative Rhetoric regards is expediency, its subjects are things good or bad, i.e. expedient or injurious,

but not all such things,

not such as do not admit of two possibilities,

nor such as depend on Nature (φύσις) or chance (τύχη).

The subjects of Rhetoric are all such things, being expedient or injurious, as are possible matters of deliberation, i.e. such as naturally depend upon our own action.

The most important of these are :—

(1) Finance.

(2) War and peace.

    (3) Defence of the country.

    (4) Imports and exports.

    (5) Legislation.

Under (1) Finance,

comes a knowledge of the resources of the State and their possible development and its channels of expenditure.

Under (2) War and Peace,

a knowledge of the actual and possible military force of the State and of other States with which it has been or may be at war and of their military history.

Under (3) Defence of the country,

a knowledge of its defensive force and the sites of its fortresses.

Under (4) Imports and exports,

a knowledge of the relation of the State to other States in respect of its necessary supplies.

Under (5) Legislation,

a knowledge of the different kinds of polities and their sources of strength or weakness.

CHAPTER V.

As all men, both individually and collectively, aim at happiness (εὐδαιμονία), it is upon happiness or the constituents of happiness that exhortation and dissuasion turn.

Various definitions of happiness :

    (a) prosperity conjoined with virtue.

    (b) an independent state of existence.

    (c) the pleasantest life conjoined with safety.

    (d) an abundance of goods and slaves with the ability to preserve them and to make a practical use of them.

Happiness implies the possession of

(1) personal goods (τὰ ἐν αὐτῷ ἀγαθά), whether of the soul or of the body;

(2) external goods (τὰ ἐκτὸς ἀγαθά), such as nobility, riches, honour.

The constituent parts of happiness are

(1) Nobility, which implies

in a State, that its citizens are indigenous or of high antiquity or have won themselves fame.

in a family, the legitimacy of its members and their good name or celebrity.

(2) The blessing of offspring,

whether of a numerous, stalwart and moral youth in a State,

or of numerous and goodly children, both male and female, in a family.

N.B. It is important to provide for the moral culture of the women as well as of the men.

(3) Wealth, in money, lands, live stock and slaves; not only the productive kinds of wealth, but luxuries. The possession of wealth should be both absolute and secure.

(4) Reputation, whether for personal character or for some prized possession.

(5) Honour, which may assume a number of different forms.

(6) Health.

(7) Beauty, which is different at different periods of life.

(8) Strength.

(9) Size, which should exceed the average size, i.e. height, stoutness and breadth, of men.

(10) Athletic excellence.

(11) A happy old age.

(12) The possession of many good friends.

(13) Good Fortune.

(14) Virtue.

CHAPTER VI.

As the end of deliberative Rhetoric is expediency and whatever is expedient (συμφέρον) is good (ἀγαθόν), it is necessary to apprehend the nature of Good.

Good may be defined as that which is desirable for its own sake, and for the sake of which we desire or choose something else, and which is sought by all things or by all sentient or intelligent things or would be sought by them, if they should acquire intelligence.

The following then are goods :

    (1) happiness.

    (2) justice, courage, temperance (σωφροσύνη), magnanimity (μεγαλοψυχία), magnificence (μεγαλοπρέπεια) and other virtues of the soul.

    (3) health, beauty etc., as being physical virtues or graces.

    (4) wealth.

    (5) friendship.

    (6) honour and reputation.

    (7) rhetorical and practical ability.

    (8) natural gifts, such as memory, sharpness of wit, etc.

    (9) all sciences and arts.

   (10) life itself, apart from the goods of life.

   (11) justice.

These are admitted to be goods; but there are other goods of a disputable kind, and in respect of them Aristotle suggests some twenty topics which may be used in syllogisms to show that a thing is a good.

CHAPTER VII.

Comparison of goods.

It often happens that two things are admitted to be expedient, but the question arises, Which is the more expedient of the two?

Hence it is necessary to consider the question of degree (τὸ μᾶλλον καὶ ἧττον).

Aristotle suggests a number of topics bearing upon the comparative greatness or goodness of things.

CHAPTER VIII.

The principal means of persuasiveness in deliberative Rhetoric is an acquaintance with the various forms of polity.

The character of a polity is determined by the character of its supreme authority (τὸ κύριον).

There are four polities, viz. Democracy, Oligarchy, Aristocracy, Monarchy.

A Democracy is a polity in which the offices of State are distributed among the citizens by lot.

An Oligarchy, one in which they are distributed among persons possessing a certain property qualification.

An Aristocracy, one in which they are distributed among the educated class.

Monarchy, or the polity in which an individual is supreme, may be

    (1)   constitutional Monarchy or Kingship (βασιλεία),

    (2)   absolute Monarchy or Tyranny.

Of these polities each has its end (τέλος).

The end of Democracy is liberty.

The end of Oligarchy is wealth.

The end of Aristocracy is education and legality.

The end of Tyranny is self-preservation.

The customs or institutions of a polity are relative to its end.

Also polities have their characters; aristocratical sentiments are suited to the character of an Aristocracy, democratical to that of a Democracy, and so on. Hence it is necessary that the deliberative orator should apprehend the characters of the several polities.

CHAPTER IX.

Epideictic Rhetoric (τὸ ἐπιδεικτικὸν γένος).

Its subjects are virtue and vice, or nobleness and shameful-ness.

Definition of moral nobleness—A thing is noble if, while it is desirable for its own sake, it is laudable, or if, while it is good, it is pleasant in virtue of its goodness.

It follows that virtue is noble ;

and the elements of virtue are justice, valour, temperance, magnificence, magnanimity, liberality, gentleness, sagacity (φρό-νησις) and speculative wisdom (σοφία).

The greatest virtues are those which are in the highest degree serviceable to others.

Taking this conception of virtue, Aristotle proceeds (1) to analyse moral actions, (2) to compare them in respect of their virtuousness.

N.B. Rhetorical artifices :

(1) To represent certain qualities as identical with other qualities which are closely allied to them, e.g. caution as subtlety, foolishness as simplicity, extravagance as liberality.

(2) To consider the qualities held in esteem by the audi-ence.

(3) To display the moral purpose (προαίρεσις) of the person who is the subject of the speech.

(Digression upon eulogy (ἔπαινος), panegyric (ἐγκώμιον), felicita-tion (μακαρισμός), congratulation (εὐδαιμονισμός) :

The subjects of eulogy are actions (πράξεις), those of panegyric are accomplished results (ἔργα).

Felicitation and congratulation are synonymous terms, em-bracing eulogy and panegyric.

The same topics, differently expressed, are suitable to eulogy and deliberative Rhetoric.)

(4) To employ the means of exaggeration (αὔξησις).

(5) To institute a favourable comparison between the person who is the subject of the speech and other persons of admitted reputation.

These artifices belong especially to epideictic Rhetoric.

In general, exaggeration is peculiarly appropriate to epideictic Rhetoric, the example to deliberative Rhetoric, the enthymeme to forensic Rhetoric.

The materials of censure may be inferred from those of eulogy.

CHAPTERS X.—XIV.

Forensic Rhetoric (τὸ δικανικὸν γένος).

CHAPTER X.

In the treatment of forensic Rhetoric, which includes accusation and defence, there are three points to be ascertained, viz.

(I) the nature and number of the objects of crime.

(II) the dispositions of the criminals.

(III) the character and condition of the victims.

Definition of crime—Voluntary injury in defiance of the law.

But law is of two kinds:

(a) particular (ἴδιος), i.e. the written law of any polity.

(b) universal (κοινός), i.e. the unwritten law which is always and everywhere recognized.

The causes of a disposition to commit crime are vice and incontinence.

(I) The objects of crime.

All human actions arise from one or more of seven causes, viz.

(1) chance
(2) nature — such actions being not due to ourselves, or involuntary.
(3) compulsion

(4) habit
(5) reasoning — such actions being due to ourselves, or voluntary.
(6) passion
(7) desire

b 2

Aristotle defines and explains these causes.

It appears then that all actions which are due to ourselves, i.e. all voluntary actions, are either good (or apparently good or pleasant or apparently pleasant.

But the good or expedient has been already discussed under the head of deliberative Rhetoric.

It remains then to consider the pleasant.

CHAPTER XI.

Definition of pleasure—A certain motion of the soul and a sudden and sensible settling (κατάστασις) of the soul into its normal and natural state.

Such being the nature of pleasure, it follows that whatever tends to promote the condition described is pleasant, and whatever tends to destroy it or produce a contrary condition is painful.

Enumeration of things pleasant and (by implication) of things painful, as being the opposites.

CHAPTER XII.

(II)   The conditions under which people commit crime.

The conditions are that they should believe the criminal action to be possible in itself and possible to them, whether as expecting to escape detection or, if detected, to escape punishment or, if punished, to endure a punishment which is not equivalent to the advantage gained by the crime.

Aristotle elaborately discusses these conditions.

(III)   The victims of crime.

Aristotle describes the classes of persons upon whom crimes are ordinarily committed.

There are certain circumstances which facilitate crime, as e.g. if the articles stolen are easily concealed, or if it is a crime of such a nature that the victim would be unwilling to publish it.

CHAPTER XIII.

Classification of actions just and unjust (δικαιώματα καὶ ἀδικήματα).

They may be classified in two ways:

    (1) relatively to the laws,
    (2) relatively to the persons affected by them.

The law may be (a) particular, i.e. the law of a particular State.
          (b) universal, i.e. the law of Nature.

The persons affected may be

      (a) the community as a whole,
      (b) some individual member or members of it.

Also crimes are committed

      either ignorantly and involuntarily,
      or knowingly and involuntarily;

and, if the latter be the case,

      either of deliberate purpose
      or under the influence of emotion.

N.B. It often happens that a fact is admitted, but the description of it or the application of the description is denied. Hence the necessity of clear definitions of crimes.

It is the purpose (προαίρεσις) which constitutes vice or criminality.

The matters which come within the province of unwritten law are

    (1) such as are instances of exalted virtue, e.g. gratitude,
    (2) such as are remedies for the deficiency of written law.

The justice which supplements the written law is equity (τὸ ἐπιεικές).

This function of equity may be

    (a) consistent with the intention of the legislator, e.g. if the terms of the law are absolute, and yet it is not absolutely applicable to all cases;

(b) contrary to his intention, if it touches upon a point which has escaped his notice.

Aristotle illustrates the province and nature of equity.

CHAPTER XIV.

The magnitude of a crime is proportionate to the magnitude of the injustice which prompts it.

Hence it is sometimes necessary to estimate the comparative magnitude of crimes.

Application of the topic of degree to criminal actions.

CHAPTER XV.

The inartistic proofs (ἄτεχνοι πίστεις), which are properly limited to forensic Rhetoric.

They are five, viz.

 (1) laws,
 (2) witnesses,
 (3) contracts,
 (4) tortures,
 (5) the oath.

(1) Laws.

Topics suitable for upsetting the authority of a law, if it tells against us, and for confirming it, if it makes in our favour.

(2) Witnesses may be

 (a) ancient,

 (b) contemporary;

and, if the latter,

 either involved in the risk of the action at law or independent of it.

 (a) Ancient witnesses are:

  poets, who testify to facts of the past,
  interpreters of oracles, who testify to facts of the future,
  proverbs.

(*b*)   Contemporary witnesses are :

living authorities, if they have pronounced judgment on
a particular point,
witnesses who appear in Court and give their evidence.

Ancient witnesses are more credible than contemporary.
Topics for confirming or invalidating the weight of testimony.
Testimony may have reference either to oneself or to one's
adversary and either to fact or to character.

(3)   Contracts.

Topics of exaggeration or depreciation in regard to contracts.

(4)   Torture.

Topics in support or depreciation of torture, as a means of
arriving at the truth.

(5)   Oaths.

Four possible cases :
(*a*)   when a person both tenders and accepts the oath,
(*b*)   when he does neither,
(*c*)   when he tenders the oath without accepting it,
(*d*)   when he accepts it without tendering it.

Also there may be combinations of two such cases.
Or there may be a further complication, if a person
his adversary has already taken the oath.
Aristotle suggests topics suitable to all these cases and
combinations of cases.

BOOK II.

CHAPTER I.

As Rhetoric is intended to be judged, there are two things—
apart from direct proof—which should be the objects of the
rhetorician's endeavour :

(1) To produce a favourable impression of his own character.

(2) To produce a favourable disposition in his audience.

Of these the former is particularly suited to deliberative, the latter to forensic, Rhetoric.

(1) The sources of personal credibility are threefold :

    (*a*) sagacity,

    (*b*) virtue,

    (*c*) goodwill, i.e. goodwill towards the audience.

The means of getting credit for sagacity and virtue may be ascertained from the analysis of the virtues in Book I.

Goodwill will be discussed under the head of the emotions (πάθη).

Definition of the emotions—Such states as are attended by pain and pleasure and produce a change or difference in our attitude as judges.

It will be proper to consider the several emotions under three heads, viz.

    (1) the conditions under which people are liable to it,

    (2) the persons who are usually the objects of it,

    (3) the causes of it.

CHAPTERS II.—XI.

Analysis of the emotions.

    (1) Anger.   }

    (2) Placability (πραότης). }

    (3) Love.   }

    (4) Hatred or Enmity. }

    (5) Fear.   }

    (6) Confidence.   }

    (7) Shame.   }

    (8) Shamelessness. }

    (9) Benevolence (χάρις).   }

        Its opposite is selfishness (ἀχαριστία). }

(10) Compassion. ⎫
(11) Virtuous indignation (νέμεσις). ⎭
(12) Envy.
(13) Emulation (ζῆλος). ⎫
(14) Contempt. ⎭

CHAPTER II.

(1) Anger.

Definition—An impulse attended with pain to a conspicuous revenge on account of a conspicuous slight shown in some offence against oneself or one of one's friends without any natural reason for the slight.

· It follows that anger is always directed against an individual, never against a class.

(There is a certain pleasure in anger, arising from the imagination of future revenge.)

A slight (ὀλιγωρία) may take three forms :

(a) contempt (καταφρόνησις),
(b) spitefulness (ἐπηρεασμός),
(c) insolence (ὕβρις).

(1) The conditions of anger—annoyance, disappointment, unsatisfied desire, etc.

(2) The objects of anger—persons who sneer at us, who disparage our accomplishments, who requite our services with ingratitude, etc.

(3) The causes of anger may be regarded as comprised under its objects and conditions.

It is the task of the rhetorician then to bring his audience into a condition of irascibility against his adversary.

CHAPTER III.

(2) Placability.

Definition—The process of becoming placable may be defined as a settling down or quieting of anger.

(1) The persons towards whom it is natural to be placable are those who do not slight us or who slight us involuntarily or

who, if they offend against us, confess their fault and are sorry for it, etc.

(2) The conditions of placability are opposed to those of anger, e.g. times of amusement, feasting, prosperity, etc.

The rhetorician will choose his topics in view of these conditions.

CHAPTER IV.

(3) Love.

Definition—To love a person is to wish him all such things as you suppose to be good, not for your own sake but for his, and to be ready so far as in you lies to effect them.

A friend is one who loves and is beloved in return (ὁ φιλῶν καὶ ἀντιφιλούμενος).

(1) Persons who are the objects of love—benefactors, liberal, brave, just people, etc.

(2) Causes of love—favours conferred, especially if conferred spontaneously and without ostentation.

N.B. Love or friendship admits of various forms, viz. companionship (ἑταιρεία), intimacy (οἰκειότης), relationship (συγγένεια), etc.

(4) Enmity or Hatred—the opposite of love.

The causes which produce it are (1) anger,
(2) spite,
(3) prejudice (διαβολή).

(Distinction between anger and hatred.

	Anger	*Hatred*
(a)	arises from personal wrongs,	is independent of personal wrongs.
(b)	is always directed against individuals,	may be directed against classes.
(c)	is curable by time,	is not curable by time.
(d)	aims at causing pain,	aims at causing evil.
(e)	is accompanied by pain,	is not accompanied by pain.
(f)	admits of compassion,	precludes compassion.)

CHAPTER V.

(5) Fear.

Definition—A species of pain or disturbance arising from an impression of impending evil which is destructive or painful in its nature.

(1) It follows that all things are formidable or inspire fear which appear to have a great power of destroying or of inflicting such injury as tends to grievous pain. Such things are the enmity or anger of powerful persons, a criminal disposition, if armed with power, etc.

Persons too are formidable, if they are in a position to commit crime or if they have been the victims of crime and are watching for their revenge, etc.

(2) Conditions of fear.—In order to feel fear it is necessary to regard oneself as capable of suffering and of suffering at the hands of particular people.

(6) Confidence—the opposite of fear.

Definition—hope accompanied by an impression of salutary things as near at hand and of formidable things as non-existent or remote.

The sources of confidence (τὰ θαρραλέα) are the remoteness of danger, the possession of remedies or means of rectification, etc.

The conditions of confidence are frequent successes in the past, frequent escapes from danger, the consciousness of innocence, etc.

CHAPTER VI.

(7) Shame.

(8) Shamelessness.

Definition—Shame may be defined as a species of pain or disturbance in regard to evil things, either past, present or future, which have an appearance of tending to ignominy; and shamelessness as a species of slight or indifference in regard to these same things.

(1) Instances of shameful action—throwing away one's shield in battle, refusing to restore a deposit, etc.

(2) Persons who inspire a feeling of shame. Those who admire us, or whom we admire, or whose admiration we desire to win, etc.

(3) Conditions of shame—When we are conscious of past achievements or actions upon which we shall bring dishonour, when we are likely to live in the presence of the witnesses of our disgrace, etc.

The rule of contraries will supply topics in regard to shamelessness.

CHAPTER VII.

(9) Benevolence.

Definition—It is benevolence in virtue of which the person in whom it resides is said to render a service to anybody in the hour of need, not in return for previous services or for any personal benefit to him who renders it but for the benefit of the recipient alone.

An act of benevolence may be enhanced by showing that it was done at a critical moment or that it has never been done before, etc.

But an act loses its benevolent character, if it is represented as having been done for selfish motives, or done by accident or under compulsion, etc.

The opposite of benevolence is selfishness.

CHAPTER VIII.

(10) Compassion.

Definition—A sort of pain at an evident evil of a destructive or painful kind, in the case of somebody who does not deserve it, the evil being one to which we may naturally expect ourselves or someone of our friends to be liable, and this at a time when it appears to be near at hand.

(1) The condition of compassion then is a capacity of similar suffering.

It follows that people, who are absolutely ruined, or who believe themselves to be supremely happy, are incapable of compassion.

N.B. Compassion presupposes a belief in human virtue; for he, who does not believe in anybody's virtue will consider that everybody is deserving of evil.

(2) The causes of. compassion are all such painful and distressing things as are destructive and ruinous, and all the evils of Fortune.

(3) The objects of compassion are familiar friends, equals in age, character, etc.

Gestures, tones, habiliments, etc., are useful to the rhetorician as means of exciting and enhancing compassion.

CHAPTER IX.

(11) Virtuous indignation (νέμεσις)—the correlative of compassion but, like it, an honourable emotion.

Definition—A feeling of pain at such prosperity as is apparently unmerited.

(Distinction between virtuous indignation and envy.

Both are painful and perturbing emotions,

both relate to the prosperity of others;

but the former relates to the prosperity of someone who is undeserving,

the latter to that of someone who is like ourselves.

N.B. Virtuous indignation, envy and malice, although different in themselves, are yet proper to the same character.)

(1) Causes of virtuous indignation—not all good things, as e.g. justice or valour, but such good things, when possessed by the bad, as seem to be rightly the possessions of the good, as e.g. wealth, power, etc.

(2) Persons who are the objects of virtuous indignation, such as the *nouveaux riches* and inferiors generally, if they contend against their superiors.

(3) Conditions of virtuous indignation. Whenever we consider ourselves to be worthy of particular things, and others to be unworthy of them.

Hence virtuous indignation is not an emotion of mean natures.

Knowing the means of exciting virtuous indignation, the rhetorician knows the means of destroying compassion.

CHAPTER X.

(12) Envy.

Definition—A species of pain felt at conspicuous prosperity on the part of persons like ourselves in respect of certain goods, and this not with any view to our personal advantage but solely because they are prosperous.

(1) Conditions of envy—People are envious if they have equals in family, age, or reputation, if they are ambitious, etc.

(2) Causes of envy—Achievements or possessions of which we covet the reputation, the gifts of Fortune, etc.

(3) Objects of envy—our equals, rivals, etc.

Envy excludes the possibility of compassion.

CHAPTER XI.

(13) Emulation.

Definition—A species of pain at the manifest presence of such goods as are highly valued and also attainable by ourselves in persons who have a natural resemblance to us, and this not because somebody else is in possession of them, but because we are not equally in possession of them ourselves.

(Distinction between emulation and envy.

Emulation is a virtuous, envy a vicious emotion, for the object of the emulous man is to acquire goods for himself, that of the envious man to deprive his neighbour of them.)

(1) Conditions of emulation—People are emulous, if they consider themselves entitled to goods which they do not enjoy;

and this is a feeling which is a result of wealth or distinguished ancestry.

(2) Causes of emulation—such goods as are held in honour, e.g. the virtues.

(3) Objects of emulation—persons who possess these goods.

(14) Contempt is the opposite of emulation.

Hence people who are in a condition to emulate others or to be themselves the objects of emulation are inclined to contemn those who are subject to such evils as are contrary to the goods which provoke emulation.

CHAPTER XII.

Varieties of character depend upon the emotions (πάθη), habits of mind (ἕξεις), times of life (ἡλικίαι), and accidents of Fortune (τύχαι).

The emotions, i.e. anger, desire, etc., and the habits of mind, i.e. the virtues and vices, have been already discussed.

The times of life are youth, the prime of life and age.

Fortune includes birth, wealth, power, etc.

Aristotle elaborately describes the character of youth.

CHAPTER XIII.

The character of age.

CHAPTER XIV.

The character of the prime of life, which is intermediate between the characters of youth and age.

N.B. The time of physical prime is from 30 to 35 ; that of mental prime about 49.

CHAPTER XV.

The character of nobility.

CHAPTER XVI.

The character of wealth.

CHAPTER XVII.

The character of power.
The character of good Fortune.
The characters of poverty, powerlessness, etc. are evident from a consideration of opposites.

CHAPTER XVIII.

Recapitulation.
Plan of the work.

CHAPTER XIX.

The four common topics (κοινοὶ τόποι), i.e. topics which are common to the three kinds of Rhetoric:

(1) Possibility.

Topics tending to show the possibility or impossibility of a thing.

(2) Fact past.

Topics tending to show that a thing either has or has not occurred.

(3) Fact future.

Topics tending to show that a thing either will or will not occur.

(4) Degree.

Topics tending to show the absolute and comparative greatness or smallness of things.

CHAPTER XX.

The common proofs (κοιναὶ πίστεις) are

(1) the example,

(2) the enthymeme.

N.B. The maxim (γνώμη) is part of the enthymeme.

(1) Examples are of two kinds, viz. :

(*a*) historical parallels,

(*b*) inventions of the rhetorician, whether illustrations (παραβολαί) or fables (λόγοι) such as the fables of Æsop.

Fables are suited to popular oratory, and, as compared with historical parallels, are easy to find.

It is proper, in default of enthymemes to make use of examples as logical proofs, but otherwise to make use of them as testimonies in support of the enthymemes.

CHAPTER XXI.

The use of maxims (γνωμολογία).

Definition of a maxim (γνώμη) : A declaration relating not to particulars but to universals, and not to all universals but to such as are the objects of human action and are to be chosen or eschewed in that regard.

The enthymeme being the form of syllogism which is appropriate to these matters, if the syllogistic form is done away, the conclusion of an enthymeme or its major premiss is a maxim.

There are four kinds of maxims; for maxims may either have or not have a logical supplement (ἐπίλογος).

Maxims have no such supplement

(*a*) when the maxim is a generally accepted opinion,

(*b*) when it is intelligible at a glance;

maxims which have it are

(*a*) parts of an enthymeme,

W. R.

c

(*b*) not parts of an enthymeme, but enthymematic in their character, where the reason of the maxim is contained in the words of the maxim itself.

Where the maxim is disputable, obscure or paradoxical, the addition of the supplement is indispensable.

Maxims are appropriate

(1) upon the lips of persons of years and experience,

(2) in contradiction of popular or proverbial sayings.

There are two important uses of maxims :

(1) That, as being general statements, they are pleasing to a vulgar audience who find in them the generalization, or, as it were, the consummation of their partial experience.

(2) That, as expressing moral predilections, they invest the speech with an ethical character.

CHAPTER XXII.

Enthymemes.

In the consideration of enthymemes it is necessary to consider

(1) the true method of looking for them,

(2) their topics.

The proper materials of enthymemes are not all opinions indiscriminately, but such opinions as commend themselves to the audience.

But it is necessary that the rhetorician should know all or some at least of the special facts of the subject with which he deals, e.g. of military matters, if it is war, of justice, if it is a judicial case, and so on.

There are two species of enthymemes, viz.:

(1) demonstrative (δεικτικά), which consist in drawing conclusions from admitted propositions,

(2) refutative (ἐλεγκτικά), which consist in drawing conclusions which are inconsistent with the conclusions of one's adversary.

The special topics of enthymemes will be derived from the special facts of each particular subject.

But there are common topics belonging to all subjects.

CHAPTER XXIII.

Aristotle gives a list of 28 topics of demonstrative and refutative enthymemes.

N.B.   Refutative enthymemes are more popular than demonstrative, as they are conclusions of opposites in a small space.

But of all enthymemes none are so much applauded as those which, although not being superficial, are immediately intelligible.

CHAPTER XXIV.

As there are not only true syllogisms but syllogisms which are apparent but not true, it follows that there are apparent as well as true enthymemes.

Aristotle gives ten topics of apparent enthymemes.

CHAPTER XXV.

Refutation (λύσις).

There are two methods of refutation, viz.:

    (1) by countersyllogism,

    (2) by objection (ἔνστασις).

The topics of countersyllogisms are clearly identical with those of syllogisms.

Objections are of four kinds, being derivable

    (a) from the enthymeme of one's adversary,

    (b) from antithesis,

    (c) from analogy,

    (d) from a previous decision.

Aristotle illustrates these four kinds of objection.

The materials of enthymemes being fourfold,

 viz. probabilities,
  examples,
  demonstrations (τεκμήρια),
 and signs (σημεῖα),

enthymemes constructed from probabilities may invariably be refuted by an objection ; but the objection must be more generally true than the fact objected to.

enthymemes constructed from signs or examples are liable to refutation, although they may be probable.

It is enthymemes constructed from demonstrations which are irrefutable, unless indeed the fact alleged as a demonstration can be disproved.

CHAPTER XXVI.

Correction of two possible errors :

(1) Exaggeration and depreciation (τὸ αὔξειν καὶ μειοῦν) are not elements (στοιχεῖα) or topics of enthymemes but actual enthymemes tending to show the greatness or smallness of things.

(2) Refutative enthymemes do not form a species distinct from constructive.

For refutation must consist either in urging positive proof or in adducing an objection ;

and in the former case it is proving the opposite of an adversary's conclusion,

and in the latter it is bringing forward an opinion to show that the adversary's reasoning is inconclusive or that there is something false in his assumptions.

The inventive part of Rhetoric may be now said to have received adequate consideration.

It remains to consider style (λέξις) and arrangement (τάξις).

BOOK III.

CHAPTER I.

Style.

It is not enough to know what to say; it is necessary also to know how to say it.

The subject admits of three divisions:

(a) the sources of persuasiveness in facts,
(b) the disposition of the facts,
(c) declamation (ὑπόκρισις);

and declamation includes

(1) the use of the voice,
(2) the use of the accents or tones (τόνοι)
(3) the use of rhythms.

Upon declamation no scientific treatise exists.

The consideration of it is necessary, if only because of the depraved character of the audience.

The capacity for declamation is a natural gift, and on its histrionic side is hardly susceptible of artistic treatment. But on its rhetorical side it may be reduced to an art.

Declamation originated among the poets, who were generally the declaimers of their own tragedies. The consequence was that a poetical style was originally adopted and admired in prose. But the styles of prose and poetry are distinct.

We confine ourselves therefore to rhetorical style.

CHAPTER II.

The principal virtues or graces (ἀρεταί) of style are

(1) perspicuity,
(2) propriety.

N.B. A certain dignity is imparted to style by the use of words which are a little out of the common. Yet upon the whole naturalness is persuasive, and artificiality of style is the reverse. Hence the use of rare or foreign words, compound words (διπλᾶ ὀνόματα), etc. should be sparing.

Prose admits in general only (1) the proper or ordinary names of things, (2) metaphors.

Metaphor has been discussed at length in the *Poetic*. But the use of metaphor is more important to prose than to poetry; as prose depends for its effect on a smaller number of artistic means. Also metaphors are sources of perspicuity, pleasure and novelty.

Metaphors, like epithets, must be appropriate; i.e. they must be (1) proportionate, (2) homogeneous, (3) not farfetched, (4) beautiful in themselves.

N.B. Good metaphors may be derived from well-constructed enigmas.

The sources of metaphors are such things as are beautiful in sound or suggestiveness or vividness of representation.

Epithets may be taken either from the lower or from the higher aspect of the things which they describe. Not unlike them in effect are diminutives (ὑποκορισμοί). But epithets and diminutives must be used with due care.

CHAPTER III.

Faults of taste may occur in four points of style, viz.

    (1) in the use of compound words,

    (2) in the use of rare words,

    (3) in the use of epithets, if they are long or unseasonable or very numerous,

    (4) in the use of metaphors, if they are inappropriate or obscure.

Aristotle quotes instances.

N.B. Compound words are suited to dithyrambic poetry.

Rare words	,,	,,	epic	,,
Metaphors	,,	,,	tragic	,,

CHAPTER IV.

The simile is a metaphor with a slight difference.

Homer's expression "He rushed on like a lion" is a simile. But "He rushed on a very lion," is a metaphor.

Aristotle quotes instances of simile.

Metaphors are always convertible into similes, and *vice versa*.

N.B. The proportional metaphor must be reciprocally transferable; if e.g. the goblet is the shield of Dionysus, then the shield may be called the goblet of Ares.

CHAPTER V.

The basis of style is purity of language.

But purity of language comprises five points, viz.

(1) the right use of connecting words or clauses ($\sigma\acute{\upsilon}\nu\delta\epsilon\sigma\mu\omicron\iota$),

(2) the use of proper or special names for things ($\acute{\iota}\delta\iota\alpha$ $\acute{o}\nu\acute{o}\mu\alpha\tau\alpha$) rather than class-names,

(3) the avoidance of ambiguous terms ($\acute{\alpha}\mu\phi\acute{\iota}\beta\omicron\lambda\alpha$),

(4) the observance of the genders of nouns,

(5) the correct expression of number.

The composition should be easy to read and—which is the same thing—easy to deliver. Hence it is necessary to avoid (1) obscurity of punctuation, (2) zeugma, (3) parenthesis.

CHAPTER VI.

Dignity of style.

Aristotle mentions seven contributing causes, viz.

(1) to employ a definition instead of the simple name of a thing,

(2) to avoid any foulness of expression by substituting the name for the definition or *vice versa*,

(3) to use metaphors and epithets as means of elucidating the subject,

(4) to put the Plural for the Singular,

(5) to repeat the article, as e.g. τῆς γυναικὸς τῆς ἡμετέρας instead of τῆς ἡμετέρας γυναικός,

(6) to use connecting particles (σύνδεσμοι),

(7) to describe a thing by negation.

CHAPTER VII.

Propriety.

The conditions of propriety are

(1) that the style should be emotional,·

(2) that it should be ethical,

(3) that it should be proportionate to the subject.

Appropriateness of language is one means of giving an air of probability to the case.

It will be emotional (παθητική) if it is angry, indignant, enthusiastic, etc. according to the subject, and, being so, it will command the sympathy of the audience.

It will be ethical (ἠθική) if it is adapted to the character of a particular class or moral state (ἕξις).

It will be proportionate, if it is elevated, when the subject is elevated, humble, when it is humble, and so on.

Opportuneness (τὸ εὔκαιρον) in the use of any rhetorical device is a rule belonging equally to all the kinds of Rhetoric.

The multiplication of compound words or epithets and the use of strange words are most appropriate to the emotional Rhetoric.

CHAPTER VIII.

The structure of the style should be neither metrical, as it would then seem artificial, nor unrhythmical, as it would then seem indefinite.

A prose composition should have rhythm, but not metre.

Of the various possible rhythms ;

the heroic is too dignified, and it lacks conversational harmony,

the iambic is deficient in dignity and impressiveness,

the trochaic approximates too much to broad comedy.

There remains the pacan, which has been used by prose writers from Thrasymachus downwards. But the paean is of two kinds, which are respectively suitable to the beginning and the end of sentences.

CHAPTER IX.

The style must be

(1)   either "jointed" (εἰρομένη) i.e. a style in which the connecting particles (σύνδεσμοι) form the only links of the sentence;

Such is the style of Herodotus ;

(2)   or "compact" (κατεστραμμένη) i.e. periodic.

A period (περίοδος) is a sentence which has a beginning and an end in itself and such a magnitude as can be easily comprehended at a glance.

A periodic style has two advantages, as being (1) agreeable, (2) easily learnt.

But the period should be marked by the completion of the sense as well as of the rhythm.

Periods may be

(1)   divided into members or clauses (ἐν κώλοις),

(2)   simple (ἀφελεῖς), i.e. consisting of a single member or clause.

The periods and the members of which they are composed, should be neither too short nor too long.

A further division of the periodic style may be made according as its clauses are (1) simply separate,

(2) antithetical.

Aristotle gives several instances of antithetical clauses.

The agreeableness of an antithetical style lies in its emphatic and syllogistic character.

Parisosis is equality of members or clauses.

Paromoiosis is similarity of extremities, whether the beginnings or the ends of sentences.

The same sentence may combine various points, e.g. antithesis, parisosis, etc.

CHAPTER X.

Clever sayings (τὰ ἀστεῖα).

Learning without trouble is agreeable to everybody.

Metaphors and similes, but especially metaphors, are instructive.

The test of a cleverly constructed enthymeme is its power of conveying rapid instruction.

Enthymemes are popular

(1) if their structure is antithetical,

(2) if their words contain a metaphor which is neither superficial nor far-fetched,

(3) if they vividly represent the subject to the eye.

In a word there are three objects to be kept in view, viz. metaphor, antithesis and vividness of representation.

Metaphors are of four kinds, proportional metaphors being the most popular.

Aristotle gives various instances of metaphor.

CHAPTER XI.

Vividness of representation shows a thing in a state of activity. It may be illustrated by Homer's treatment of inanimate objects as animate.

Metaphors should be derived from objects which are closely related to the thing itself, but which are not immediately obvious.

Another instrument of clever sayings is surprise or deception (παρὰ προσδοκίαν), as it gives people the sense of having learnt something. Hence too the pleasure of good apophthegms, riddles, and puns.

A proper enunciation is requisite in all such sayings. But their chief merit is their appropriateness to the things described.

Metaphor, especially proportional metaphor, antithesis, parisosis and vividness are all means of giving point to a sentence; and the larger the number of these means, the more cleverly pointed the sentence appears.

'Similes, as has been said, are always in a sense popular metaphors.

Proverbs are metaphors from one species to another.

Hyperboles of an approved kind are also metaphors.—There is however a character of juvenility in hyperboles.

CHAPTER XII.

Every kind of Rhetoric has its own appropriate style.

There is a difference between the literary (γραφική) and controversial (ἀγωνιστική) styles and in the controversial style between the political (δημηγορική) and forensic (δικανική). But the rhetorician should be familiar with both.

It is the literary style which is the most finished and the controversial which is the best suited to declamation.

Controversial oratory is (1) ethical, (2) emotional.

Hence such artifices as the use of asyndeton and the repetition of the same word, although alien from the literary style, are favourites among controversial orators.

The style of political oratory resembles scene-painting, for as the view is more distant, where the crowd is greater, a finished style becomes inappropriate.

The style of forensic oratory, especially when addressed to a single judge, is most finished.

The epideictic style is best suited to literary purposes.

CHAPTER XIII.

A speech has two parts. It is necessary first to state the case and then to prove it.

The exposition of the case and the proof—these are the only indispensable parts of a speech. But if more parts are added, they must not exceed four, viz. exordium, exposition, proof and peroration.

CHAPTER XIV.

The exordium (προοίμιον).

The exordium of a speech corresponds to a prologue in poetry and to a prelude in a musical performance.

The sources of exordia in epideictic speeches are eulogy, censure, exhortation, dissuasion and appeals to the audience.

The exordia of forensic speeches resemble the proems of epic poetry.

The exordia of epideictic speeches resemble the proems of dithyrambic poetry.

The essential function of the exordium is to explain the end or object of the speech itself.

Exordia of other kinds, whether derived from the speaker himself or from the audience or from the subject or from the adversary, are merely the means of remedying certain defects in the audience; they would not be used, if the audience were not corrupt.

The art of exciting attention belongs equally to all the parts of a speech, perhaps to other parts rather than to the exordium. But the topics appropriate to the exordium may all be used as means of exciting attention. No means however is so effective as character.

In political speeches exordia are rare, as the subject is generally familiar to the audience.

In the exordia of epideictic speeches the audience should be led to fancy themselves participators.

CHAPTER XV.

Calumny or prejudice (διαβολή).

Aristotle enumerates the topics which are useful as means of creating or dissipating prejudice.

CHAPTER XVI.

Narrative (διήγησις).

(1) In epideictic speeches the narrative should be not continuous but fragmentary. But if the facts are notorious, it is

proper merely to recall them to the memory of the audience; there is no need to dwell upon them.

(2)   In regard to forensic speeches it is absurd to lay down the rule that the narrative should always be rapid.   Here too it is proper to observe the rule of the mean.

The orator may slip into his narrative anything which tends either to prove his own virtue or to gratify the jury.

On the side of the defence the narrative part of the speech may be abbreviated, as the facts upon which it turns are already known.

But the narrative should be ethical; and it will be ethical

,   (a) if it indicates a moral purpose,

(b) if it contains such characteristic marks as accompany particular characters,

(c) if it seems to proceed not from policy but from the heart.

It is possible to derive topics from emotional signs by describing the familiar features of emotion.

N.B.   The narrative should be distributed over the speech.

(3)   In political speeches, as referring to the future, there is the least room for narration.   It can be introduced only because a knowledge of the past facilitates a judgment of the future.

CHAPTER XVII.

Proofs (πίστεις).

The proofs should be demonstrative (ἀποδεικτικαί).

In forensic speeches, as there are four points on which the issue may turn, viz. the fact, the injury, the magnitude of the injury or the criminality the proof should be directed to the particular point at issue.

In epideictic speeches the facts must be generally taken on trust, and amplification (αὔξησις) used to emphasize their moral or utilitarian character.

In political speeches it must be urged that the policy of one's adversary is impossible or unjust or inexpedient or that it will not have the important results which he anticipates.

Examples are especially appropriate to political Rhetoric.

Enthymemes are especially appropriate to forensic Rhetoric.

The enthymemes, which should be chosen with discrimination, should not be put forward in a continuous series, but intermingled with various other topics.

Enthymemes are out of place in the pathetic or ethical passages of a speech.

Maxims, as possessing an ethical character, should be used both in narrative and in proof.

Political Rhetoric is more difficult than forensic, as it relates to the future, and the future cannot be known; nor does it equally allow of digressions or appeals to the emotions.

In epideictic speeches eulogies should be introduced by way of episodes.

In default of proofs the speech should be both ethical and demonstrative ; in default of enthymemes it should be exclusively ethical.

Refutative enthymemes are more popular than demonstrative.

The reply to the adversary is not a separate branch of the speech.

The arrangement of the speech will vary according to circumstances. In deliberative and forensic Rhetoric, if you speak first, you should begin with a statement of your own proofs and then meet the arguments on the other side. (But if the case on the other side is of a varied character, you should begin by meeting the opposing arguments and then make your own statement.) If you speak last, you should begin with the answer to the arguments on the other side.

As to character, things which would be invidious or tedious, if you said them of yourself, or which would be calumnious or coarse, if you said them of others, may be conveniently put into the mouth of a third person.

Enthymemes should sometimes, by a change of form, be expressed as maxims.

CHAPTER XVIII.

(1) Interrogation (ἐρώτησις).

The interrogation of one's adversary is a device which may be opportunely used as a means of landing him in an absurdity or contradiction.

(2) Reply (ἀπόκρισις).

In replying to ambiguous questions it is proper to proceed by distinction or definition, and not to use too concise a mode of expression. Where the adversary's conclusion is put in the form of a question, the reply to the question should be made at once.

*(3) Jokes (τὰ γελοῖα).

It is necessary that they should be such as are suited to gentlemen.

N.B. Irony (εἰρωνεία) is more gentlemanly (ἐλευθεριώτερον) than buffoonery (βωμολοχία), as the former is used simply for its own sake and the latter for some ulterior object.

CHAPTER XIX.

The peroration (ἐπίλογος).

There are four elements of the peroration, viz.

(1) to inspire the audience with a favourable opinion of oneself and an unfavourable opinion of one's adversary,

(2) to amplify or depreciate the subject,

(3) to excite the emotions of the audience,

(4) to recall the facts to their memory.

In the recapitulation it is a good rule to repeat the points several times for the sake of intelligibility.

Comparison, irony, interrogation are all suitable elements of recapitulation.

An asyndeton forms an appropriate conclusion.

THE RHETORIC OF ARISTOTLE.

BOOK I.

RHETORIC is a counterpart of Dialectic. For both are concerned with such subjects as fall in a sense within the cognizance of all men, and neither is limited to any definite science. Accordingly we are all in a sense dialecticians and rhetoricians; for everybody essays up to a certain point the criticism and support of a thesis, defence and accusation. It is true that most people do this either without any method at all or by a familiarity which is the result of habit. But the possibility of proceeding in both these ways is itself a proof that the processes may be systematized; for it is possible to investigate the causes of such success as is attained by familiarity or at random, and such an investigation will be universally admitted to be essentially a function of an [1] art.

[1] Aristotle's conception of a τέχνη or art is clearly expressed in the first chapter of the *Metaphysics*. γίγνεται δὲ τέχνη (he says) ὅταν ἐκ πολλῶν τῆς ἐμπειρίας ἐννοημάτων μία καθόλου γένηται περὶ τῶν ὁμοίων ὑπόληψις.

Criticism of existing rhetorical handbooks.

As it is, the compilers of our "¹arts" or rhetorical handbooks have supplied but a fragment of an art. For while it is the proofs alone which form the proper subjects of artistic treatment, and everything except the proofs is a mere accessory, they omit all mention of enthymemes, which are the soul of proof, and occupy themselves almost exclusively with such things as lie outside the actual issue. For ²prejudice, compassion, anger and such emotions of the soul have no bearing upon the point at issue; they merely affect the minds of the jury. Our rhetoricians then would not have a word to say, if the practice in all trials were the same as at this moment exists in some few States, especially States which are well ordered; for it is universally allowed that there ought to be, even if there is not actually, a provision in the laws by which a veto is set upon "travelling out of the record," as e.g. in the Court of Areopagus. There is reason in this practice; for it is improper to warp the judg-

¹ The connexion between τέχνη and αἱ τέχναι τῶν λόγων can hardly be preserved in translation. It is well known that τέχνη in the language of the rhetoricians came to mean (1) Rhetoric, as the supreme art, (2) a rhetorical treatise or handbook. (Dr Thompson's *Gorgias* of Plato, *Introduction*, p. v.) The Latin writers use *ars* in much the same sense, e.g. Juvenal *Sat.* vii. 177, *artem scindes Theodori*, where see Prof. Mayor's note.

² Nothing can be clearer than that διαβολή is here in Aristotle's view a πάθος τῆς ψυχῆς. When Spengel says διαβολή "non est quidem πάθος sed efficit πάθος," he separates it generically from ἔλεος (compassion) and ὀργή (anger) with which it is joined. Perhaps it has the sense not of διαβάλλειν but of διαβάλλεσθαι, and means a "prejudice" or "preconceived hostility." Cp. p. 64, l. 6, where ὀργή, ἐπηρεασμός, διαβολή are described as ποιητικὰ ἔχθρας.

ment of a juror by exciting him to anger or jealousy
or compassion, as this is like making the rule, which
one is going to use, crooked. It is evident too that
one who is a party to a legal suit has nothing to do
except to show that the fact alleged is or is not so,
or has or has not occurred, and that its magnitude
or triviality, its justice or injustice, except in cases
where the legislator has determined this, is a
point which the juror should presumably decide for
himself and not learn from the statements of the
parties.

It is best, we may observe, where the laws *Reasons for*
preferring
are enacted upon right principles, that everything *the autho-*
rity of the
should, as far as possible, be determined absolutely *laws to the*
decisions of
by the laws, and as little as possible left to the dis- *particular*
judges.
cretion of the judges. For in the first place it is
easier to find an individual or a few than a number
of people who are sensible and capable of exercising
legislative and judicial functions ; and secondly, while
legislative enactments are the results of mature deliberation, judicial decisions are given on the spur of
the moment, so that it is difficult for the judges in
particular cases duly to deliver such a sentence as is
just and expedient. But the point of principal importance is this ; that, while the legislator's decision
is not particular but prospective and universal, the
members of the Public Assembly or the Court of
Law from the nature of the case decide upon actual
definite issues, in which feelings of affection or ill-
will and private interests are necessarily often [1]in-

---

[1] Reading συνήρηται, which has the support of the *Vetusta*
Translatio (ad quos...annexa sunt) and agrees better than συνήρη-

volved, so that they lose the power of adequately studying the truth, and their judgment is clouded by a consideration of their personal pleasure or pain.

It is then, as we say, a general rule that we should limit as far as possible the authority of the judge. But such questions as whether a fact has or has not occurred in the past, or will or will not be so in the future or is or is not so *at present*, are necessarily left to the decision of the judges, as they lie beyond the prescience of the legislator. This being the case, it is clear that to lay down definite rules, as is sometimes done, upon a number of other points, e.g. upon the proper contents of the exordium, the narrative or any other part of a speech, is to make an art of things which are foreign to the issue ; for the authors of such rules have no other object than to produce a certain disposition in the judge, while they give no explanation of the [1]artistic proofs, which are the materials of all enthymematic reasoning.

Hence it is that, although the same mode of treatment is applicable to the oratory of public life and to that of the Law Courts, and the study of political oratory is more elevated and statesmanlike than a study which limits itself to the ordinary dealings of man with man, they disregard political oratory altogether and set themselves with one consent to make

p. 11.
p. 13.

Forensic rhetoric the principal subject treated in rhetorical handbooks.

ται with Aristotle's usage. (See the *Index Aristotelicus* of Bonitz s. v. συναρτᾶν.)

[1] Aristotle is scarcely justified in using the expressions, αἱ ἔντεχνοι πίστεις and ἐνθυμηματικός, as if they would be intelligible at this point of his treatise. It is not until the second chapter that he defines them.

an art of pleading in Court, because it does not pay so well to "travel out of the record" in political questions, and political oratory, as [1]involving wider interests, offers fewer opportunities of chicanery. For while in politics, where the judges are personally interested in the questions which come before them, all that the advocate of a certain policy has to do is to demonstrate that the facts are as he alleges, in forensic cases such a procedure is insufficient, and it is worth while to conciliate the audience. For as they have no personal interest in the decision, they consider their own gratification and, as they do not listen to the case impartially, are carried away by the parties instead of judging between them. The result is that there are many places, as we said before, where the p. 2. law forbids all "travelling out of the record." In political matters however the judges themselves look to this sharply enough.

It is clear then that the only proper subjects of artistic treatment are proofs. But proof is a species of demonstration [2](for we regard a demonstration as the highest form of proof), and a rhetorical demon-

Rhetorical proofs.

[1] It seems clear from the following words (ἐνταῦθα μὲν γὰρ ὁ κριτὴς περὶ οἰκείων κρίνει) that κοινότερον refers to the personal interest of the audience collectively in the subjects of political debate. The jury, who would be the audience in a legal case, would not be personally interested in its result. But it is to be noticed that the ἐκκλησιασταί as well as the δικασταί are called κριταί or judges of the arguments addressed to them.

[2] The alleged reason is in fact little more than another way of saying ἡ πίστις ἀπόδειξίς τις; but it would be more natural to argue that demonstration is a species of proof than that proof is a species of demonstration.

stration takes the form of an enthymeme, which may
be broadly described as the most powerful form of

The enthy-
meme.
rhetorical proof. Again, the enthymeme is a species
of syllogism, and it falls within the province of ₁Dia-
lectic, either as a whole or in some one of its branches,
to make a complete examination of the syllogism in
all its forms. [1]From all this it appears that the
most competent judge of the materials and constructive principles of a syllogism will also be the
most complete master of enthymemes, if only he is
further acquainted with the proper subjects of enthymemes and with the differences between enthymemes
and [2]logical syllogisms. For as it is the same faculty
which discerns what is true and what resembles truth,
and as men have a sufficient natural aptitude for
truth and in a majority of instances attain it, it
follows that the most sagacious judge of truth will
be at the same time the most sagacious judge of
probabilities.

Although it is clear then that the matters, which
all other writers upon Rhetoric reduce to an art, are
irrelevant to the issue, and it is clear why they have
inclined by preference to forensic oratory, still Rhe-

The four
uses of
Rhetoric.
toric is not without its value. *It is valuable, firstly,*
because truth and justice possess a natural superiority

---

[1] The MSS. reading δῆλον δ' ὅτι may be retained, if the δὲ
is regarded as apodotic. It is in Aristotle's manner to build up
a protasis of a number of clauses, not all equally influencing the
conclusion.

[2] The λογικὸς συλλογισμός, which is complete in all its parts, is
here opposed to the ἐνθύμημα, which is an imperfect or rhetorical
syllogism.

to their opposites, and therefore, if judgments are not given as they should be, it must be the speakers themselves who are responsible for the defeat; and this is itself a state of things which is reprehensible. Secondly, there are audiences which, even if we possess the most exact scientific knowledge, it is not easy to persuade by scientific arguments. For scientific argument implies [1]instruction; but it is impossible to instruct such people as we are supposing, and we necessarily find the instruments of our proofs and arguments in the generally accepted notions of mankind, as we remarked in the [2]*Topics*, in discussing the [3]method of dealing with ordinary people. Again, in Rhetoric no less than in syllogistic reasoning it is right to be capable of arguing on both sides of a case, not for the sake of doing both (as we have no right to argue in favour of anything that is wrong), but that the true state of the case may not escape us and that, if another party makes an unfair use of his arguments, we may be able in our turn to refute them. There is

----

[1] Aristotle uses "instruction" (διδασκαλία) in a special sense, as implying exact or syllogistic proof. See the passage quoted by Mr Cope in his *Introduction*, p. 75, περὶ σοφιστικῶν ἐλέγχων, p. 165 A₃₈—B₂, where after dividing οἱ ἐν τῷ διαλέγεσθαι λόγοι into four classes, διδασκαλικοὶ καὶ διαλεκτικοὶ καὶ πειραστικοὶ καὶ ἐριστικοί, Aristotle adds διδασκαλικοὶ μὲν οἱ ἐκ τῶν οἰκείων ἀρχῶν ἑκάστου μαθήματος καὶ ἐκ τῶν τοῦ ἀποκρινομένου δοξῶν συλλογιζόμενοι.

[2] Τοπικά i. ch. 2, p. 101, A₃₀₋₃₄.

[3] ἔντευξις passes from the sense of "intercourse" in general to "specially dialectical or argumentative intercourse," as the passages quoted by Mr Cope seem to show.

no art, it may be observed, which *possesses this characteristic of* drawing opposite logical conclusions *with equal ease*, except Dialectic and Rhetoric, which are both equally ready to take opposite sides. Still it is not the fact that the subject-matter is indifferent to them; on the contrary whatever is true or expedient may be said generally to be always in its nature more easily susceptible of proof and more persuasive. Lastly, it would be a paradox that there should be something disgraceful in the inability to defend oneself by bodily strength, and not in the inability to defend oneself by speech, when speech is more characteristic of man than the use of the body. And *if it is urged* that the unjust use of this rhetorical faculty would be exceedingly mischievous to the world, this is a charge which may be brought against all good things, save virtue only, and most of all against the things of highest utility, such as strength, health, riches and military skill, which may all prove the greatest blessings in the hands of one who uses them with justice, and the greatest curses in the hands of one who uses them unjustly.

The function of Rhetoric.

[1]It is evident then that Rhetoric is not limited to a particular definite class of subjects, but like Dialectic *is universally applicable*, and that it has certain uses *which have already been described*. [2]It

---

[1] Of the three points which are here said to be "evident," the first and second have been already made good; the third is new.

[2] Aristotle is glancing at the passage in Plato's *Gorgias*, where Socrates says to Gorgias εἰ τι ἐγὼ συνίημι, λέγεις ὅτι πειθοῦς

is evident also that its function is not to persuade but to discover the available means of persuasion in any subject. And in this respect Rhetoric is like the other arts. It is not the function e.g. of Medicine to restore a person to perfect health but only to bring him to as high a point of health as possible; for even people who can never possibly recover their health may still be scientifically treated. Further, *it is evident* that it falls within the scope of the same art to discern the real and the *sham* or apparent means of persuasion, as in Dialectic the real and the apparent syllogism. For it is not the faculty but the moral purpose which constitutes the sophistical character. But *there is this* [1] *difference between Rhetoric and Dialectic, that,* while in the former the name "rhetorician" is descriptive either of the science or of the moral purpose, there is in the latter the name "sophist" to describe the moral purpose, and "dialectician" to describe not the purpose but the faculty.

The fallacious branch of Rhetoric.

But it is now time to endeavour to state the actual system, *or in other words* the means and materials which will enable us to attain the objects

δημιουργός ἐστιν ἡ ῥητορική, καὶ ἡ πραγματεία αὐτῆς ἅπασα καὶ τὸ κεφάλαιον εἰς τοῦτο τελευτᾷ, p. 453 A. But the definition of Rhetoric as πειθοῦς δημιουργός is said not to have been Plato's own, but to have descended from Corax and Tisias or Isocrates (Dr Thompson's note *ad loc.*).

[1] The point, which is somewhat obscurely put, seems to be this: There are sophistical rhetoricians as well as sophistical dialecticians; but while the latter are called by the special name of "sophists," the former, having no special name, are simply called "rhetoricians."

proposed. Let us start afresh then, as it were, and, before we proceed, define the actual nature of Rhetoric itself.

CHAP. II.
Definition
of Rhetoric.

p. 7.

Rhetoric may be defined as a faculty of discovering all the possible means of persuasion in any subject. For this is exclusively the function of Rhetoric, as every other art, [1]whether instructive or persuasive, deals with a subject-matter peculiar to itself, Medicine e.g. with the conditions of health and disease, Geometry with the properties of magnitudes, Arithmetic with number, and so on through the list of arts and sciences. Rhetoric on the other hand may be said to possess the faculty of discovering the means of persuasion in any given subject; and accordingly we hold that the rules of the rhetorical art are not limited in their application to a certain special definite class of subjects.

Rhetorical
proofs.
(1) inar-
tistic,

Rhetorical proofs are either artistic or inartistic. By "inartistic proofs" I mean all such as are not provided by our own skill but existed before and independently, e.g. witnesses, tortures, contracts and the like; by "artistic," such as admit of being constructed systematically and by our own skill; in fine, the former we have only to apply and the latter we have to invent.

(2) artistic.

The proofs provided through the instrumentality

---

[1] The distinction between arts as "instructive" or "persuasive," i.e. in other words as exact or inexact, depends upon the special sense in which Aristotle uses "instruction." See note on ch. i. Cp. Plato *Gorgias*, p. 455 A, οὐδ' ἄρα διδασκαλικὸς ὁ ῥήτωρ ἐστὶ δικαστηρίων τε καὶ τῶν ἄλλων ὄχλων δικαίων τε πέρι καὶ ἀδίκων, ἀλλὰ πειστικὸς μόνον.

of the speech are of three kinds, consisting either
in the moral character of the speaker or in the production of a certain disposition in the audience or
in the speech itself by means of real or apparent
demonstration. The instrument of proof is the moral
character, when the delivery of the speech is such
as to produce an impression of the speaker's credibility; for we yield a more complete and ready
credence to persons of high character not only ordinarily and in a general way, but in such matters as
do not admit of absolute certainty but necessarily
leave room for difference of opinion, without any
qualification whatever. (It is requisite however that
this result should itself be attained by means of the
speech and not of any antecedent conception of the
speaker's character.) For so far from following the
example of some authors of rhetorical handbooks,
who in their "art" of Rhetoric regard the high
character of the speaker as not being itself in any
sense contributory to his persuasiveness, we may
practically lay it down as a general rule that there
is no proof so effective as that of the character.
Secondly, proof may be conveyed through the audience, when it is worked up by the speech to an
emotional state. For there is a wide difference in our
manner of pronouncing decisions, according as we
feel pleasure or pain, affection or hatred; and indeed
the power of working upon the emotions is, as we p. 2.
assert, the one end or object to which our present
professors of the rhetorical art endeavour to direct
their studies. This is a part of the subject which
will be elucidated in detail, when we come to discuss

the emotions. *Lastly,* [1]the instrument of proof is the speech itself, when we have proved a truth or an [2]apparent truth from such means of persuasion as are appropriate to a particular subject.

Qualifica-tions of a rhetorician. Such being then the channels of rhetorical proofs, it is evident that no one can make himself master of all three, unless he is competent to reason logically, to study human characters and virtues, and thirdly to study the nature and quality of the several emotions, the sources from which they spring and the methods of exciting them.

Relation of Rhetoric to Dialectic and Ethics. It follows that Rhetoric is, so to say, an offshoot of Dialectic *on the one hand* and *on the other* of the study of Ethics [3]which may fairly be described as political. Hence it is that Rhetoric and its professors assume the mask of Politics, whether from ignorance or imposture or any other human infirmity. For it is *really* a branch **p. 1.** or copy of Dialectic, as we said at the outset, neither being a science which deals with the constitution of any definite subject-matter, but both being mere faculties of supplying arguments.

Enough has perhaps been said as to the faculty and mutual relations of Rhetoric and Dialectic. But taking the proofs conveyed by real or apparent demonstration, *we find that,* as in Dia-

---

[1] Omitting πιστεύουσιν.

[2] There is no need to insert ἀληθές after φαινόμενον as in Bekker's text; see e.g. p. 25, l. 22 ἀγαθὸν ἢ μεῖζον, p. 37, l. 13 τῶν λυπηρῶν ἢ φαινομένων.

[3] The view of Politics as the architectonic science, embracing Ethics as a subordinate or ancillary science, is expounded in *Nicom. Eth.* i. ch. 1.

lectics there are three modes of proof, viz. induction, syllogism and apparent syllogism, so in Rhetoric there is the example corresponding to induction, the enthymeme to syllogism and the apparent enthymeme to apparent syllogism. I call an enthymeme a rhetorical syllogism and an example a rhetorical induction. The universal means of demonstrative proof *in Rhetoric* are examples or enthymemes, and there is no other; hence if it is assumed to be absolutely necessary that [1] whatever is proved should be proved either by syllogism or by induction—and this we see clearly from the [2] *Analytics*—it is a necessary conclusion that the enthymeme and example are respectively identical with the syllogism and induction. The difference between example and enthymeme *on the one hand and induction and syllogism on the other* is clear from the [3] *Topics*. For as syllogism and induction have been already discussed, it is clear

Example and enthymeme.

[1] The words ἢ ὁντινοῦν are rightly omitted in Bekker after ὁτιοῦν; they are at best, I think, nothing more than a marginal note, showing that either ὁτιοῦν or ὁντινοῦν would make good sense.

[2] There are several passages of the *Analytics* which may have been in Aristotle's mind, as Mr Cope says (*Introduction*, p. 153); perhaps the clearest is *Analyt. Pri.* ii. ch. 23, p. 68 B₈₋₁₄.

[3] The meaning, as Mr Cope saw, should be not so much that the difference is stated in the Τοπικά as that it may be inferred from the definitions of syllogism and induction given in the Τοπικά. A syllogism is there defined as λόγος ἐν ᾧ τεθέντων τινῶν ἕτερόν τι τῶν κειμένων ἐξ ἀνάγκης συμβαίνει διὰ τῶν κειμένων, Bk i. ch. 1, p. 100 A₂₅; an induction as ἡ ἀπὸ τῶν καθ' ἕκαστον ἐπὶ τὰ καθόλου ἔφοδος, Bk i. ch. 12, p. 105 A₁₃. But the passage remains obscure, unless ἐκεῖ is altered to ἐπεί, and φανερὸν supplied before ὅτι τὸ μὲν ἐπὶ πολλῶν καὶ ὁμοίων δείκνυσθαι ὅτι οὕτως ἔχει.

that the proving of a rule in a number of similar instances is an induction in Dialectic and an example in Rhetoric, while the conclusion from certain premisses that something else which is different from them results as a consequence of them by reason of their being what they are, whether universally or generally, is called a syllogism in Dialectic and an enthymeme in Rhetoric. It is clear that there is an advantage in either kind of Rhetoric. For the remark which has been made in the [1]*Methodics* is not less applicable here; there are some rhetorical efforts in which the example and others in which the enthymeme predominates, and rhetoricians are similarly distinguishable by a predilection for the one or the other. It may be added that speeches which make use of examples are fully as persuasive as the others, but enthymematic speeches are more applauded. The sources of examples and enthymemes and the proper uses of them both we will state hereafter. Let us now however define more explicitly these *logical processes* themselves.

[2]Persuasiveness then is a relative conception, and a fact is persuasive and credible either immediately and in its own strength or as seeming to be proved by facts which are persuasive and credible. But no art takes particular cases into consideration. Thus

The limitations of Rhetoric.

---

[1] A logical treatise of Aristotle, now lost.

[2] I have broken up the long protasis of the sentence; for the conclusion οὐδὲ ἡ ῥητορικὴ τὸ καθ᾽ ἕκαστον ἔνδοξον θεωρήσει follows not from all the three preceding clauses, but, as Mr Cope says, from the third only, or perhaps more accurately from the first and third.

Medicine does not consider what is wholesome to Socrates or Callias *as individuals* but what is wholesome to a person or persons of a certain constitution; for it is this *generalization* which is characteristic of an art, whereas particulars are infinite in number and cannot be known. Similarly Rhetoric will not investigate what is probable to each individual, as e.g. to Socrates or Hippias, but what is probable to persons of a certain character; and the same is true of Dialectic. *Both are practically limited in respect of the subjects with which they deal.* For Dialectic no less than Rhetoric does not employ any and all opinions indiscriminately as materials of syllogisms (for even people who are out of their minds have certain fancies); but the materials of Dialectic are such subjects as need discussion, and those of Rhetoric are the ordinary and recognized subjects of deliberation. The function of Rhetoric is limited to matters about which we deliberate [1] and do not possess artistic rules *for our guidance in determining them,* and the audience to which it addresses itself consists of persons who are unable to comprehend a number of arguments in a single view or to follow out a long chain of reasoning. Now the proper subjects of deliberation are such as appear to admit of two possibilities; for if things cannot possibly either have happened or happen or be otherwise *than in one particular way,* nobody deliberates about them, at least upon that supposition, *i.e. so long as he regards them as absolutely certain;* for what would be the advan-

---

[1] The rules of medicine, e.g., would not be the proper subjects of rhetorical argument.

tage of deliberation? (But the materials of syllogistic and inferential reasoning may be either the actual conclusions of previous syllogisms or propositions which have not been syllogistically proved and at the same time need such proof, as lacking probability. Syllogisms of the first class will be necessarily difficult to follow from their length, as the judge is assumed to be a simple sort of person; and those of the second class will fail to carry conviction, as the premisses on which they rest are neither *practically* admitted nor *intrinsically* probable.) [1]We conclude then that the enthymeme and example are necessarily applied to such things as are in general indeterminate; the

The enthy-meme. example being an induction and the enthymeme a syllogism, with its constituent parts only few and generally fewer than those of the [2]primary *or normal* syllogism; for if one of them is well known, it need not be stated, as the audience supplies it of its own accord. *If we wish* e.g. *to prove* that Dorieus has been victorious in a contest in which the prize of victory is a crown, it is enough to say that he has won an Olympic victory; there is no need to add that the prize of an Olympic contest is a crown, as the fact is universally known.

---

[1] The conclusion is not justified by the sentences which immediately precede it, but follows as a natural consequence from ll. 4—6, βουλευόμεθα δὲ περὶ τῶν φαινομένων ἐνδέχεσθαι ἀμφοτέρως ἔχειν κ.τ.λ. Accordingly I regard the intervening sentences as parenthetical, and should put a full stop, instead of a comma, after ἐνδόξων.

[2] For the primary syllogism, or syllogism of the first figure, see *Analyt. Pri.* i. ch. 4, or Grote's *Aristotle*, vol. i. pp. 213—221.

[1]The propositions then which are the materials The mate-
rials of en-
of rhetorical syllogisms are seldom necessary.   The thymemes.
ordinary subjects of our judgments and investigations are indeterminate ; for it is human action
which is the sphere of deliberation and inquiry ; and
all such action is of an indeterminate character, it
may be said to be practically never necessary.
Further, the premisses of such conclusions as are
generally true or only possible must themselves be
general and possible, and those of necessary conclusions necessary, as in fact we saw in the [2]*Analytics.* It is evident then from these considerations
that the propositions which form the materials of
enthymemes, although sometimes they are necessary,
are for the most part only generally true.   For the
materials of enthymematic reasoning are probabilities Probabili-
ties, signs
and signs ; and [3]it follows that these are respectively and demon-
strations.
identical with the propositions which are generally
and necessarily true.   A probability is something
that usually happens, although the definition must

---

[1] This is another case in which there is no strict conclusion
from the protasis ; the conclusion is in fact only a re-statement of
part of the protasis.

[2] The reference is to *Analyt. Pri.* i. ch. 8, p. 29 B$_{29-35}$.

[3] This clause, if I rightly understand it, is somewhat incorrectly
expressed.   It is true that the materials of enthymemes may be
described either as signs (σημεῖα) and probabilities (εἰκότα), or as
propositions which are sometimes necessarily and sometimes only
generally true.   But the inference that the signs are the necessary,
and the probabilities the generally true propositions is an unsound
one.   For although the probabilities are never necessary, the signs
may be either necessary (τεκμήρια) or not.

As to εἰκὸς, σημεῖον and τεκμήριον, see Mr Cope's *Introd.* pp.
160—163 and *Analyt. Pri.* ii. ch. 27.

W. R.   2

not be stated, as it sometimes is, without qualification, but something that usually happens in such
matters as are indeterminate ; and it stands to the
thing which is to be proved in the relation of the
universal to the particular.   A sign on the other
hand bears *to the thing which is to be proved* the
relation either of an individual to the universal or
of an universal to the particular.   Such signs as are
necessary *or conclusive* are called [1]demonstrations ;
the others have no distinctive name.   By "necessary
signs" I mean the propositions of which a syllogism
in its strict sense is composed.   Hence a sign of this
kind is called a demonstration ; for it is when we
suppose the statement we make to be irrefutable that
we think we adduce a demonstration, meaning that
it has been *logically* proved and concluded, as
[2]demonstration and conclusion are in old parlance
identical.   It would be a case of a sign standing *to
the thing which is to be proved* in the relation of
the individual to the universal, if one were to urge
e. g. as a sign that the wise are just, "Socrates was
wise and just."   This is a sign, but it may be refuted,
even if the fact alleged is true ; for it is incapable
of expression in the form of a syllogism.   But such
a statement as "A person is feverish ; therefore
he is ill," or "A woman is giving milk ; therefore

[1] The Greek word is τεκμήρια, which is rendered "infallible
proofs," as is well known, in *Acts of the Apostles* i. 3.

[2] It is difficult in translation to preserve the point that τέκμαρ
or, as it is in Homer, τέκμωρ (which is here identified with
τεκμήριον) means (1) a limit or conclusion, (2) a demonstrative sign
or demonstration.

she has lately become a mother," is an instance of
a necessary sign. This is the only kind of sign which
is a demonstration, as it is the only one which, if
true, is irrefutable. As an instance of a sign which
stands *to the thing to be proved* in the relation of
the universal to the particular, one may say, "It
is a sign that so-and-so has a fever; his breathing
is hard." This again however admits of refutation,
even if it is true; for a person may breathe heavily
without having a fever.

The nature of a probability, a sign and a demonstration, and the difference between them have been
here stated; but a more explicit description of them
and of the reason why some of them can and others
cannot be expressed in the form of syllogisms will
be found in the *¹Analytics.*

As to the example, we have stated that it is an Example.
induction and have described the character of the p. 13.
subjects with which it deals. It stands *to the thing
which is to be proved* in the relation not of part
to whole nor of whole to part nor of whole to whole,
but of part to part, of similar to similar, *and is
employed* when both the example and the thing exemplified fall under the same general head, but the
one is more familiar than the other. Thus, *if we
are arguing* that Dionysius in asking for his body-
guard has a design of attempting to gain tyrannical
power, *we may urge that* Pisistratus once asked for
a bodyguard with this design and, as soon as he had
obtained it, made himself tyrant, and that the same
was true of Theagenes at Megara; in fact every other

---

¹ *Analyt. Pri.* ii. ch. 27.

case with which we are acquainted constitutes an example applicable to Dionysius, whose object in making this request is not yet known to us. All these are instances falling under the same universal rule, viz. that a person who aspires to tyrannical power asks for a bodyguard.

So much then for the materials of the proofs which are commonly regarded as demonstrative. But in the case of enthymemes there is a most important distinction, which is equally true of the dialectical system of syllogisms, although it has been practically almost entirely overlooked. It is that some enthymemes are proper to Rhetoric, [1]as *some syllogisms* to Dialectic, and others to other arts and faculties, whether actually existing or not yet established. Accordingly [2]rhetoricians ignore this distinction and, in proportion as they handle subjects in the manner of specialists, over-step the province of Rhetoric or Dialectic. But the point will be clearer, if I express it at greater

Topics, general and special.

length. I mean that the proper subjects of dialectical and rhetorical syllogisms are the topics, as we call them *par excellence*, i.e. such as are equally suitable to questions of justice, physics or politics, and to many questions of many different kinds. Such is e.g. the topic of "the more or less," *or of degree*, which will serve equally well to construct a syllogism or enthymeme about justice, physics or anything else, although these are subjects differing in kind. Special topics on the other hand are such as spring from the propositions appropriate to a particular species or class of subjects.

---

[1] Omitting μέθοδον τῶν συλλογισμῶν.

[2] Omitting τοὺς ἀκροατάς.

Thus there are propositions in physics from which it is impossible to form an enthymeme or syllogism upon ethics, ethical propositions again from which it is,impossible to form an enthymeme or syllogism upon physics, and so on through the whole range of subjects. The general topics, as having no *special* subject-matter, will not convey a practical knowledge of any class of subjects. But in regard to the special topics *it may be remarked that*, in proportion as a rhetorician is specially skilful in the choice of his propositions, he will imperceptibly construct a science different from Dialectic and Rhetoric; for if he lights upon first principles, *i.e. the principles or axioms of the special sciences*, it will cease to be Dialectic or Rhetoric and will be the science to which the principles in question belong. The materials of enthymemes however are in the great majority of cases the particular and private topics, comparatively seldom the common ones. Accordingly here as well as in the *Topics* it is necessary to draw a distinction between the special and general topics from which enthymemes may be derived. I mean by special topics such propositions as are proper to a particular class of subjects, and by *general* topics such as are common to all alike. We will begin then with a discussion of the special topics. But let us first ascertain the different kinds of Rhetoric, that after determining their number we may ascertain the ¹elements and propositions of each separately.

---

¹ What is meant by an "element" (στοιχεῖον) of Rhetoric is clear from ii. ch. 22, where Aristotle says στοιχεῖον δὲ λέγω καὶ

CHAP. III.
The three
kinds of
Rhetoric.

There are three kinds of Rhetoric, corresponding to the three kinds of audience to which speeches are naturally addressed. For a speech is composed of three elements, viz. the speaker, the subject of the speech and the persons addressed; and the end *or object* of the speech is determined by the last, viz. by the audience. Audiences are necessarily either [1]critics or judges; and if the latter, they may be judges of things lying either in the past or in the future. A member of the Public Assembly may be taken as an instance of a judge of the future, a member of the Courts of Law as an instance of a judge of the past; while one who judges merely of the ability *displayed in a speech* is the critic. It follows that there must necessarily be three kinds of rhetorical speeches, the deliberative, the forensic and the [2]epideictic.

The subdivisions of each.

Deliberative Rhetoric is partly hortatory and partly dissuasive; for people who counsel their friends deliberatively on private affairs and people who address popular meetings on matters of State are alike in this, that they always exhort or dissuade. Forensic Rhetoric may be divided into accusation and defence; for the parties to any legal action necessarily adopt either one or other of these lines. To the epideictic

τόπον ἐνθυμήματος τὸ αὐτό, p. 95, l. 26. The term itself is discussed by Mr Cope, *Introd.* pp. 127, 128.

[1] The difference, as appears in the next sentence, is that the "critic" regards a speech merely as an intellectual effort, the "judge" as an argument in which he is personally interested.

[2] As ἐπίδειξις is a set rhetorical display, so epideictic oratory is the oratory of display.

orator belong eulogy and censure. Again, there are Their times.
times belonging to the several kinds of Rhetoric ;
to deliberative Rhetoric the future, as deliberative
counsel, whether hortatory or dissuasive, has reference
to things which lie in the future; to forensic Rhetoric
the past, as the subject of accusation or defence is
always something which has been already done ; and
to epideictic Rhetoric most properly the present, as
it is always existing facts which form the grounds
of eulogy or censure, although epideictic orators often
amplify their resources by appealing to the past
in the way of reminiscence and to the future in the
way of anticipation. There are three ends too appro- Their ends.
priate respectively to the three kinds of Rhetoric.
The end which the deliberative orator has in view is
expediency or injury ; for if he exhorts to a particular line of action, he recommends it as being better,
i.e. more advantageous, if he dissuades from it, he
does so on the ground that it is worse, and every
other consideration, whether justice or injustice,
honour or disgrace, he embraces merely as something
secondary and subservient to this. The end of the
parties to a legal action *or in other words of forensic
orators* is justice and injustice ; and if they too introduce other considerations, it is always as subordinate
to these. Orators of the panegyrical and depreciatory
style take honour and disgrace as their end and again
refer all other considerations to these. As a sign
that the end of Rhetoric is in each case such as we
have stated, it may be noticed that an orator will
sometimes forbear to argue any point in the case
except this one. Thus a person who is a party to

a legal suit will sometimes not care to contend that the action with which he is charged has not occurred or that it did no damage ; but the injustice or criminality of the action he will never for a moment allow, as, if he did, there would be no need of a suit at all. Similarly deliberative speakers, while they frequently abandon every other point, will never admit that the course which they recommend is inexpedient or that the course from which they dissuade is advantageous ; but the injustice of reducing their neighbours, even if absolutely unoffending, to slavery is often a point about which they do not trouble themselves in the least. So too in eulogy or depreciation the speakers, instead of considering the expediency or hurtfulness of a person's actions, often go so far as to reckon it meritorious that he did some noble deed at the sacrifice of his own interest, as when they eulogize Achilles for having avenged his friend Patroclus, although he knew he must perish and he might have saved his life, *if he had chosen.* But in this case, although it was more honourable so to die, yet his personal interest was to live.

The remarks we have made clearly show that these, *viz. expediency, justice, honour and their opposites,* are the subjects about which propositions are primarily indispensable to the rhetorician. By rhetorical propositions I mean demonstrations, probabilities and signs. For a syllogism consists of propositions, and the enthymeme is a syllogism composed of the propositions described, *viz. demonstrations, probabilities and signs.* Again, as things which are impossible

The propositions indispensable to a rhetorician.

cannot have been done in the past or be done in the future, and things which have not occurred or will not occur cannot have been done or be done hereafter, it is indispensable that the rhetorician, whether deliberative, forensic or epideictic, should be master of certain propositions as to possibility and impossibility and as to the occurrence or non-occurrence of events in the past or in the future. And further, as all speakers, whether in eulogy or depreciation, exhortation or dissuasion, accusation or defence, are not contented with trying to prove the points I have mentioned, but try also to prove the greatness or smallness of the good or evil, the honour or disgrace, the justice or injustice *which is the subject of their speech*, either absolutely or in comparison with something else, it will clearly be necessary to be supplied with propositions respecting greatness and smallness both absolute and comparative, whether universally or in reference to particular cases, as e.g. to the greater or less of two good things or of two actions either just or unjust ; and the same is true of every other subject.

So much then for the subjects in regard to which it is right that the rhetorician should acquire his propositions. We must now proceed to distinguish them individually, *i.e. to distinguish* the proper subjects of deliberative, of epideictic, and in the third place of legal oratory.

The first step is to ascertain the character of the good or bad things in regard to which the deliberative orator gives his counsel. For he does not concern himself with all things which are good or

Chap. IV.
Deliberative Rhetoric.
Nature of its subjects.

bad, but only with such as either may or may not come to pass; whereas, if a thing either is or will be necessarily or cannot possibly be or come to pass, it is not a proper subject of deliberative counsel. Nor again does he concern himself with all things which either may or may not come to pass; for there are some good things of the kind which are the gifts of Nature or the results of chance, and about these it is entirely useless to offer counsel. It is clear that his subjects are all such things as are possible matters of deliberation, i.e. all things which are naturally referred to our own agency and [1]whose production depends in the first instance on our own will. For we always carry back our investigations to the point of discovering whether the act in question is or is not within our power.

Now any attempt at an exact and particular enumeration and classification of the ordinary subjects of public business and at an accurate definition of them, so far as such is possible, would be inappropriate on the present occasion; for such a task belongs not so much to the rhetorical art as to an art of a more intellectual and authentic character, and a great deal more has already [2]been assigned to Rhetoric than its own proper subjects of investigation. For

p. 12.

---

[1] For the meaning of the phrase ἡ ἀρχὴ τῆς γενέσεως ἐφ᾽ ἡμῖν ἐστίν, see *Metaphysics* vi. ch. 8, p. 1033 A_{24} ἐπεὶ δὲ ὑπό τινός τε γίγνεται τὸ γιγνόμενον (τοῦτο δὲ λέγω ὅθεν ἡ ἀρχὴ τῆς γενέσεώς ἐστι) κ.τ.λ.

[2] Aristotle is alluding to the practice of preceding writers on Rhetoric. See marginal reference. As Rhetoric is there said to be an offshoot of Dialectic and Ethics, it is clear that "the analytical science" must be Dialectic. See Mr Cope's note *ad loc.*

the truth is, as indeed we have already remarked, that Rhetoric is composed of the analytical science and of the ethical branch of Politics and bears a certain resemblance to Dialectic on the one hand and to the sophistical arguments on the other. But the more one attempts to set either Dialectic or Rhetoric on the footing of sciences rather than of *simple* faculties, the more will one imperceptibly obliterate their nature by transgressing *their proper limits* in the reconstructive process and passing from a science of mere words to sciences of certain definite subject-matters. Still so far as an analysis *of the subjects of public business* has a practical value *and is possible* without encroachment upon the studies proper to political science, it is one upon which we may now proceed to enter.

The most important subjects of general deliberation and deliberative oratory are practically five, viz. finance, war and peace, the defence of the country, imports and exports, and legislation. Thus to speak in the first instance of finance: one who aspires to be a deliberative *or political* speaker will need to be acquainted with the nature and number of the resources of the State, so that any resource which is neglected may be added to them and any which is defective may be increased, as well as with all the items of the public expenditure, so that whatever is superfluous may be abolished and whatever is excessive may be cut down; for it is possible to enrich a State not only by adding to its resources but also by curtailing its expenses. But it is not only from experience at home that a comprehensive view

The five principal subjects of deliberation.

(1) Finance.

of these questions may be derived; it is indispensable, if one is to deliberate and advise respecting them, that he should be equally familiar with the discoveries made in other lands. Under the head of war and peace he must know the strength and character of the existing military force in the State and of the force which can be called into existence, also the wars in which the State has been engaged and its success or failure in them. Nor must his knowledge of these points be limited to his own State; it must extend to neighbouring countries [1] or even *to all countries* with which there is a prospect of war, his object being to conclude a peace with the superior powers and to have the option of fighting or not with the inferior. He must know too whether the forces of the States are similar or dissimilar, as this is a point in which one may have an advantage or disadvantage as compared with the other. With the same view it is necessary that he should have studied the issues of the wars not only of his own State but of other States as well; for similar causes naturally produce similar results. Nor again should he be ignorant of the means of defence possessed by his country; he should know the strength and character of its defensive force and the sites of its fortresses (which is impossible without a practical knowledge of the country) in order to strengthen the force, if it is inadequate, or to abolish any part of it, if superfluous, and to concentrate the attention of the

(2) War and peace.

(3) Means of defence.

---

[1] It seems best to place only a comma after εἰδέναι, so that the sentence, if fully expressed, would run τῶν ὁμόρων ταῦτα ἀναγκαῖον εἰδέναι, ἢ καὶ πάντων πρὸς οὓς ἐπίδοξον πολεμεῖν.

citizens upon the most favourable localities. In regard to the question of supplies, *the deliberative* (4) Sup-
orator ought to understand the total expenditure
plies.
which is adequate for the State, the nature of the
supplies produced at home and imported from abroad
and the requisite exports and imports, with the view
of making conventions and commercial treaties with
the exporting and importing countries. For there are
two classes of persons in regard to whom it is necessary that the citizens should always be kept clear of
offence, viz. those who are superior *in military strength*
and those who control the supplies. But while it is
necessary, as a means of safety, that our orator
should be a competent observer of all the points
we have described, it is especially necessary that he
should understand legislation. For as the safety of (5) Legisla-
the State depends upon its laws, he must know all
tion.
the different kinds of polities, the nature of the
measures beneficial to each and the natural causes
of its destruction whether inherent in the polity
itself or antagonistic to it.

[1]When I speak of the destruction of a polity by
causes which are inherent in itself I mean that all
polities, except the ideally best polity, are liable
to destruction either by relaxation or by intensification ; a democracy e.g. is not only enfeebled by
relaxation so as to issue actually in an oligarchy but
may be destroyed also by a marked intensification,

---

[1] There is a passage of the *Politics* so closely resembling this,
even in the illustration drawn from the characteristics of the
nose, that the two should be read side by side. It is VIII (V)
ch. 9, and will be found on pp. 377—379 of my Translation.

in the same way as not only does the aquiline or snub character *of a nose* become regular by relaxation, but, if the nose becomes excessively aquiline or snub, it acquires such a shape that it ceases to look like a nose at all. It is useful too for legislative purposes not only to understand the nature of the proper polity by a study of the past but to be familiar with the polities of other countries and to know the particular politics suitable to particular peoples. It is clear then that from a legislative point of view there is a value in the accounts of travels round the world, as from them we may learn the laws and customs of foreign nations, and from the point of view of political counsel there is a value in historical compositions, although all this is the province of Politics rather than of Rhetoric.

These then are all the principal topics which the deliberative *or political* orator should [1] understand. But the proper materials of exhortation or dissuasion upon these or upon any other topics remain to be discussed ; and the discussion of them will be a fresh branch of our inquiry [2].

CHAP. V.
The object
of human
actions.

It may be said that all men both individually and collectively have a certain object at which they

[1] I can hardly believe in the absolute use of ἔχειν, without an object or with τὰς προτάσεις to be mentally supplied. Nor does Spengel's λέγειν commend itself as an emendation. Is it possible that the true reading is περὶ ὧν μὲν οὖν νοῦν ἔχειν δεῖ τὸν μέλλοντα συμβουλεύειν ? Cp. Plato *Republic*, p. 534 B.

[2] It is perhaps worth while to quote M. St Hilaire's remark upon this chapter: Il est fait pour étonner beaucoup ceux qui croient non-seulement à notre supériorité mais en outre à une différence radicale entre nous et les Grecs.

aim in all that they choose and in all that they avoid.
This object may be summarily defined as happiness
and the constituents of happiness. Let us then by Happiness.
way of illustration ascertain what is in general
terms the nature of happiness and what are the
elements of its constituent parts, as it is upon happiness and all that is conducive or prejudicial to
happiness that exhortations and dissuasions always
turn. For whatever procures or augments happiness
or one of its constituents is a thing to be done, and
whatever destroys or impedes happiness or creates
its opposite is a thing to be left undone.

Happiness then may be defined as prosperity Its defini-
conjoined with virtue, or as an independent state of tion.
existence, or as the pleasantest life conjoined with
safety, or as an abundance of goods and slaves with
the ability to preserve them and make a practical
use of them ; for it would be pretty generally admitted that happiness is one or more of these
things.

Such then being the definition of happiness, it Its constitu-
follows that its constituent parts are nobility, the ent parts.
possession of many and excellent friends, wealth,
a goodly and numerous family and a happy old age ;
also such physical excellences as health, beauty,
strength, stature, and athletic power, *and finally*
fame, honour, good fortune and virtue[1]. For the

---

[1] After ἀρετήν most MSS. contain the words ἢ καὶ τὰ μέρη αὐτῆς,
φρόνησιν ἀνδρίαν δικαιοσύνην σωφροσύνην. But not to say that
such an analysis of ἀρετή is, as Spengel says, rather Platonic than
Aristotelian, it is clear from the concluding words of this chapter
that a specification of the "constituents" of ἀρετή would here be

only way to be absolutely independent is to possess both personal and external goods, as there are no other kinds of goods than these. Personal goods are those of the soul or of the body; nobility, friends, riches and honour are external goods. We hold that resources too and fortune should not be wanting, if the life is to be perfectly secure. Let us ascertain then in the same way as before the nature of these several *constituents of happiness.*

(1) Nobility.   Nobility in the case of a nation or a State implies that its members are indigenous or of high antiquity, that its first rulers were illustrious persons and that many of its sons have been illustrious on the score of qualities which excite admiration. The nobility of a private family on the other hand may be derived either from the male or the female side ; it implies legitimacy on both sides and, as in the case of a State, the distinction of its founders for virtue or wealth or something else which is held in honour among men and the celebrity of many members of the family, men and women, young and old.

(2) Offspring.   What is meant by the blessing of a goodly and numerous race is not at all difficult to understand. [1]It implies in a community a large and sterling body of youth, sterling physically, i.e. in stature, beauty, strength and athletic powers, *as well as in regard to* the virtues of the soul, which in a young man are temperance and courage. It implies in an indi-

premature. What Aristotle understands by these "constituents" appears from p. 29, ll. 28—30.

[1] Omitting εὐτεκνία.

vidual that his own children, both sons and daughters, are numerous and goodly. *It may be observed that in a woman the excellences or graces of the body are beauty and stature, those of the soul are self-command* and an industry which never degenerates into vulgarity. Nor is it less our duty as members of a State than as individuals to try to ensure these virtues among women as well as among men; for where the condition of the women is vicious as at Lacedæmon, it may be said that there is no happiness in half the State.

The constituents of wealth are plenty of money, (3) Wealth. the possession of landed property and estates and also of chattels, live-stock and slaves of exceptional number, size and beauty; all these are safe, [1] gentlemanly and useful kinds of property. But, while it is the productive kinds of property which are the more useful, it is the means of luxury which are the more gentlemanly; I mean by "productive kinds" the ordinary sources of income, and by "luxuries" such kinds as produce nothing worth speaking of beyond the actual enjoyment of them. The criterion of security *in the case of property* is the possession of it in such a place and in such a manner that you enjoy the power of using it as you like; that of ownership or the reverse is your power of aliena-

---

[1] When Aristotle speaks of certain kinds of property as "liberal" or "gentlemanly," his words are intelligible, if it is borne in mind that the Greeks looked upon trade and all the property which comes of trade as being essentially unnatural and illiberal. This view is familiar to every reader of Plato's *Laws* or Aristotle's *Politics*. See Mr Cope's note.

tion, i.e. of giving it away or selling it. It is indeed the general rule that wealth consists not so much in possession as in use ; for it is the active exercise or use of such things as have been mentioned which constitutes wealth.

(4) Reputation. To have a high reputation is to be regarded by everybody as a man of honour or to be the possessor of something which is an object of desire to all or most people or to the good or the wise.

(5) Honour. Honour is a sign of a reputation for beneficence. It is especially paid, as indeed is right, to past benefactors, although it is sometimes paid too to persons capable of beneficent action. Such action may affect either personal safety and the various causes which conduce to existence or wealth or some other good which is difficult of acquisition either universally or at a particular place or time ; for it often happens that people receive honour for services of an apparently insignificant kind, but the explanation lies in the places or seasons at which they were rendered. The elements of honour are sacrifices, memorials in verse and prose, special distinctions, allotments of land, the foremost seats on public occasions, sepulchral monuments, statues, maintenance at the public charge, barbaric compliments, as e.g. the prostrating oneself before a person or giving him place, and such presents as are valued in the particular country where they are made. For the present, as being a gift of property and a sign of honour, is equally an object of desire to the avaricious and the ambitious. For to both it offers something that they need, as on the one hand it is a property, which is the desire of the

avaricious, and on the other hand it confers honour, which is the desire of the ambitious.

Of the physical excellences one is health; and by this I mean that a person is free from disease and has the use of his bodily faculties; for there are many persons who keep themselves in health in such a manner as is attributed to [1]Herodicus and who would not be congratulated by anybody upon their health, as they deny themselves all or nearly all human pleasures. <small>(6) Health.</small>

Beauty varies with the different periods of life. A young man is beautiful, if his body is adapted to exercises of speed and strength, and if he is a pleasant and delightful object to look upon. This is the reason why [2]pentathletes are most beautiful; they are equally ready for feats of strength and of speed. A man in the prime of life [3]*is beautiful, if his body is adapted* to military exercises and if his appear- <small>(7) Beauty.</small>

---

[1] The best account of Herodicus will be found in Plato, *Republic* iii. p. 406, where it is said that he was a training-master (παιδο-τρίβης) who fell into ill-health and invented such a compound régime of gymnastics and medicine as to worry himself and a great many other people to death.

[2] The πένταθλον, as its name implies, comprised five exercises,

ἄλμα, ποδωκείην, δίσκον, ἄκοντα, πάλην,

but it is not certain whether the successful pentathlete was necessarily victorious in all or only in three of the exercises.

[3] Victorius is probably right in saying that the elliptical sentence would, if fully expressed, be ἀκμάζοντος δὲ κάλλος τὸ πρὸς μὲν πόνους τοὺς πολεμικοὺς χρήσιμον ἔχειν τὸ σῶμα κ.τ.λ.

It should be remembered that the ἀκμὴ or "prime" of physical life was, according to Aristotle, attained at the age of 37 or thereabouts. See *Politics* IV (VII), ch. 16 (p. 213 of my Translation).

ance combines grace with sternness; an old man, [1]if his body is equal to such exertions as are inevitable and if it is not repulsive, as having none of the disfigurements of age.

(8)Strength.
Strength is a power of moving somebody else at will; and as a person must be moved either by pulling or pushing or lifting or pressing or compressing, it follows that a strong man is strong either in all or in some of these respects.

(9) Size.
In respect of size excellence consists in superiority to ordinary people in height, stoutness and breadth, although not to such an extent that the movements are retarded in consequence of the excess.

(10) Athletic excellence.
Athletic excellence is composed of size, strength and speed[2]; for a man who can move his legs about and take long rapid strides is a good runner, one who can pound an adversary and hold him down a good wrestler, one who can drive him from his ground by his blows a good boxer, one who is a master both of wrestling and of boxing a [3]pancratiast, and one who is a master of [4]all the exercises a pentathlete.

---

[1] In full : γέροντος δὲ κάλλος τὸ πρὸς μὲν πόνους τοὺς ἀναγκαίους ἱκανὸν ἔχειν τὸ σῶμα κ.τ.λ.

[2] I cannot help thinking that the clause καὶ γὰρ ὁ ταχὺς ἰσχυρός ἐστιν is spurious, having been introduced by a copyist who noticed that, while ἀγωνιστικὴ ἀρετή consists of three elements, size, strength and speed, the first two only have been described, but not the third.

[3] The παγκράτιον comprised wrestling and boxing.

[4] There is some little difficulty in πᾶσι, as boxing was not a part of the πένταθλον, and quoit-throwing, javelin-hurling and (possibly) leaping, which were included in the πένταθλον, have not been mentioned in this sentence. But probably the word πᾶσι

A happy old age is one which approaches gradu- (11) A happy old age. ally and without pain ; for if its approach is rapid, or painful although slow, it is not a happy old age. It is dependent too on physical excellences and on fortune ; for a person will not be exempt from suffering, unless he is healthy and strong, nor will he enjoy a painless and protracted life, ¹unless he is fortunate. It is true that there is such a thing as a faculty of long life even without health and strength, for many people are long-lived who have no physical excellences ; but a precise consideration of this subject would not be serviceable to our present purpose.

What it is to possess numerous friends and good (12) Friend-ship. friends is evident at once from the definition of a friend as one who, if he considers anything to be good for another, is ready to do it for the other's sake. Thus one who has many such persons about him has a number of friends, and one who has worthy persons has good friends.

Good fortune implies the acquisition and posses- (13) Fortune. sion of either all or nearly all or the most important of the good gifts which F rtune bestows. But while there are some of Fortun :'s gifts which are equally the gifts of various arts, there are many too which are independent of art, e.g. the various gifts of Nature ²(although Fortune's gifts may also be unnatural);

would convey to a Greek the idea of an "all-round" athlete, without any special reference to the exercises named in the context.

¹ Omitting οὔτ' before ἄνευ τύχης.
² The clause ἐνδέχεται δὲ καὶ παρὰ φύσιν εἶναι is strictly paren- .

for health may be a product of art, but beauty and stature can only be gifts of Nature. It is a general rule that all such blessings as excite envy are gifts of Fortune. Fortune again is the author of exceptional blessings, as e.g. if all your brothers are ugly and you are handsome, or if everybody else failed to perceive a particular treasure and you discovered it, or if a shot hit your neighbour instead of yourself, or if although you were always in the habit of going *to a particular spot* you were *one day* the only person who did not go to it, and other people, although it was the only time that they ever went there, were killed. All such cases may be regarded as instances of good Fortune.

(14) Virtue.   We have still to speak of virtue; but as the most convenient place to discuss it will be when we come to treat of panegyrical Rhetoric, we will postpone the definition until then[1].

CHAP. VI.   It is evident then what are the points to be kept in view, [2]as being consequent or as already existing,

thetical. The gifts of Fortune (says Aristotle) are sometimes such as art or science can produce, e.g. health, and sometimes such as Nature bestows, e.g. beauty. But it then occurs to him that the gifts of Fortune may also be unnatural or abnormal; hence the parenthetical words. If he were speaking here exactly, he would not call anything unnatural or abnormal a gift of Fortune (τύχη), ὅταν γὰρ γένηταί τι παρὰ φύσιν, τότε οὐκ ἀπὸ τύχης ἀλλὰ μᾶλλον ἀπὸ ταὐτομάτου γεγονέναι φαμέν, (φυσικὴ ἀκρόασις, ii. p. 197 B$_{24}$). But compare p. 36, l. 25.

    [1] See ch. 9.

    [2] Although it is true that the future is in Aristotle's view the "time" which especially belongs to deliberative Rhetoric (p. 11, l. 23), yet an appeal to present or existing facts will not be out of

in a hortatory and on the other hand in a dissuasive
speech; for the latter are the opposites of the former.
[1]But as in deliberative Rhetoric it is expediency
which is the end proposed, the subject of deliberation
being not the end but the means to the end or in
other words whatever is expedient in actions, and
as what is expedient is good, it is necessary to apprehend certain elementary propositions respecting
what is good or expedient in general.

Good then may be defined as that which is de- Description
sirable for its own sake and for the sake of which we   of Good.
desire or choose something else, and which is sought
by all things or by all sentient or intelligent things or
would be sought by them, if they should acquire intelligence. Again, whatever [2]intelligence would assign to
each individual or the intelligence of each individual
assigns to himself, this is good relatively to him. Or
again, that which by its presence produces a good
condition and a state of independence, or independence *in the abstract*, or that which is productive
or preservative of such things, or that upon which
they are consequent, or that which tends to hinder
or destroy their opposites *is also a good.* [3]Conse-

place. His exhortation may e. g. assume the form "Show yourselves men, or you will lose the blessings you have," as well as
"Show yourselves men, and you will gain greater blessings."

[1] This is another sentence which is logically irregular. The
clause βουλεύονται δὲ οὐ περὶ τοῦ τέλους......κατὰ τὰς πράξεις has no
bearing upon the conclusion and should be regarded as virtually
parenthetical.

[2] The supreme or Divine Intelligence.

[3] This and the next sentence form a sort of explanatory note
which slightly interrupts the sequence of the argument.

quence however may be either subsequent or simultaneous; knowledge e.g. is consequent upon learning subsequently but life upon healthiness simultaneously. Also a cause may be productive in three senses; as ¹healthiness e.g. is productive of health in one sense, food is productive of it in another and gymnastic exercise, as generally producing health, in a third.

These principles being laid down, it necessarily follows that any acquisition of what is good and any rejection of what is evil is good, as the enjoyment of the good is consequent upon the former subsequently and the deliverance from the evil upon the latter simultaneously. So also is the reception of a greater good in lieu of a less and of a less evil in lieu of a greater; for the excess of the greater over the less is in effect the measure of the good received or of the evil rejected. The virtues too necessarily constitute a good, as it is in respect of them that the virtuous are in a good case, and they are productive of what is good and also ²practical. But the nature

---

¹ It is curious that Aristotle speaks here of τὸ ὑγιαίνειν as producing ὑγίεια and in *Nicom. Eth.* x. ch. 4, p. 1174 B₂₆ of ὑγίεια as producing τὸ ὑγιαίνειν. Perhaps his meaning is the same in both passages, although his language is practically inverted. A healthy condition of body (he seems to say) is productive of health as a visible objective fact.

² The distinction between ποιητικός and πρακτικός, which is necessary to the understanding of this passage, is nowhere perhaps more clearly expressed than in *Politics* i. ch. 4, τὰ μὲν οὖν λεγόμενα ὄργανα ποιητικὰ ὄργανά ἐστι, τὸ δὲ κτῆμα πρακτικόν· ἀπὸ μὲν γὰρ τῆς κερκίδος (which is an ὄργανον) ἕτερόν τι γίγνεται παρὰ τὴν χρῆσιν αὐτῆς, ἀπὸ δὲ τῆς ἐσθῆτος καὶ τῆς κλίνης (which are κτήματα) ἡ χρῆσις μόνον.

and character of the several virtues deserve a separate
discussion. Pleasure again must be a good, as all
living things naturally desire it; and if so, all that
is pleasant or noble must be good, as what is pleasant
is productive of pleasure, and what is noble is either
pleasant or intrinsically desirable. But, to parti- Goods.
cularize, it results *from the definition* that the following are goods. Happiness, as being something intrinsically desirable and independent and for the sake of
which we choose many things. Also justice, courage,
temperance, magnanimity, [1] magnificence and other
such habits, as being virtues of the soul. Health,
beauty and the like, as being virtues *or graces* of the
body and as being productive of many things *which
are good;* for health e.g. produces pleasure as well as
life and is therefore in the popular view the best
of blessings, as being the source of the two things
most highly esteemed in the world, viz. pleasure and
life. Wealth again *is a good,* as being [2] a virtue *or
successful result* of acquisition and as something which
is productive of many *good* things. Also a friend and
friendship; for not only is a friend intrinsically desirable, but he is productive in a number of ways.
Honour and reputation again, as being pleasant,
variously productive and generally attended by the
actual possession of the qualities which are the

---

[1] The virtue which is called by Aristotle μεγαλοπρέπεια is discussed in *Nicom. Eth.* iv. ch 4, where ὁ μεγαλοπρεπής is defined
as one who is able δαπανῆσαι μεγάλα ἐμμελῶς. Cp. p. 30, l. 12,
μεγαλοπρέπεια δὲ ἀρετὴ ἐν δαπανήμασι μεγέθους ποιητική.

[2] It is rather, I should say, the accumulation of wealth than
wealth itself which would be strictly called an ἀρετὴ κτήσεως.

grounds of the honour so paid. Rhetorical and practical ability *are good,* as these and all similar *faculties* are productive of good. Natural gifts again, [1]memory, aptness to learn, sharpness of wit and the like, all these faculties being productive of what is good. Similarly, all sciences and arts and life itself; for life if unattended by any other good is yet intrinsically desirable. And lastly, justice as tending to promote the interest of the community at large.

This is a fairly exhaustive catalogue of such things as are generally admitted to be good. There are other goods of a disputable kind, and in regard to these the materials of syllogism will be as follows. A thing is good if its opposite is evil. Or if its opposite is advantageous to our enemies ; as if it is of high advantage to our enemies that we should be cowards, it is clear that valour is highly beneficial to our country. It is in fact a general rule that, whatever our enemies desire or rejoice at, the opposite of this is clearly beneficial to ourselves. Hence the point of the lines

" Sure [2]Priam would rejoice," &c.

But this is only a general and not an invariable rule ; for there is no absolute reason why our own interest should not in some instances coincide with

---

[1] Reading μνήμη, with Spengel.

[2] The passage referred to is the beginning of the speech in which Nestor tries to reconcile Achilles and Agamemnon. *Iliad,* i. 255 sqq.

> ἦ κεν γηθήσαι Πρίαμος, Πριάμοιό τε παῖδες,
> ἄλλοι τε Τρῶες μέγα κεν κεχαροίατο θυμῷ,
> εἰ σφῶϊν τάδε πάντα πυθοίατο μαρναμένοιϊν.

that of our enemies. Hence the saying " Misery acquaints a man with strange bedfellows," when the same danger threatens two people. Again, [1]if a thing is not, in excess, it is a good ; but if there is more than the proper amount of it, it is an evil. It is a good too, if it is a thing for which a great deal of trouble or expense has been incurred ; for it is proved thereby to be an apparent good, and an apparent good is assumed to be an end and *not only so but* an end of various actions, and an end is *ex hypothesi* a good. Hence [2] the lines *beginning*

" Yea, after Priam's heart "

and

" 'Twere shame to tarry long "

and [3]the proverb " to break the pitcher at the door."

---

[1] It seems from the correspondence of the clauses οὐ μή ἐστιν ὑπερβολή and ὃ δ' ἂν ᾖ μεῖζον ἢ δεῖ that the former means not "that which does not admit of excess" but rather "that which is not in excess."

[2] Both quotations are from the Second Book of the *Iliad*, vv. 176 and 298. The point lies not in the mere words quoted but in the context. In the first passage Athene is speaking of the noble lives sacrificed for Helen's sake.

κὰδ δέ κεν εὐχωλὴν Πριάμῳ καὶ Τρωσὶ λίποιτε
Ἀργείην Ἑλένην, ἧς εἵνεκα πολλοὶ Ἀχαιῶν
ἐν Τροίῃ ἀπόλοντο, φίλης ἀπὸ πατρίδος αἴης.

In the second it is Odysseus who speaks

ἡμῖν δ' εἴνατός ἐστι περιτροπέων ἐνιαυτὸς
ἐνθάδε μιμνόντεσσι· τῷ οὐ νεμεσίζομ' Ἀχαιοὺς
ἀσχαλάαν παρὰ νηυσὶ κορωνίσιν· ἀλλὰ καὶ ἔμπης
αἰσχρόν τοι δηρόν τε μένειν, κενεόν τε νέεσθαι.

[3] The pitcher broken at the door after so much trouble in carrying it was a proverbial instance of labour thrown away.

Again, that which is an object of general desire or
that which is clearly an object of contention is a
good, for we defined a good as an object of universal
desire, and the general opinion is regarded as *virtually* universal. That which is an object of praise
too *is a good*, as nobody praises anything which he
does not regard as a good. Or again that which is
praised by our enemies[1], for it is an universal admission *that a thing is a good*, if it is admitted even by
those who are the sufferers by it. For 'it may be
argued that, if they admit it, the reason must be that
it is indisputable, as *it may be equally argued ex
contrario that* people must be vicious, if their enemies praise them. It was thus that the Corinthians
considered themselves to have been insulted by
Simonides in the line

"The men of Corinth Ilium blameth not."

Again, a thing is a good, if it has been preferred
by some sagacious or good man or woman, as
Odysseus by Athene, Helen by Theseus, Alexander
by the goddesses and Achilles by Homer. The
objects of deliberate choice in general are good,
these being such things as have been already described or such as are injurious to our enemies or
good for our friends or such as are practicable. But
what is practicable may be either just[3] possible or
easily done, i.e. done either without trouble or in

---

[1] Omitting καὶ οἱ φαῦλοι.

[2] Upon the whole it seems best to follow Spengel in omitting
the words οὓς οἱ φίλοι ψέγουσι καὶ ἀγαθοί.

[3] The ἂν should certainly be retained in the text. It is clear

a short time ; for the difficulty of a thing is determined either by the trouble it gives or by the length
of time it takes. Again, things are good, if they
happen in accordance with our desires ; for the
object of our desire is either not an evil at all or
is an evil which is more than compensated by the good
which follows from it, as e. g. if the *consequent*
penalty is either imperceptible or insignificant. They
are good too, if they are special or unique or pre-
eminent gifts, as in such case they are held in
greater honour. Or if they are appropriate to
ourselves, i. e. suitable in regard to our birth or
influence. Or if they are things of which we feel
the deficiency, even though *in themselves* they are
insignificant ; for it is none the less our deliberate
choice to attain them. Or if they are things which
are easy of accomplishment ; for if they are easy,
à fortiori they are possible—I mean things in which
all or most men or our own equals or inferiors have
been successful. Or things by which we shall gratify
our friends or annoy our enemies. Or things which
persons whom we respect deliberately choose as
objects to be attained. Or things for which we are
fitted by nature or experience, as then we anticipate
that success will be the easier. Or things which
are unattainable by any bad person, as such things
are more loudly applauded. Or such things as are
in fact the objects of our desire ; for these are in our
eyes not only pleasant but actually better. *And*

that the distinction is between such things as may conditionally
and so by implication rarely come to pass and such as are easy or
ordinary occurrences.

finally, whatever it is upon which we are especially bent, *it is this that we regard especially as a good*, e.g. victory, if we are bent upon victory, honour, if upon honour, money, if upon money, and so on.

CHAP. VII.   In regard then to what is good and expedient these are the sources from which it is proper to derive our proofs. But as it often happens that people, while they admit two things both to be expedient, differ as to the more expedient of the two, it will be Comparison proper, as our next point, to consider the greater of goods. good or the more expedient *of two things which are both admittedly good or expedient*.

A thing which exceeds another may be defined as so much and something more ; a thing which is exceeded by another as something included in the other. Also while the terms "greater" and "more" have always a reference to something less, "great" and "small," "much" and "little" are relative to the average size of things, that which is called "great" being in excess of this average, that which falls short of it being called "small"; and similarly the words "much" and "little."

p. 30.   Now[1] by a good we mean that which is desirable for its own sake and not for the sake of something

---

[1] It is necessary in considering the Greek of this sentence, to observe that here, as often in Aristotle, the conclusion does not follow from the clauses of the protasis. The ἀνάγκη, p. 23, l. 17, has nothing to do with the statements that "a good is something desirable for its own sake," &c. which are only the definitions given at the beginning of the last chapter; but it is a result of the new definition ἔστω δὴ ὑπερέχον μὲν τοσοῦτον καὶ ἔτι, ὑπερεχόμενον δὲ τὸ ἐνυπάρχον, although it is not grammatically connected with it.

else and that which is sought by all things or which would be chosen by all things, if they should acquire intelligence and sagacity, and that which is productive and preservative of such things or is attended by then?. Also the object *of things* is their end, and the end is the object of everything else, and the absolute good is that which is an end and. object to itself. It follows then that the larger number of things is a greater good than a single thing or than the smaller number of things, if the single thing or the smaller number be reckoned as part of the larger; for then *the larger number* is in excess *of the smaller*, and that which is included *in the larger* is exceeded by it.

Again, if the largest member *of one class of things* exceeds the largest member of another, then the first class exceeds the second; and *conversely*, if one class exceeds another, the largest member of the first exceeds the largest member of the second. Thus if the tallest man is taller than the tallest woman, so are men generally taller than women, and if men are generally taller than women, so is the tallest man taller than the tallest woman; for the excess of one class over another is proportional to the excess of the greatest member of the one over the greatest member of the other. Again, if A is consequent upon B but B is not *necessarily* consequent upon A, B *is greater than A*, whether the consequence is simultaneous or subsequent or potential[1]; for then the use of the consequent A is involved in the use of B. (Life,

---

[1] The "potential" is a third sort of consequence, not mentioned, p. 20, l. 9.

it may be said, is consequent upon health simultaneously, although the converse is not true, knowledge upon learning subsequently, and cheating upon sacrilege potentially, as a man who was guilty of sacrilege would not hesitate at cheating.) Again, if there are two things in excess of a third, the one which exceeds it by the greater amount is the greater, [1]as it is necessarily in excess of the greater as well as of the less *of the other two things*. Things too which are productive of a greater good are greater; for[2] this is involved, as we have seen, in the conception that a thing is productive of something greater. Similarly, if that which is productive of a thing is greater, *the thing itself is greater;* thus if what is wholesome is more desirable and a greater good than what is pleasant, so is health greater than pleasure. Again, a thing which is more desirable in itself *is a greater good* than a thing which is not desirable in itself, as e.g. physical strength than wholesome food ; for strength is, and food is not, desirable for its own sake, and this is our definition of a good. Or again, if one of two things is an end, and the other is not, *the former is the greater good*, as being

p. 39.

---

[1] If this is the meaning of the clause ἀνάγκη γὰρ ὑπερέχειν καὶ τοῦ μείζονος, the reason alleged is hardly more than a re-statement of the point to be proved, and there is an obscurity in τοῦ μείζονος denoting "the greater of the other two things" viz. of τὸ ὑπερεχόμενον and of the less of τὰ ὑπερέχοντα. Is it possible that the words καὶ τοῦ μείζονος should be omitted, as being a repetition of καὶ τὰ μείζονος?

[2] The argument, which is a little obscure, is that, if τὸ ποιητικὸν ἀγαθοῦ is ἀγαθόν, as appears from p. 23, l. 14, τὸ ποιητικὸν μείζονος ἀγαθοῦ must be μεῖζον ἀγαθόν.

desirable for its own sake and not for the sake of something else, like gymnastic exercise for the sake of a good condition of body. Or if there is one thing which stands less in need of external help than some other thing or things, *it is a greater good*, as being more independent ; and this is the case, when its needs are fewer or more easily supplied. Or if *A* does not exist or cannot come into being without *B*, but the converse is not true, *B is then the greater good*, the thing which does not require something else being more independent and therefore, as is clear, a greater good. The same is true, if *B* is an ¹originating principle and *A* is not, or if *B* is a cause and *A* is not, for the same reason, as without a cause or a principle it is impossible that anything should exist or come into being. Again, if there are two such principles or causes, the result of the greater principle or cause is greater ; and conversely, if there are two results, the principle or cause of the greater result is greater. It is clear then from what has been said that a thing may be *shown to be* greater *than something else* in either of two ways ; for it will appear greater, if it is an originating principle and the other is not, and again, if it is not an originating principle and the other is, as the end of anything is greater and is not an originating principle. It was thus that Leodamas in his accusation of Callistratus argued that he who advised a conspiracy was a greater criminal than he who executed it, on the ground that

---

¹ The Aristotelian word ἀρχή is discussed at considerable length in Mr Cope's note. The classical passage relating to it in Aristotle himself is *Metaphysics*, iv. ch. i.

it would never have been executed, if he had not devised it, whereas in his accusation of Chabrias he argued that he who executed it was a greater criminal than he who advised it, on the ground that it would never have taken effect without somebody to execute it, as it is the execution which is the object of any conspiracy. Again, that which is rarer *is greater or more valuable* than that which is plenteous, e.g. gold than iron, although it is not so useful; for the acquisition of it, as being more difficult, is something greater. But there is another sense in which what is plenteous *is greater* than what is rare, as being more abundantly useful; for frequency of use is superior to rarity, whence the saying [1]"The best of things is water." It is in fact a general rule that the more difficult of two things, as being the rarer, is greater than the easier, although in another sense the easier, as gratifying our wishes, may be said to be greater than the more difficult. Again, a thing is greater, if its opposite is greater, or if the deprivation of it is greater. [2]Virtue is greater than non-virtue, vice than non-vice; for virtue and vice are, and the others are not, ends *or complete states*. Again, if the functions of things are nobler or baser, they are themselves greater. Or if the vices and virtues of things are greater, so are their functions, as results

---

[1] Pindar, *Olympians*, i. 1.

[2] Rhetoric, as Aristotle says, p. 4, l. 13, τἀναντία συλλογίζεται, and the superiority of virtue to non-virtue or of vice to non-vice, i.e. of the positive or complete state to the negative or incomplete, is only, as it were, a rhetorical thesis in which the moral point of view is disregarded.

correspond with their causes or originating principles and *vice versa.* *Things are greater* too, if superiority in them is more desirable or nobler ; and [1] conversely, if things are themselves better and nobler, the excesses of them are also better and nobler. Thus keenness of sight is more desirable than keenness of smell, as sight itself is more desirable than smell ; and as it is nobler to be excessively fond of friends than to be excessively fond of money, the love of friends is itself nobler than that of money. Again, the objects of the nobler or better desires are nobler or better ; for the greater impulses are directed to greater ends. So too the desires of nobler and better objects are for the same reason themselves nobler and better. Or if the science which deals with particular subjects is nobler and more moral, so are the subjects ; for as is the science, so is the truth *at which it aims,* and every science is supreme in its own province. Similarly the higher and more moral the subjects, the sciences which deal with them are proportionately more moral and nobler for the same reason. Again, that which would be decided or has been decided by sagacious people, whether by all or almost all or the majority or the ablest of them, to be a good or the greater of two goods, must necessarily be such, either absolutely or in so far as their decision was the result of their sagacity. This is a rule which is applicable to everything else as well as to goods ; for the nature, quantity and quality of things are always such as science and sagacity would pronounce. But it is only in respect

---

[1] I cannot doubt that the words καὶ ἀντικειμένως δὲ...καλλίους should be transposed so as to precede the illustrations.

of goods that we have laid it down ; for a good has been defined to be that which would be desired or chosen by each individual thing, if it should acquire sagacity. It is clear then that a thing is a greater good, if it is more strongly pronounced to be so by sagacity, or if it is the property of a superior class either ¹absolutely or in so far as the class is superior, as e.g. valour is a greater good than strength, or again if it is that which would be desired by a superior either absolutely or in so far as he is superior, as e.g. to suffer wrong rather than to commit wrong, this being the part which the juster person would choose. Again, that which is pleasanter *is a greater good* than that which is less pleasant, as all things pursue pleasure and covet it for its own sake, and these are the criteria of the good or the end. But *of two pleasant things* the pleasanter is that which is the less accompanied by pain and the more permanent. Again, that which is nobler *is a greater good* than the less noble ; for what is noble is either what is pleasant or what is intrinsically desirable. Anything which we are particularly anxious to effect for ourselves or our friends is a greater good, as anything which we are least anxious to effect is a greater evil. Also whatever is more permanent or secure *is a greater good* than what is less so ; for if

---

¹ Perhaps Aristotle's meaning will be explained by an illustration. If man is superior to the other animals, then it will be true either absolutely that the qualities of a man are higher than those of an animal or in particular that any especial quality which contributes to his superiority, such as valour, will be higher than one, such as strength, which he shares with the animals.

a thing is more permanent, it is longer ours to enjoy, and if it is more secure, it is more an object of desire, as the desire of a thing implies an expectation that the enjoyment of it will be comparatively secure. [1]Further, in accordance with the rule of co-ordinates or of inflexions of the same roots, what is true of any one such word is true of all. Thus if the term "valiantly" is nobler and more desirable than the term "temperately," so is "valour" more desirable than "temperance" and "to be valiant" than "to be temperate." The object of universal choice is a greater good than the object of a choice which is not universal. The object of the choice of the majority is a greater good than that of the choice of the minority ; for we defined a good as the object of universal desire, and it follows that the object of greater universal desire is a greater good. A thing is a greater good also, if it is judged to be so by our rivals or enemies or by connoisseurs or by a jury selected by connoisseurs ; for in the one case there is a recognition which is virtually universal and in the other the recognition of authorities and specialists. It sometimes happens that that which all men possess alike is a greater good, as there is a certain disgrace in not possessing it, and at other times that that which is possessed by nobody or by a few only is a greater good, as being rarer. Again, the objects of

---

[1] The meaning is made plain by the illustrations given here and p. 96, ll. 25—29. See Mr Cope's notes. It is to be noticed that although τὰ σύστοιχα and αἱ ὁμοίαι πτώσεις are virtually identical expressions, the former refers to the logical conception, the latter to the grammatical form.

higher praise, as being nobler, are greater goods. So too are all things of which the honours are greater; for the honour paid to a thing may be regarded as being in some sense its valuation. Things for which the penalties are greater *are themselves greater*. The same is true of things which are greater than other things confessedly or apparently great. Again, the same things may be made to look greater by being divided into their parts; for then [1] the points of superiority seem to be multiplied. Accordingly [2] the poet makes Meleager's *wife* induce him to arise by reciting:

> "The ills of men whose city has been ta'en,
> Their townsfolk perishing, fire-wasted homes
> And children carried far to servitude."

Accumulation too and climax, of which Epicharmus was a master, *are means of magnifying a subject*, partly for the same reason as division—for the accumulation shows great superiority—and *partly* because *the subject* thus assumes the appearance of being an originating principle and cause of great results. And as a thing is greater in proportion to its difficulty and its rarity, the greatness may be due to particular seasons, ages, places, times and faculties. For if an

---

[1] Grammatically, πλειόνων is, 1 think, governed by ὑπερέχειν. The result of the division into parts is that instead of one ὑπεροχή there is, so to say, a succession of ὑπεροχαί, and the effect of the "superiority" is increased.

[2] Homer, *Iliad*, ix. 588 sqq.; but the quotation does not correspond with the ordinary text. Probably the reading here should be ὁ ποιητής φησι πεῖσαι τὴν γυναῖκα τὸν Μελέαγρον ἀναστῆναι λέγουσαν.

action exceeds a person's faculty, age or stature, or
is performed in a particular manner or at a particular
place or time, it will acquire a high degree of nobleness, goodness, justice or the contrary. Hence the
epigram on the Olympian victor

> "Once on my back I bore a heavy yoke
> And carried fish to Tegea from Argos."

[1] Iphicrates too was wont to eulogize himself by describing from what he had risen to his present position. Again, a natural talent is *a greater good* than
an acquired accomplishment, as being more difficult.
Hence [2] the poet's lines

> "Self-taught am I, &c."

A thing is magnified too, if it is the greatest part
of something great, as when Pericles [3] in his funeral
oration said that the cutting off of the youth from the
State was like taking the spring out of the year.

---

[1] τὸ τοῦ Ἰφικράτους ἐξ οἵων εἰς οἷα, is quoted p. 32, l. 22. It is
said that Iphicrates was the son of a cobbler.

[2] Homer, *Odyssey*, xxii. 347. It is Phemius who speaks to
Odysseus; but the point of the quotation lies not so much in
the words quoted as in their context

> θεὸς δέ μοι ἐν φρεσὶν οἵμας
> παντοίας ἐνέφυσεν· ἔοικα δέ τοι παραείδειν
> ὥστε θεῷ· τῷ μή με λιλαίεο δειροτομῆσαι.

[3] It is well known that this famous simile, which is quoted
again p. 127, l. 22, is not found in the funeral oration which
Thucydides (Bk. ii. ch. 35—46) has put into the mouth of Pericles.
Some commentators, e.g. Göttling and Westermann, think that it
is taken from the funeral oration delivered by Pericles after the
Samian War, B.C. 440. There are other references, which cannot
now be verified, to passages in the speeches of Pericles, p. 118,
ll. 15 sqq., p. 128, l. 1, p. 146, l. 2.

The same is true of such things as are useful when the necessity is greater, e.g. such things as are useful in old age or in times of sickness. Again, of two things that which is nearer to the end is the greater. That which is good ¹ relatively to the individual as well as absolutely *is greater than that which is good only in one of these senses.* Possibilities are greater goods than impossibilities, as the possible is good relatively to the individual, and the impossible is not. Such things as are inherent *or implied* in the end of life *are greater goods;* for all that approximates to the end is in a higher degree participant in the character of the end. Genuineness of any kind is a greater good than pretence, the test of pretence being that a person would not choose the thing, if there were no chance of his being known to have it. And from this it would seem that it is more desirable to receive benefits than to confer them, as one would choose to receive benefits, even if they were quite unknown, but would probably not choose to confer benefits without getting credit for them. Again, anything of which the reality is preferable to the appearance is a greater good, as being more genuine. This is the reason why justice itself in the eyes of some people is a poor thing, because it is

---

¹ Spengel's interpretation, which I have accepted, lays the stress upon the καί in the phrase τὸ αὑτῷ (ʔαὑτῷ) καὶ ἁπλῶς, the good which is useful *both* absolutely and relatively to the individual being preferred to the good which is useful either absolutely or relatively to the individual. But if this is the meaning, it would more naturally be expressed by some such words as καὶ τὸ καὶ αὑτῷ καὶ ἁπλῶς τοῦ ἢ αὑτῷ ἢ ἁπλῶς.

more desirable to appear just than to be so, whereas the contrary is the case with health. A thing is a greater good, if it is more conducive to various ends, e.g. to life, excellence of life, pleasure and the performance of noble deeds. Accordingly wealth and health are esteemed so highly important, because they fulfil all these conditions. So too if a thing involves comparatively little pain and affords pleasure, *it is a greater good*, as there is a double advantage in the attainment of two goods, viz. pleasure and the absence of pain. Again, if we take any two things, the greater is that which by addition to the same thing makes the total greater. Things are greater, if their presence cannot be concealed than if it can; for in this case they have more the character of reality. Accordingly wealth, [1]if it is apparent, must be clearly a greater good. So too is any gift, if it is dearly prized or if it is our all, while our neighbours have other gifts as well. Hence the punishment is greater for destroying the eye of a one-eyed man than of a man who has two eyes, as the one-eyed man is deprived of something which he dearly prizes.

The proper sources of proofs in exhortation and Chap. VIII. dissuasion have been now pretty exhaustively described. But the greatest and most authoritative of all, as a means of persuasion and good counsel, is an acquaintance with all the various forms of polity and an analysis of their several customs, institutions and interests. For it is self-interest which is the dominant force in the world, and whatever is preser-

---

[1] Reading τῷ δοκεῖν, unless it is permissible to alter μεῖζον to μεῖον.

vative of a particular polity is its interest. Further, it is the [1]expressed will of the supreme authority which is supreme *in any State,* and the supreme authorities are different in the different polities, being as numerous as the politics themselves. [2]There are four polities, viz., Democracy, Oligarchy, Aristocracy and Monarchy; consequently the supreme or decisive authority in each case is either some particular part of these polities or the whole.

Classification of polities.

A Democracy is a polity in which the offices of State are distributed among the citizens by lot, an Oligarchy one in which they are distributed among the persons who possess a certain property qualification, an Aristocracy one in which they are distributed among the educated class. *In speaking of the educated class,* I mean such education as is prescribed by the law of the land; for it is such persons as have been ever faithful to their institutions who constitute the official class in an Aristocracy. Such persons will necessarily appear the best ($\mathring{a}\rho\iota\sigma\tau o\iota$); hence 'Aristocracy' *or the government of the best* is the name which has been given to this polity. Monarchy, as its name implies, is the polity in which an individual is universally supreme; but it may be (1) constitutional Monarchy or Kingship, or (2) absolute Monarchy or Tyranny.

The ends or objects of the polities.

It is especially necessary to be acquainted with the end *or object* of each several polity, as it is the means conducive to this end which are the objects

---

[1] Reading $\mathring{a}\pi\acute{o}\phi av\sigma\iota s$.

[2] This rapid classification of polities may be compared with *Politics,* iii. ch. 7.

of the citizens' choice. The end of Democracy is liberty, that of Oligarchy wealth, that of Aristocracy the means of education and the institutions of the State, that of Tyranny self-preservation. It is clearly necessary then to distinguish such customs, institutions and interests as are appropriate to the end of each polity, as it is to these that the choice of the citizens has reference. But as ethical no less than demonstrative Rhetoric is an instrument by which proofs are conveyed—for we believe a speaker in virtue of his appearing to possess a certain character, i.e. if he appears to be good or well disposed to us or both—it will be proper that we should apprehend the character of each particular polity, as the character of each will necessarily be the most potent instrument of persuasion in dealing with it. The characters of the several polities will be ascertained by the same means *as those of individuals;* for characters are displayed in the moral purpose, and the moral purpose is relative to the end.

The objects then, whether future, or actually existing, at which we should aim in Rhetoric of a hortatory kind, the sources from which we should derive our proofs in regard to expediency, and lastly the means and method of acquiring ample materials in regard to the characters and institutions of the different polities have been described, so far as was appropriate to the present occasion; a full and exact discussion of them will be found in the *Politics*[1].

We have next to discuss virtue and vice, or what is noble and shameful, as these are the objects of CHAP. IX.
Epideictic
Rhetoric.

[1] The reference is to the 3rd and 4th Books of the *Politics*.

eulogy and censure. For the discussion of them will incidentally serve to indicate the means by which we shall ourselves be regarded as persons of a certain

p. 11.

moral character, (which, as we saw, is a second species of proof), since the same means will enable us to represent both ourselves and others as deserving of confidence in respect of virtue. And further, as eulogy is often jocular as well as serious, its subjects being not only men or gods but even inanimate things or any animals however insignificant, it is right to provide ourselves in the same manner with other propositions respecting these. Let us then treat of them too sufficiently for the purpose of illustration.

Definition of moral nobleness.

A thing is noble if, while it is desirable for its own sake, it is laudable, or if, while it is good, it is pleasant in virtue of its goodness.

Virtue.

This being the definition of nobleness, it follows that virtue is noble ; for, while it is good, it is also laudable[1]. By virtue is meant according to the popular idea a faculty of providing and preserving good things and a faculty of conferring many great benefits and indeed benefits of all kinds on all occasions. The elements of virtue are justice, valour, temperance, magnificence, magnanimity, liberality, gentleness, sagacity and speculative wisdom.

The several virtues.

Assuming then that virtue is a faculty of bene-

---

[1] It is only necessary to compare this off-hand definition of virtue with the definition given in *Nicom. Eth.* vi. ch. 10 and the discussion of particular virtues which follows it, to see how unphilosophical is Aristotle's treatment of ethical questions in a popular work like the *Rhetoric*.

ficence, we conclude at once that the greatest virtues are those which are in the highest degree serviceable to others. Accordingly none are so highly esteemed as valour and justice, the former being serviceable to others in war, and the latter both in war and in peace. Liberality comes next, as liberal people are always lavish and never contend with their neighbours in the race for wealth, which is the principal object of other men's desire. Justice is the virtue to which it is due that individuals possess their own property and possess it in accordance with the law, whereas to injustice it is due that they possess the property of others illegally. Valour is the virtue which inspires people to perform noble deeds and such as the law enjoins in the face of perils; its opposite is cowardice. Temperance *or continence* is the virtue which leads them to regard all bodily pleasures in the spirit enjoined by the law; and its opposite is licentiousness *or intemperance.* Liberality is the virtue of the beneficent use of money and is opposed to illiberality. Magnanimity is the virtue which inspires beneficent actions on a large scale[1], magnificence the virtue which produces grandeur in matters of expenditure, their opposites being pusillanimity and meanness. *Lastly,* sagacity is an intellectual virtue, rendering people capable judges of the things good and evil which I have described in their relation to happiness.

Virtue and vice in their general character and their constituents have now been discussed sufficiently for our present purpose. Nor is it difficult

Elements of moral nobleness (τὸ καλόν).

---

[1] Omitting μικροψυχία δὲ τοὐναντίον.

in the remaining cases to see the truth. It is clear
that whatever is productive of virtue, as tending
in a virtuous direction, and whatever results from
virtue must itself be noble; and by these I mean
the signs of virtue and its effects. And as the signs
and all such things as are the effects of good, ¹whether
active or passive, are noble, it follows that any effect
or sign of valour or any deed valiantly done must
be noble, and that just deeds and active effects of
justice must be noble too, not its passive effects
however: for justice is unlike all other virtues in
this, that the *adverb* "justly" has not always a noble
sense, but in the case of punishment inflicted it is
more disgraceful to be punished justly than unjustly.
It follows also that the same is true of the other
virtues. Again, a thing is noble, if its prize is
honour; or if its prize is honour rather than money;
or if it is a desirable thing and yet is not done from
selfish motives; or if it is good absolutely, like ²a
deed done for one's country without regard to oneself. *It is noble too*, if it is in its nature good, or

¹ Aristotle illustrates his own meaning by the examples
which follow. To inflict punishment justly would be an ἔργον
ἀρετῆς or "active effect of virtue"; to suffer it justly would be a
πάθος ἀρετῆς or "passive effect of virtue."

² Reading ὑπὲρ τῆς πατρίδος. The passage, as it stands, can
only be regarded as a striking example of the Greek way of
looking upon the individual as properly and absolutely a part of
his State. But it may be doubted whether services rendered to
the State should not constitute a special class of moral actions.
The true text ought then to be καὶ ὅσα ὑπὲρ τῆς πατρίδος τις
ἐποίησε, παριδὼν τὸ αὑτοῦ. καὶ τὰ ἁπλῶς ἀγαθά. καὶ τὰ τῇ φύσει
ἀγαθά, κ.τ.λ.

if it is not good only in relation to the individual, as individual interests are always selfish. Or again if it is something capable of enjoyment after death rather than in life; for there is more of selfishness in the enjoyments of life. Or if it is any work undertaken for the sake of others, as being less selfish. Or any service rendered to one's neighbours and not to oneself. Or a service rendered to one's benefactors, as being a just return. Or any beneficent action, as being unselfish in its object. Or the opposite of anything of which one is ashamed; for we are ashamed of saying or doing or intending to say or do anything shameful, as may be illustrated by the lines of Sappho in reply to the confession of Alcaeus that he would "fain speak, but shame forbade."

> "[1] If thou would'st say aught good or wise
> Nor meditate to speak some ill,
> Shame should not sit upon thine eyes
> But thou should'st rightly say thy will."

Or again anything about which we distress ourselves although without a sense of fear; for this is our natural attitude in regard to all such good things as conduce to reputation. The virtues and functions of the class which is naturally higher in the moral scale are themselves nobler, those of a man e.g. than those of a woman. The virtues which

Comparison of virtues.

---

[1] The reading of this Fragment, as given by Bergk, seems to be best.

αἰ δ' ἦχες ἔσλων ἵμερον ἢ κάλων,
καὶ μή τι Ϝείπην γλῶσσ' ἐκύκα κακόν,
αἴδως κέ σ' οὐ κίχανεν ὄμματ'
ἀλλ' ἔλεγες περὶ τῶ δικαίως.

afford gratification to our neighbours rather than
to ourselves *are the nobler;* hence the nobleness
of just conduct and of justice in the abstract. It
is nobler too to avenge ourselves upon our enemies
instead of making up our quarrels with them, partly
because retaliation is just and just conduct is noble,
and partly because a brave man should never be
beaten. Victory and honour may both be reckoned
as noble ; for they are desirable in spite of their
unproductiveness and are evidences of superiority in
virtue. Such things too as are memorable are noble,
and the nobler in proportion as they are more
memorable. [1]Such things as survive one's death,
or such as are attended by honour, or such as are
exceptional *are also noble.* Things of which one
is the sole possessor are nobler, as being more easily
remembered. So are all unproductive properties,
as being more gentlemanly. Again, a thing is noble
if it is a speciality of a certain class, or if it is an
indication of something admired among a particular
people as e.g. the practice of wearing the hair long
at Lacedaemon, as a sign of gentility ; for if a person
has long hair, he cannot easily do any menial work.
It is noble to abstain from all mechanical arts, as
gentility is incompatible with dependence upon
another. It is a good plan, if a person is in possession of certain qualities, to represent the qualities
which are nearly allied to these as being identical
with them, whether the object we have in view is

Rhetorical
artifices.

[1] These are not the same things as are mentioned, p. 30, l. 34,
but rather things, as e.g. glory, which, although they may be
enjoyed during life, are yet not terminated by death.

eulogy or censure, e.g. to represent a cautious person as cold and designing, a simpleton as a good worthy fellow, and a phlegmatic person as easy-tempered. [1] In fact, in every case we may take the nearest qualities and on the strength of them represent a person in the best light; if he is passionate e.g. or furious, calling him an honest fellow, if he is churlish, [2] proud and dignified, *and so on.* One who has any quality in excess *may be represented* as having the corresponding virtue, a foolhardy person e.g. as courageous, or a spendthrift as liberal ; for the statement will commend itself to ordinary minds and will at the same time lead to a fallacy by confusion of motives, since if a person shews a venturesome spirit without necessity, it will seem that he will do so *à fortiori* where his honour is concerned, and, if he is lavish in his dealings with strangers, *it will seem that he will be still more lavish* in his dealings with friends, as it is an excess of virtue to be everybody's benefactor.

Another point is to consider the audience in a panegyrical speech, for, as [3] Socrates said, it is easy enough to be the panegyrist of the Athenians

---

[1] Although it is convenient to begin a fresh sentence here, the construction is unbroken, and there should perhaps be a comma, instead of a full stop, after πρᾶον.

[2] Mr Cope naturally wishes for μεγαλόψυχον here, in place of μεγαλοπρεπῆ. Still Aristotle's definition of μεγαλοψυχία, p. 30, l. 10, would not suit the present passage. In the Platonic ὅροι μεγαλοπρέπεια is defined as ἀξίωσις κατὰ λογισμὸν ὀρθὸν τὸν σεμνότατον, and μεγαλοψυχία itself as μεγαλοπρέπεια ψυχῆς μετὰ λόγου.

[3] Plato, *Menexenus*, p. 235 D.

at Athens. It is proper to attribute *to the subject of the speech* such qualities as are held in honour among the particular people *to whom it is addressed*, whether they are Scythians or Lacedaemonians or philosophers. It is a good general rule to invest the qualities so held in honour with a character of moral nobleness, as what is honourable and what is noble seem to be closely allied.

A deed is noble, if it accords with expectation, e.g. if it is worthy of a person's lineage and antecedents, as there is a source of happiness and an element of nobleness in the acquisition of additional honour. It is the same if it exceeds expectation by attaining to a higher standard of goodness or nobleness, as when a person behaves with moderation in prosperity or preserves his elevation of mind in adversity or is better and more conciliatory as he increases in importance. Witness the saying of Iphicrates :

"How low I was! how great am I become!"

or the epigram upon the Olympian victor,

[1] "Once on my back I bore a heavy yoke,"

or [2] that of Simonides *upon the lady*,

"Whose father, husband, brethren all were kings."

---

[1] It may be doubted from this passage whether Aristotle would have agreed with some ancient authorities in attributing this epigram to Simonides.

[2] The epigram is given in full by Thucydides, vi. 59. Archediæ, who is the subject of it, was one who had preserved her moderation in prosperity,

ἣ πατρός τε καὶ ἀνδρὸς ἀδελφῶν τ' οὖσα τυράννων
παίδων τ' οὐκ ἤρθη νοῦν ἐς ἀτασθαλίην.

Again, as the subjects of eulogy are actions and it is characteristic of a virtuous person that he acts in accordance with a moral purpose, we must make it our endeavour to prove that the hero of our speech has a moral purpose in his actions. To this end it is useful that he should be shewn to have frequently acted *in the same way*. Accordingly mere coincidences and happy accidents should be represented as actions of deliberate purpose; for if a large number of similar actions are alleged, there will seem to be here a sign of virtue and moral purpose.

Eulogy is speech setting forth magnitude of virtue. It is the business then *of an orator in eulogy* to demonstrate that the actions of his hero are virtuous. But a panegyric has reference to accomplished results, and the attendant circumstances, such as rank and education, are merely confirmatory from the natural presumption that the children of virtuous parents will be virtuous, and that the recipient of a good education will be good. [1] Hence when we pronounce a panegyric upon anyone, we pronounce it for something that he has already done. But the accomplished results are *praised as being* indications of the moral state; for we should eulogize a person even without his actual performance of the deeds, if we believed him to be capable of performing them. Felicitation and congratulation, *it may be observed*, although themselves identical, are not identical with eulogy and panegyric; still,

Definition of eulogy.

Distinction between eulogy and panegyric.

Felicitation and congratulation.

[1] The διὸ follows from the words τὸ δ' ἐγκώμιον τῶν ἔργων ἐστίν, the intervening words being unnecessary to the conclusion.

5—2

as virtue is included in happiness, so are these included in congratulation.

There is a community in kind however between eulogy and counsel, inasmuch as the suggestions which you would make in giving counsel may by a change of expression be rendered panegyrical.   Thus as we have ascertained the points of good conduct and character, it is only necessary to change and shift the form of expression in order to put them forward as suggestions. Let us take as an ¹example the sentiment that we ought not to be proud of what Fortune has done for us but only of what we have done for ourselves. Put it so, and it is virtually a suggestion. But put it in this way, "Proud not of what Fortune has done for him but of what he has done for himself," and the sentence becomes eulogistic. We arrive then at the following rule, that, if eulogy is your object, you should consider what you would suggest, if suggestion, you should consider what you would eulogize. But the expression will be contradictory *in the two cases*, ²when the prohibitive and the non-prohibitive elements are interchanged.

Again, there are various means of exaggeration to be employed. It may be said e.g. that our hero is the only person or the first to have done a particular deed or has been almost single-handed or the chief agent in doing it, all these being points which enhance

¹ The example is taken from two passages of Isocrates, *Panath.* § 35 and *Evag.* § 52.

² In the "suggestive" form of expression pride is prohibited, in the "eulogistic" it is not prohibited but rather enjoined.

the nobleness of the deed.　Then there are the circumstances of time and opportunity, if they exceed
reasonable expectation.　There may be the fact that
he has been often successful in the same undertaking ; a fact which not only increases its importance but is calculated to convey the impression
that the success has not been an accidental result
but has been due to his own exertions.　Or it may
be the case that especial incentives and distinctions
have been devised or were instituted in his honour.
Or that he is the first person who was the subject
of a panegyric, like [1] Hippolochus, or the *first for whom
some special compliment was devised, like* the erec-
tion of a statue in the market-place for Harmodius
and Aristogiton.　And what is true of signal distinctions is not less true of their opposites.

Further, if you cannot find much to say about Compari-
your hero himself, it is proper to contrast him with son.
other people, after the manner which [2] Isocrates
adopted owing to his inexperience in forensic oratory.　But the persons with whom you compare him
must be persons of reputation, as superiority .to
persons who are *confessedly* virtuous lends new
dignity and nobleness to the character.　Exaggeration naturally finds a place in eulogies ; for it is a
means of establishing superiority, and superiority
is one kind of nobleness.　It follows that, even if
you cannot compare your hero with persons of

---

[1] Nothing is known, except from this passage, of Hippolochus.

[2] It seems most probable that Aristotle regarded Isocrates
as having introduced into his forensic speeches the habit of comparison which was better adapted to panegyrical orations.

reputation, yet it is best to compare him with some other persons, as superiority is taken to indicate virtue.

The characteristics of the three kinds of Rhetoric. It may be laid down as a general rule that, of the characteristics which are common to the three styles of Rhetoric, exaggeration is most appropriate to the epideictical style—for as the facts are taken for granted *in this style*, it only remains to invest them with grandeur and dignity—examples to the deliberative style, as in this we divine and infer the future from the past; and enthymemes to the forensic style, as in this the obscurity of the facts leaves the largest room for deduction and demonstration.

So much then for the general materials of eulogy and censure, the proper objects to be observed in both and the sources of panegyric or abuse. For having ascertained the one we can at once see their opposites, as the materials of censure are exactly opposed to those of eulogy.

Chap. X. Forensic Rhetoric. Accusation and defence. The three points. Coming now to accusation and defence, we have next to describe the number and nature of the materials proper for the construction of the syllogisms. There are three points which we have to ascertain, viz. (1) the nature and number of the objects of crime, (2) the dispositions of the criminals, and (3) the character and condition of the victims. But in the first instance it is necessary to define crime.

Definition of crime. Crime may be said to be injury voluntarily inflicted in defiance of the law. But law may be either particular or universal. I mean by "particular" the

written law which regulates the life of the citizens Particular and uni-
in any polity and by "universal" the unwritten prin- versal law.
ciples which may be said to be universally recognized.

Voluntary action is all such action as is performed Voluntary action.
with knowledge and not under compulsion. Now an
action may be voluntarily performed without being
deliberately purposed; but if it is done of deliberate
purpose, it is always done knowingly, as nobody is
ignorant of his own purposes.

The causes of a deliberate purpose to commit Causes of a disposition
injury and to do evil in defiance of the law are vice to commit crime.
and incontinence. For if there are certain people
who have vicious habits, whether one or several, it
is in the particular respect in which they are vicious
that they are apt to commit crimes,—an illiberal
person e.g. in respect of money, a licentious person
in his sensual pleasures, an effeminate person in his
luxuries, a coward in dangers, by leaving his com-
rades in the lurch from personal fear, an ambitious
person from the love of honour, a passionate person
from anger, an emulous person from the love of
victory, a vindictive person to gratify his revenge, a
foolish person from his mistaken notion of justice and
injustice, a shameless person from disregard of public
opinion, 'and so each individual in respect of his own
particular subject.

This is a matter however which will be sufficiently
clear partly from the description already given of the p. 60.
several virtues and partly from the remarks which we
shall have occasion to make when we come to discuss pp. 115 sqq.
the emotions. It remains for us now to describe the

---

1 Putting only a comma after δόξης.

objects of crime, the conditions under which people commit it and its victims.

(I) The objects of crime.

Let us begin with a classification of the objects, the attainment or avoidance of which is the motive inciting to crime. For it is clearly the duty of the prosecutor to consider the nature and number of such of these objects as are present to his [1] adversary and that of the defendant to consider the nature and number of such as are not present to him.

Causes of human action.

All our actions are either due to ourselves or not. If they are not, they are either due to chance or else arise from necessity, and, if necessary, are done either under compulsion or by nature. The result is that all such actions as are not due to ourselves are done either by chance or by nature or under compulsion. Actions on the other hand which are due to ourselves and of which we ourselves are the authors may be due either to habit or to impulse and, if to the latter, either to rational or irrational impulse. [2] The one of these is the wish, which is an impulse towards good; for nobody wishes a thing, unless he conceives it to be good; the irrational impulses are e.g. anger and desire.

[3] To sum up then; all our actions are necessarily due to seven causes, viz. chance, nature, compulsion,

----

[1] Omitting as unnecessary the words ὧν ἐφιέμενοι πάντες τοὺς πλησίον ἀδικοῦσι.

[2] There is no need to insert βούλησις δ' as in Bekker's text, although it makes the meaning a little plainer.

[3] It would be better to put a full stop after ἐπιθυμία, as the sentence beginning ὥστε πάντα ὅσα πράττουσιν sums up the results of the two preceding sections.

habit, [1] reasoning, passion and desire. It is superfluous to make a further classification of actions
according to periods of life or moral states or any
other occurrences ; for if it happens as a matter of
fact that the young have quick tempers and strong
desires, yet it is not their youth but anger or desire
which is the cause of their passionate and sensual
actions. Nor again can wealth and poverty be described as causes of action ; it happens as a matter of
fact that the poor from their indigence are desirous of
money and that the rich from their abundance desire
the pleasures of luxury, but in these cases as before
the cause of the actions will be not wealth and
poverty but their desire. The same is true of persons
who are just or unjust and of others whose actions are
said to be regulated by their moral states; it will be
either reason or emotion which is the cause of their
actions, although in some cases good characters and
emotions, and in others the reverse. Still it is the
fact that particular qualities are the accompaniments
of particular moral states. No sooner, it may be
said, is a person temperate than in virtue of his
temperance good opinions and desires in regard to
pleasures wait upon him, while contrary opinions
and desires in regard to pleasures wait upon one
who is destitute of self-restraint. It is right therefore, while we abandon such classifications as have
been mentioned, to consider the connexion of particular qualities with particular classes; for although
a person may be fair or dark, tall or short without
any of the qualities in question regularly following,

---

[1] λογισμός is equivalent to λογιστικὴ ὄρεξις of l. 20.

yet it does necessarily make a difference whether
he is young or old or just or unjust. And it is right
to consider generally all such accidental circumstances
as produce differences of moral character. It will
make a difference e.g. to a person whether he believes
himself to be rich or poor, fortunate or unfortunate.
Postponing then this question for the present, let
us first proceed to the points which still remain.

The causes of actions considered: (1) chance, [1]A thing is the result of chance, if its cause is
indeterminate and if it is not directed to any object
or does not occur invariably or usually or by any
regular law, as indeed is evident from the definition
of chance.

(2) nature, It may be said to occur by nature, if its cause
is self-contained and regular; for then it happens
invariably or usually in the same way. For we need
not endeavour to determine accurately whether vio-
lations of the law of Nature happen in accordance
with some natural law or with another cause, although
the more probable view is that such occurrences are
also caused by chance.

(3) compulsion, Again, a thing is said to be done under compulsion, if it is done against the desire or rational faculties of the agents themselves.

(4) habit, It is done by habit, if the reason for doing it
is that it has been often done by the same person
before.

---

[1] The early chapters of the Second Book of the φυσικὴ ἀκρόασις should be studied in connexion with this passage. The
distinction between ἡ τύχη and τὸ αὐτόματον, which is there emphasized, would be out of place in a popular treatise like the
Rhetoric.

To the influence of reason may be ascribed all such actions as have an air of expediency in accordance with the catalogue of goods already given, whether as ends or as means to ends, when it is the expediency which is the cause of the action—*a limitation which is necessary*, inasmuch as it sometimes happens that the actions of persons who have no self-restraint are expedient, although the cause of them is not their expediency, but pleasure. *(5) reason, pp. 39 sqq.*

Passion and anger are the causes of revengeful acts. There is a distinction, *it may be observed*, between revenge and punishment; for the object of punishment is the reformation of the sufferer, and that of revenge the gratification of the agent. *(6) anger,*

The nature of anger will be seen in our treatment of the emotions. *p. 115.*

Desire is the cause of all such actions as appear pleasant, and among them of actions with which we are familiar or to which we are habituated; for there are many things, even such as are not naturally pleasant, which we do with pleasure after habituation. *(7) desire.*

In a word then all such actions as are due to ourselves are either good or apparently good or pleasant or apparently pleasant. And further, as actions which are due to ourselves are done voluntarily and actions which are not due to ourselves are done involuntarily, it follows that all voluntary actions must be either good or apparently good or pleasant or apparently pleasant; for I reckon as a good the deliverance from evils either real or apparent or the exchange of a greater evil for a smaller one, as being events which are in a certain sense desirable, and on the same principle I reckon as a pleasure the deliverance from painful things whether real or apparent, or the exchange of a greater pain for a smaller one. It is necessary then to ascertain the number and character of such things as are expedient or pleasant. It follows that, as expediency has been already discussed under the head of deliberative oratory, we have now to discuss pleasure. But we must regard our definitions as satisfactory, if upon any point they are neither obscure nor yet exact.

CHAP. XI.
Definition of pleasure.

Let us assume that pleasure is a certain motion of the soul and a sudden and sensible settling *of the soul* into its normal and natural state; and that pain is the opposite.

Pleasures and pains.

Such being the nature of pleasure, it is evident that everything which tends to produce the condition described is itself pleasant, and everything which tends to destroy it or produce a settling of an opposite kind is painful. It follows at once then that the return to the natural condition is generally pleasant, [1] and never so pleasant as when the processes of nature have attained their full natural development. It follows also that habits *are pleasant;* for that to which we are habituated becomes, as being so, virtually natural, as habit is in a certain sense a second nature, owing to the close connexion between the usual, which is the sphere of habit, and

[1] The meaning is apparently that the pleasure is keenest when not only the general laws of Nature but the bye-laws of one's own individual nature have been satisfied.

the invariable, which is the sphere of Nature. Again, anything that is not done under compulsion *is pleasant*, as compulsion is a violation of Nature. Accordingly all necessity is painful, as has been truly said [1]

> "Need-be is evermore a thing of pain."

Acts of attention too or serious effort or strong exertion must be painful, as they involve necessity and compulsion, unless one is habituated to them, in which case habit renders them pleasant. The opposites of these are pleasant. Accordingly all conditions of ease, comfort or inattention, amusements, recreations and sleep may be reckoned as pleasures, none of these having a character of necessity. Anything of which we have a natural desire is pleasant ; for desire itself is an impulse to pleasure. But desires may be either rational or irrational. I describe as irrational desires all such as do not spring from any definite theory, meaning all natural desires, as they are called, such as those of which the body is the necessary instrument, e.g. the desire of food, viz. hunger and thirst [2] and so on, or desires of the taste, of sexual love and of the touch in all its forms or of the smell, the hearing and the sight. Rational desires on the other hand are all such as originate in conviction, as there are many things which we are desirous of seeing and acquiring from the report of them and from a conviction *of their excellence*. *Rational and irrational desires.*

---

[1] The saying is attributed to Evenus of Paros.
[2] Omitting τροφῆς and in l. 14 εὐωδίας.

As pleasure then consists in the sensation of some emotion, and impression is a kind of feeble sensation, [1]memory or anticipation must be attended by a certain impression of the object remembered or anticipated. If this is so, it is clear that, as there is sensation, there are accompanying pleasures also in memory and anticipation. Consequently, all pleasant things must consist either in the sensation, if they are present, or in the memory, if they are past, or in the anticipation, if they are future; for the present is the object of sensation, the past of memory and the future of anticipation. Now the objects of recollection are pleasant not only if they were pleasant at the actual time at which they happened but in some cases even if they were not pleasant, provided that the consequence of them has been noble and good.

Pleasures of anticipation or memory.

Hence the lines

[2]"Tis pleasant to remember ills survived"

and

[3]"For there is after-pleasure e'en in woes
For one remembering toils and troubles past,"

---

[1] Upon the whole there seems to be no sufficient reason for changing the reading or punctuation of the passage. It is true that the apodosis, κὰν τῷ μεμνημένῳ κ.τ.λ. is not a legitimate conclusion from the clauses of the protasis; but this is often, if not generally, the case in Aristotle. It is his object here to extend the meaning of pleasure from the actually pleasurable sensation of the moment to the remembrance of past or the anticipation of future sensations. Cp. φυσικὴ ἀκρόασις, vii. ch. 3, p. 274 A sqq.

[2] From the *Andromeda* of Euripides.

[3] Homer, *Odyssey*, xv. 400—1; but in the Homeric text the second line runs thus :

ὅστις δὴ μάλα πολλὰ πάθῃ καὶ πόλλ' ἐπαληθῇ.

the reason being that the mere deliverance from evil is pleasant. The objects of anticipation are pleasant, if their presence appears to be a source of great delight or benefit and of such benefit as is unattended by pain. In fact it is a general rule that whatever by its presence is a source of delight is usually a source of delight in anticipation or recollection. It is thus that there is a pleasure in being angry, as appears e. g. from Homer's description of passion

[1]" Far sweeter than the flowing stream of honey."

For nobody is angry with those who are evidently beyond the reach of revenge or greatly superior to himself in power; [2] or, if we are angry with them at all, our anger is mitigated. In the great majority of desires too there is some attendant pleasure, as we experience a certain sort of pleasure either from the recollection of past, or from the anticipation of future enjoyment. Thus fever-patients derive a pleasure from their thirsty moments by the recollection of past, or the anticipation of future draughts. Lovers too find a pleasure in talking or writing about the object of their love or in ever doing something of which he is the object, as in all this their recollection of him seems to them to amount to actual sensation. It is indeed ever the beginning of affection to find pleasure not only in a person's presence but in the recollection of him too when he is away. And accordingly even when the loss of his presence is pain-

---

[1] *Iliad*, xviii. 108—110. The word which Homer uses is not θυμός but χόλος.

[2] It is necessary to insert ἀλλ', as in Bekker's text.

ful to us, there is still a kind of pleasure arising
in our very regrets and lamentations; for although
there is pain in the loss of him, yet is there a
pleasure in recollecting him and almost seeing him
and his very actions and the manner of man that
he was. Hence the appropriateness of the words

[1]" He spake and in them stirred the love of tears."

Other
pleasures.
Again, there is a pleasure in revenge. For where
failure is painful, success is pleasant; and as angry
men are pained beyond all measure by the failure
to gratify their revenge, they are equally delighted by
the anticipation of it.

Victory too is pleasant, pleasant to us all, not
only to those who always hate to be beaten. The
reason is that we experience an impression of superiority, and superiority is an object of desire to all
in a less or a greater degree. And from the pleasure
of victory follows the pleasure of all amusements
which are contests of strength or wit, as they afford
many opportunities of victory, games of knuckle-
bones or tennis or dice or draughts. The same remark applies to serious amusements; they either
become pleasant by habit or are pleasant from the
first, as e.g. the chase and every variety of field-
sports; for wherever there is competition, there is
victory. This too is the explanation of the pleasure
which the Bar and the Debating Society afford to
all experienced and able speakers.

---

[1] A line which occurs more than once in the Homeric poems,
e.g. *Iliad*, xxiii. 108, when Achilles has seen and sought to hold
the shade of Patroclus, *Odyssey*, iv. 113 when Menelaus has told
to Telemachus the tale of his sorrow for Odysseus.

Again, there are few things so pleasant as honour and a good reputation; for the consequence of possessing them is an impression that one is a virtuous sort of person, especially if this is the opinion of those in whose judgment one has confidence, i.e. of neighbours rather than of those who live at a distance, of friends and fellow-citizens rather than of strangers, of contemporaries rather than of posterity, of sensible people rather than of fools, of a number of people rather than of a few, as these classes of people are more likely to form a true judgment than their opposites. *It is necessary however that the classes should be capable of judging;* for if they are such as one regards with a strong contempt, e.g. as children or animals, there is no regard paid to their respect or opinion, at least for its own sake or unless for some independent reason.

There is pleasure too in a friend; for love [1] is pleasant—nobody e.g. can be said to be a lover of wine who does not find pleasure in it—and it is pleasant to be the object of another's love, as here again one has an impression of possessing a good character, which is the desire of every sentient being. But to be loved is to be esteemed for one's own sake.

Again, it is pleasant to be an object of admiration, if only for the esteem which it implies.

Again, there is a pleasure in flattery and in a flatterer, as a flatterer is ostensibly an admirer and friend. Or in frequent repetition of the same actions; for habit, as has been already said, is pleasant. Or p. 76.

---

[1] There is a difficulty here, as elsewhere, in translating φιλεῖν, where it varies between "loving" and "liking."

again in change, as being a return to Nature; for perpetual uniformity produces an excess of the normal state. Hence the saying[1], "Change ever is delight." This is the reason why occasional visitors or occasional events are always pleasant, as not only do they imply a change from the existing condition, but the occasional is *necessarily* rare *and therefore pleasant.* Wonder and learning too are generally pleasant; wonder, because it necessarily involves the desire of learning, and therefore the wonderful is an object of desire, and learning, because it involves a settling[2] into a person's proper natural condition. Again, it is pleasant to receive benefits or to confer them; for the former implies the satisfaction of our desires, and the latter implies possession and superiority, which are both natural objects of ambition. And as the power of conferring benefits is pleasant, it follows that there is a pleasure in setting up our neighbours again *after a failure* and in[3] supplying such deficiencies *as are seen in them.* From the pleasure of learning and wonder it results that there is a pleasure in such things as the imitative[4] arts, e.g.

---

[1] Euripides, *Orestes*, 228.

[2] The reason assigned here for the pleasure found in learning accords with the definition of pleasure at the beginning of the chapter. But it strikingly shews the Aristotelian sense of φύσις as "the perfect or normal state of anything," the fifth of the senses of φύσις distinguished by Sir A. Grant in his note on *Nicom. Eth.* ii. ch. 1.

[3] Perhaps the words καὶ τὸ τὰ ἐλλιπῆ ἐπιτελεῖν are not in place here; they occur again p. 41, l. 25.

[4] It can hardly be doubted that τὸ μιμούμενον is transitive and not, as Mr Cope supposes, passive in its meaning. The first

painting, sculpture and poetry, or in any successful imitative work, even if the actual object of imitation is not pleasant; as it is not the pleasantness of the object which produces the pleasure but an inference[1] from the copy to the original and in consequence of it a kind of learning. Catastrophes *in tragic plays* and hairbreadth escapes from perils are all pleasant, as being all wonderful.

Further, as what is natural is always pleasant, and things which are cognate have a natural relation to each other, it is a general rule that all such things as are cognate and similar are pleasant to each other, e.g. a man to a man, a horse to a horse, and a youth to a youth. Hence the proverbial sayings, "Crabbed age and youth," "Like to like[2]," "One beast knows another," "Birds of a feather" and the like. But as things which are similar and cognate are pleasant to each other, and every[3] one stands in this relation preeminently to himself, the result is that all people are lovers of self in a higher or lower degree; for all the conditions of self-love exist preeminently in the relation of an individual to himself. And all people being lovers of their own selves, the result is that

chapter of the *Poetic* illustrates the conception of Poetry as an imitative art.

[1] For the nature of the inference see *Poetic*, ch. 4. It is not, I think, the discovery of some new quality or feature in the object imitated, but the recognition that the copy is the same thing as, or in other words is an imitation of, the original.

[2] The Homeric line (*Odyssey* xvii. 218) is in full

ὡς αἰεὶ τὸν ὅμοιον ἄγει θεὸς ὡς τὸν ὅμοιον.

[3] The words πρὸς ἑαυτὸν ἕκαστος τοῦτο πέπονθεν are equivalent to ἕκαστος ἑαυτῷ ὅμοιος καὶ συγγενής ἐστι.

they all find pleasure in such things as are their own, their own works, their own sayings *and so on.* This[1] is the reason why people are generally so fond of flattery or love or honour or again of their children as being their own works. Hence too the pleasure of supplying the deficiencies of others; for then the work becomes what it was not before, our own.

Again, as it is an especial pleasure to be a ruler, a reputation for wisdom is pleasant; for practical wisdom is a commanding faculty, and speculative wisdom the knowledge of many marvels. Again, as ambition is an almost universal quality, it follows that there is a certain pleasure in censuring[2] others, *as censure necessarily implies superiority,* or[3] in dwelling upon the points in which one appears to the best advantage, according to the lines[4] of Euripides

> "To that he presses,
> To that he gives the flower of every day,
> Wherein himself doth show most excellent."

Similarly, as amusement and relaxation of every kind

---

[1] Although the four objects of natural affection or desire are placed as parallels, there is really a difference between the first three and the last. A man is fond of his children, because, as Aristotle says, they are in a sense his productions, his works. But he is fond of flattery or love or honour as being a recognition or appreciation of himself and his works.

[2] The etymological play upon the words φιλότιμοι and ἐπι-τιμᾶν, which constitutes the point or argument of the sentence, can hardly be preserved in English.

[3] Changing the full stop after εἶναι to a comma.

[4] The lines here quoted from the *Antiopa* of Euripides appear, although not without some slight variation, in the *Gorgias* of Plato, p. 484 E, where a full discussion of them will be found in Dr Thompson's note.

and humour are pleasant, it is clear that what is humorous, whether a person or tale or circumstance, is also pleasant. But the subject of humour has been separately treated in my book[1] on *Poetry*.

We may content ourselves then with this discussion of pleasures, and it is easy to discover pains by a consideration of their opposites.

The objects of crime being such as I have described, it remains to consider the conditions under which crime is committed and its victims.

CHAP. XII.
Crime
continued.

As to the agents, the conditions under which we commit crime are when we believe that the deed is possible and possible to us, whether it is our belief that we shall escape detection or that, if detected, we shall not be punished or that we shall be punished, but the penalty will not be equivalent to the advantage gained by ourselves or by our friends.

(II) The conditions under which crimes are committed.

The character of such deeds as are apparently possible or impossible *in the abstract* will be described hereafter, [2]as it is a subject equally appropriate to all the three kinds of Rhetoric. But taking the personal view, we believe we are most likely to succeed in committing crimes without incurring any penalty, if we are able speakers and men of action and large forensic experience and if we have a great number of friends and large property. This belief is strongest, if we are ourselves in possession of the advantages I have described; but, failing this, *it*

---

[1] Not in the *Poetic*, as it exists at present; but perhaps in a Second Book, which has been lost.

[2] τὸ δυνατὸν καὶ ἀδύνατον is the first of the κοινοὶ τύποι discussed in Bk. ii. ch. 19.

exists also, if we have friends or subordinates or associates who possess them, as we are thereby enabled to commit crimes and to escape detection and punishment. It is the same if we are the personal friends of our victims or of the judges ; for our friends are not on their guard against criminal injury at our hands and, *when the crime has been committed*, are disposed to reconciliation without prosecuting us on account of it, and the judges show partiality to their friends and either absolutely acquit them or inflict a merely nominal penalty.

Persons are likely to escape detection, if their character or condition is inconsistent with the crime alleged, as e.g. an invalid in a case of assault and battery, or an ugly pauper in a case of adultery. *Actions are likely to escape detection*, if they are excessively patent and public, as nobody would anticipate them and consequently nobody is on his guard against them ; or if they are of a magnitude and character passing anybody's audacity, as in this case too nobody is on his guard ; for everyone is on his guard against ordinary crimes as against ordinary illnesses, but nobody takes precautions *against extraordinary crimes any more than* against an illness which has never yet attacked any human being. Again, *people think to commit crimes with impunity*, if they have no enemies or a great number of enemies ; for in the first case they hope to escape detection, because nobody is on his guard against them, and in the second they actually do escape it, because nobody suspects them of being likely to make an assault upon people who are already on

their guard and they are able to plead in their
defence the improbability of their having attempted
such a thing. The same is the case, if they have
any plan[1] or place of concealment or any easy means
of disposing *of their stolen goods*. Or if in case of
detection they are able to evade or postpone the
trial or in some way or other to corrupt the judges.
Or if, when mulcted in a certain sum, they can evade
the payment or postpone it for a considerable time.
Or[2] if they are so poor that they have nothing to
lose. Or if, while their gains are clear or considerable or immediate, their penalties are trifling or
uncertain or remote. Or if there is no penalty com-
mensurate with the *prospective* advantage, as e.g.
in the case of tyranny. Or if the result of the crime
is pecuniary gain, and the punishment nothing but
disgrace. Or, conversely, if the crime is such as is
calculated to win a certain measure of applause, as
e.g. if in committing it one had the fortune, like Zeno[3],
to exact vengeance for one's father or mother, but
the punishment takes the form of a fine or exile
or something of the kind. Both these are objects
and conditions of criminal action ; only in persons
not of the same but of different characters.

Again, people are guilty of crimes, if they have
often escaped detection or punishment. Or if they

---

[1] Reading ἢ τρόποις ἢ τόποις upon the best MSS. authority.

[2] The insertion of εἰ is unnecessary, if this sentence is grammatically connected with the last, as εἴ τις may well be supplied
as a subject of ἕξει from the preceding οἷς, which is equivalent to
εἴ τισι.

[3] Nothing is really known about the case of Zeno.

have often been unsuccessful ; for in crime as well as in war there are some people who are ever ready to renew the battle. Or if the pleasure is immediate and the pain is subsequent, or the gain immediate and the punishment subsequent ; for such is the natural conduct of all incontinent people, and there is incontinence about any object of human ambition. Or on the other hand if the pain or punishment is immediate *and momentary*, and the pleasure and profit subsequent and more lasting ; for this is the aim of all such people as are continent and comparatively sagacious in character. Or if it is possible that their actions[1] will appear to be the result of chance or necessity or nature or habit and in general to be errors rather than crimes. Or if there is a prospect of their receiving an equitable consideration *from the judges*. Or if they feel a deficiency, whether it is a necessity of life that they lack, like the poor, or a superfluity, like the rich. Or if their reputation stands exceedingly high or exceedingly low, as in the one case they will not be suspected of the crime and in the other will not be more strongly suspected than before.

Such then being the conditions under which criminals attempt to commit crimes, I come now to consider the victims and the crimes themselves.

(III) The victims of crime.

The victims of crime are people who are in possession of the advantages which we ourselves require,

---

[1] It will be noticed that this passage differs from p. 35, ll. 14 sqq. in distinguishing compulsory actions (δι' ἀνάγκην) from natural (διὰ φύσιν) and in apparently classing habitual actions (δι' ἔθος) among those which are there regarded as involuntary.

whether in the way of the necessaries of life or of
excess or luxury. Nor does it matter whether they
are near to us or far removed ; for in the one case
the acquisition is speedy and in the other the vengeance is slow, as e.g. if we plunder the Carthaginians.
Or people who are trustful rather than cautious or
suspicious, as it is always easy to escape their notice.
Or indolent people, as a person must be ready to
take trouble, if he wishes to prosecute a criminal. Or
sensitive people, as they are not disposed to fight for
gain. Or people who have been the victims of many
crimes without revenging themselves, such people
being in the proverbial phrase "Mysians' prey[1]." Or
people whom we have never injured before or have
often injured ; for both will be off their guard, the
former from an idea that they will never be injured,
and the latter from an idea that they could not be
injured any more. Or people who have become un-
popular or who are liable to unpopularity, as such
people have neither the will to prosecute for fear of
the judges nor, *if they do prosecute*, the power of
convincing them ; and among such people are those
who are the objects of hatred or envy. Or again
people whom we have an excuse for injuring, because
they or their ancestors or friends either inflicted or

---

[1] It is clear that the contempt felt for the Mysians, as for the
Carians, shows itself in this proverb. Yet the origin of it is
involved in obscurity. M. St Hilaire understands it as meaning
literally "people so feeble that even the Mysians could prey
upon them." The usual explanation, which has the authority of
Suidas and Harpocration, is that the Mysians, owing to their
feebleness or defencelessness, were themselves the prey of their
enemies.

intended to inflict injury either upon ourselves or our ancestors or those who are dear to us; for villainy, according to the proverb, only waits for an excuse. Or our enemies, because it is so pleasant, or our friends, because it is so easy, to injure them. Or people who have no friends. Or people who are not great as orators or as men of action; for such people either make no attempt to prosecute or *soon* come to terms or, *if they do prosecute*, achieve no success. Or people whom it does not pay to waste their time in waiting either for trial or for payment, such as foreigners and peasant proprietors; for they are ready to patch up a quarrel on easy terms and make no difficulty about abandoning *the prosecution*. Or people who have committed many crimes or crimes akin to those of which they are the victims; for it is hardly regarded as a case of criminal action, if a person is the victim of a crime such as that of which he was himself habitually the author, as e.g. if an assault[1] is committed upon a man who has been habitually guilty of outrageous insolence. Or people who have either done or intended or intend to do or will in the future do us injury; for then the criminal action has an element not only of pleasure but of morality and looks almost as if it were not a crime at all. Or people whose[2] injury will be a gratification either to

---

[1] αἰκία and ὕβρις are both offences recognized by Attic law, the former, which was the less serious, being the subject of a δίκη or civil action, the latter of a γραφή or public prosecution.

[2] The construction is harsh; for οἷς must be taken as an instrumental dative. It is, as Spengel says "idem ac si dixisset καὶ οὒς ἀδικοῦντες χαριοῦνται ἢ φίλοις."

our friends or to the objects of our respect or affection or to our masters or to any one upon whom our own life depends. Or people in relation to whom we may hope for an equitable consideration *from the judges*. Or people against whom we have a cause of complaint and with whom we have had a difference before, as in the example of Callippus[1] in the case of Dion ; for a crime so committed seems to approximate to not being a crime at all. Or if people would soon be the victims of the crimes of others, unless they were the victims of ours, *we commit the crimes* on the plea that no time is left for deliberation, in the spirit of Ænesidemus who, as the story[2] goes, sent the cottabus-prize to Gelo after his success in reducing *Gela* to slavery, implying that Gelo had only forestalled him, as it had been his own intention to do the same. Or again if after injuring people criminally we shall have many opportunities of treating them justly, *we commit the crime* in the belief that we shall soon make amends, according to the saying of the Thessalian[3] Jason that it is a duty to do some acts of injustice in order to have the power of doing many acts of justice.

A crime is natural, if it is universal or *at least* usual ; for then we may expect to be pardoned for Circumstances which facilitate crime.

[1] The story is told in Mr Cope's note; but if it is the story which Aristotle had in mind, it would hardly seem that Callippus had any good reason for regarding himself as "having a cause of complaint" against Dion.

[2] See Mr Cope's note. This passage would naturally suggest that speed as well as skill was an element of the popular game known as κότταβος.

[3] Jason of Pheræ.

committing it. Or if *the articles stolen* admit of easy concealment, e.g. if they are such as are rapidly consumed, like eatables. Or if they can be easily disguised by new shapes or colours or mixtures, or easily put out of sight in many different places, e.g. if they are portable and can be hidden away in holes and corners. Or if the criminal has already many things indistinguishable from them or closely resembling them in his possession. Or if the deed is one which the victims are ashamed to publish, such as an outrage committed upon the women of one's family or oneself or one's sons. Or if it is a case in which a prosecutor would be looked upon as litigious, e.g. if the act in question is unimportant or pardonable.

CHAP. XIII. Classification of actions.

Such then being the usual conditions of crime, the nature of criminal actions and the victims and motives, let us now proceed to the classification of all actions whether just or unjust.

Our first consideration is the following. Just and unjust actions admit of a twofold division, according as they are considered relatively to the laws[1] or to the persons affected by them.

Particular and universal law.

[2]I regard law as either particular or universal,

[1] Omitting δύο.

[2] There is a discrepancy of language, which deserves to be cleared up, between this passage and the beginning of ch. 10. Aristotle there describes law as either (a) particular (ἴδιος) or (β) universal (κοινός), defining "particular" law as the statutes of any given state, and "universal" law as the unwritten but universally recognised principles of morality (ὅσα ἄγραφα παρὰ πᾶσιν ὁμολογεῖσθαι δοκεῖ. Cp. Sophocles, *Antigone*, 450 sqq.). The "universal" or "unwritten" law of ch. 10 is the "universal" law or "law of

meaning by 'particular' the law ordained by a particular people for their own purposes, and capable of subdivision into written and unwritten law, and by 'universal' the law of Nature. For there exists, as all men divine more or less, a natural and universal principle of right and wrong, independent of any mutual intercourse or compact; the principle to which Antigone in Sophocles is made to appeal, when she avows that it is right to bury Polynices in defiance *of Creon's edict*, because this is right according to the law of Nature

> "Not of to-day nor yesterday
> Is this a law, but ever hath it life,
> And no man knoweth whence it came or how."

It is in the same sense that Empedocles[1] lays down his prohibition of putting any living thing to death; this (he says) is not right in one land and wrong in another

> "But the law universal evermore
> Pervades the omnipotent heaven and boundless earth."

So too Alcidamas[2] in his Messenian oration.

Nature" here, but "particular" law is here subdivided into (*a*) "written" law, which is, as before, the statutes of a particular State, and (*b*) "unwritten" which is such equitable considerations, derived from custom, social relations, &c., as are recognized for the time being in a community and serve as corrections or adjustments of the written law. (See infra, p. 47, l. 12, and cp. Plato, *Laws*, vii. p. 793, c and D.) For the "laws of custom" (οἱ κατὰ τὰ ἔθη νόμοι) are ἔτι κυριώτεροι καὶ περὶ κυριωτέρων τῶν κατὰ γράμματα νόμων (*Politics*, iii. ch. 16, p. 1287 B_5).

[1] In his didactic poem Περὶ Φύσεως.

[2] The sentence is apparently incomplete; but if the words quoted by the Scholiast are the true ones, ἐλευθέρους ἀφῆκε πάντας ὁ Θεός, οὐδένα δοῦλον ἡ φύσις πεποίηκεν, they form an ex-

Again, there is a twofold division of actions relatively to the persons affected by them. Actions proper to be done or left undone may have reference either to the community or to some individual member of it. And accordingly just and unjust actions may be also of two kinds, referring either to a particular individual or to the community; for adultery and assault are crimes against particular persons, but the refusal of military service is a crime against the State.

All unjust or criminal actions then may be classified and distinguished as relative either to the community or to some individual or individuals. But, before we proceed, let us define once again what it is to be the victim of a crime. It is to suffer criminal injury at the hands of a voluntary agent; for the p. 70. voluntary character of crime has been already determined. We have seen too that the victim of crime must suffer injury and must suffer it involuntarily. The various kinds of injury are evident from the p. 71. remarks we have made; for we have already analysed things good or bad in themselves and have shown that knowledge is a necessary condition of voluntary action. It follows that every crime alleged against a person is relative either to public or to individual interests and is committed either ignorantly and involuntarily or voluntarily and knowingly and, if the latter, either of deliberate purpose or under the in-

cellent instance of a general principle, especially in comparison with *Politics*, i. ch. 3 *ad fin.*

The "Messenian oration" of Alcidamas was according to the Scholiast an exhortation to the Lacedaemonians not to reduce the Messenians to slavery.

fluence of emotion. Passion is a subject which will
be discussed in the general treatment of the emotions, ^{pp. 115 sqq.}
and the object and conditions of deliberate purpose
have been already described. But it often happens ^{pp. 72 sqq.}
that people, while admitting a particular fact, re-
fuse to admit either the description of it or the application of the description ; a person will admit e.g.
that he took an article, but not that he stole it,
or that he struck the first blow, but not that he
committed an outrage, or that there was intercourse, but not that there was adultery, or that
there was theft, but not that there was sacrilege,
as the article stolen was not consecrated property,
or that there was trespass but not that there was
trespass on the State lands, or that there was communication, but not that it was communication of
a treasonable nature, with the enemy. From this
we see the necessity of definitions of theft or outrage or adultery, if we are to succeed in putting our
case in the strongest light, whether we are anxious
to prove or disprove a certain allegation. In all such
cases the point at issue is the criminality and wickedness or the reverse of the person accused, as it is
the purpose which constitutes vice or crime, and all
such terms as "outrage" or "theft" have a certain
connotation of the purpose. For if it *is admitted
that* a person dealt a blow, it does not necessarily
follow that he committed an outrage, unless he had
a particular object in dealing the blow, i.e. to insult
the person struck or to gratify himself ; nor again, if
it is admitted that a person took an article by stealth,
does it necessarily follow that he was guilty of theft,

unless the purpose of his taking it was the injury of somebody else and the appropriation of it to himself. The same is the case with every other crime that may be alleged.

p. 93.

[1] We have seen then that cases of justice and injustice may be divided into two classes, viz. unwritten and unwritten. So far as the law expressly declares them, they have been already discussed. The unwritten law on the other hand comprises (1) such points as are indications of a high degree of virtue or vice and are the subjects of reproaches, compliments, degradations, honours and presents, e.g. gratitude to benefactors, the repayment of kindnesses received, a disposition to serve one's friends and the like, (2) such points as supply the deficiencies of the special or written law. For equitable conduct is admitted to be just ; and the justice which supplements the written law is equity. But this *function of equity* may be either contrary to or consistent with the *legislator's* intention—the former, if the point is one which has escaped his notice, the latter, if it is impossible to specify *all the possible cases which may arise,* and it is necessary *therefore* to lay down a rule as universal, although it is *properly* not universal but only general, or [2] again if it is difficult to specify

Two kinds of unwritten law.

Equity.

---

[1] The present passage, although it seems only to recapitulate the result arrived at in an earlier part of the chapter, yet so far departs from it as (1) to show that the "universal" law is itself unwritten, (2) to explain the characteristics of this universal unwritten law, (3) to define the nature of that other unwritten law which is a part of the "particular" law of States.

[2] It is better to connect this sentence closely with the preceding one.

all possible varieties of a case, as they are infinite
in number, e.g. all the various sizes and kinds of
iron instruments with which a wound may be inflicted,
as human life is too short for a complete enumeration of them. Hence if an exact specification is
impossible, and yet it is indispensable to legislate,
it is necessary to employ general language, the result
being that if e.g. you are only wearing an iron ring
when you lift your hand against a person or deal him
a blow, according to the letter of the law you are
guilty of a crime, yet in reality you do not commit a
crime, and it is in this *merciful interpretation of your
action* that equity consists. And from this definition Its province.
of equity we see at once the kind of actions which
do or do not deserve equitable consideration and
the kind of persons who are not equitable. For all
such cases as deserve indulgence are proper subjects
of equity. Again, it is equitable not to treat errors
and crimes or errors and accidents alike. I mean
by an "accident" anything which cannot be foreseen
and does not proceed from vice, by an "error"
anything which might have been foreseen and yet
does not proceed from wickedness, and by a "crime"
anything which might have been foreseen and is
itself a result of wickedness ; for all such actions
as are due to desire proceed from wickedness. Equity Its nature.
consists too in making allowance for human infir-
mities, in regarding the legislator rather than the
law, the intention of the legislator rather than his
language, the purpose of an act rather than the act
itself and the whole rather than the part, in considering not so much what is a person's character

at a particular moment as what it has invariably or usually been, in remembering benefits more than injuries and benefits received more than benefits conferred, in suffering injustice patiently, in consenting to settle disputes by agreement rather than by a trial of strength, in wishing to resort to arbitration rather than to law ; for an arbitrator always takes the equitable, whereas a juror takes the legal view, of a case, and indeed the object with which arbitration was devised was to ensure the triumph of equity.

Such then may be regarded as a sufficient description of the nature and province of equity.

CHAP. XIV.
The magnitude of crimes.

The magnitude of a crime is proportionate to the magnitude of the injustice which prompts it. Hence the smallest crimes may be actually the greatest, as e.g. the crime alleged by Callistratus against Melanopus, viz. that he had defrauded the temple-builders of an obol and a half of consecrated money. [1]But in regard to justice the contrary of this is true ; *for the greater the temptation to commit a crime, the greater is the justice shewn in resisting it.* The reason *of the extreme criminality of petty crimes* is that the greater crime is potentially included *in the less;* for he who stole an obol and a half of consecrated money would be ready to commit any crime. The degree of criminality is determined sometimes in this way and at

---

[1] If it may be permitted to put Aristotle's meaning into other words, it is that the magnitude of criminality is determined by the smallness of the temptation which was not resisted, the magnitude of the justice by the greatness of the temptation resisted.

other times by consideration of the actual injury. *A crime is the greater*, if there is no possible punishment adequate to it ; or if there is no remedy for it, [1]*as in such a case it is grievous and even incurable* ; or if the victim has no hope of redress, as it is then irremediable ; for legal justice and punishment are remedial processes. *It is the greater* again, if the victim *in consequence of it* inflicted a heavy punishment upon himself ; for then the perpetrator seems to deserve still heavier punishment, as Sophocles argued in pleading the cause of Euctemon after his committing suicide in consequence of the outrage inflicted upon him, when he said he would not estimate the proper penalty less highly than the victim had estimated it for himself. Or if the perpetrator of the crime is the only person or the first who has so acted or has had but few associates in his action. Again, an offence is magnified, if it is constantly repeated ; or if it is one which has led to the desire and discovery of particular deterrents and penalties, as when at Argos a penalty is inflicted upon any individual on whose account a law has been passed or upon the [2]persons on whose account the prison was built. Again, a crime is the greater in proportion as it is more brutal or more deliberate or as it inspires the audience with sentiments of terror rather than of pity. There are other rhetorical means of exaggeration, as e.g. *the assertion* that the accused has subverted or transgressed many obligations *at*

---

[1] Perhaps the MSS reading χαλεπὸν γὰρ καὶ ἀδύνατον may stand, the infinitive ἰᾶσθαι being supplied with ἀδύνατον.

[2] The indicative mood implies that some definite persons are meant ; but the circumstances are not known.

once, such as oaths, pledges, securities and covenants of intermarriage; for so a crime is intensified by multiplication. Again, *it is an aggravation of a crime* that the scene of it should be the spot where criminals are brought to justice, as in the case of perjured witnesses; for where (*it may be argued*) would they be likely to refrain from crime, if they commit it actually in a Court of Law? A crime is magnified too, if it is one of a particularly shameful character; or if the victim of it has been a benefactor of the criminal, as there is then a multiplication of the crime in that not only the injury is done, but the service *which might have been expected* is not done; or if it is an offence against the unwritten principles of justice, as it is an indication of superior virtue to be just without the need of external compulsion. Now while written laws have a character of compulsion, the laws which are unwritten are not compulsory. Yet in another sense a crime is the greater, if it is a violation of the written law, as *it may be contended that* one who is guilty of such crimes as are dangerous to him and render him liable to punishment will not hesitate to commit those crimes to which no punishment is attached.

CHAP. XV.
The inartistic proofs.
p. 10.

Having now determined the comparative magnitude of crimes, we have next to take a rapid survey of the inartistic proofs as they are called. *We consider them last,* as [1]they belong exclusively to forensic

---

[1] This is generally, but not quite strictly, true, as appears from the words καὶ προτρέποντα καὶ ἀποτρέποντα, l. 17, and again εἰ συμφέρον ἢ ἀσύμφορον, p. 51, l. 12, which are appropriate to deliberative oratory.

Rhetoric. They are five in number, viz. laws, witnesses, contracts, tortures and the oath.

We will begin by discussing the proper means of (1) laws.
employing laws whether in exhortation and dissuasion or in accusation and defence. It is clear that,
if the written law is unfavourable to our case, we
must appeal to the universal law and to the principles
of equity as expressing justice of a higher order.
[1]*We must contend* that the formula "[2]according to
the best of my judgment" implies that the juror is
not to be absolutely bound by the letter of the law.
We must urge that, while equity and universal law,
as being conformable to Nature, are perpetual and
invariable, written laws are liable to frequent change.
Hence the lines in the *Antigone* of Sophocles, where
she pleads that in burying *her brother* she had violated
Creon's law but not the unwritten law *of Nature.*

> "[3]Not of to-day nor yesterday
> *Is this a law* but ever *hath it life;*
> This should not I for fear of mortal man
> *Dare violate.*"

---

[1] It is necessary to supply λεκτέον or some such word before ὅτι.

[2] The Athenian δικασταί promised on oath to judge γνώμῃ τῇ
ἀρίστῃ or, more correctly, γνώμῃ τῇ δικαιοτάτῃ. But the promise
so made, as is clear from many passages, was applicable only
where there was no law or where it was obscure.

[3] This quotation is made somewhat loosely, as though the
passage of the *Antigone* would be familiar to everyone. Cp. p. 45
l. 28. The lines are

> οὐ γάρ τι νῦν γε κἀχθές, ἀλλ' ἀεί ποτε
> ζῇ ταῦτα, κοὐδεὶς οἶδεν ἐξ ὅτου 'φάνη.
> τούτων ἐγὼ οὐκ ἔμελλον, ἀνδρὸς οὐδενὸς
> φρόνημα δείσας, ἐν θεοῖσι τὴν δίκην
> δώσειν.

Again, *we must argue* that justice is something which is genuine and beneficent, but that the sham justice *which consists in a rigorous interpretation of the law* is quite the contrary; hence the written law is neither genuine nor beneficent, as it does not discharge the proper function of law. Or that a judge is like an assayer of coin, whose business it is to distinguish base justice from genuine. Or that a higher virtue is displayed in loyalty and obedience to unwritten than to written laws. Again, [1] it may happen that the law *against which we are contending* is inconsistent with some other law of high repute or with itself; it is sometimes the case, e.g. that, while there is one law which enacts the validity of all contracts, there is another which prohibits the forming of any such contract as is illegal. Or it may happen that the law is ambiguous; then it will be proper to turn it about, and to consider to which of the two possible constructions either the justice or the expediency, as it may be, of our case will adapt itself and, after so considering it, to adopt that construction. Again, if the circumstances which the law was intended to meet have altered but the law remains in force, we must do our best to prove this to be the case and so to contend against the law. But if the letter of the law is on our side, it must be urged that the words "according to the best of my judgment" were never meant to justify illegal procedure on the

---

[1] The construction is again irregular or elliptical; the true apodosis would be found in some such words as χρηστέον αὐτῇ τῇ ἐναντιότητι. Similarly in the next sentence there is some such suppressed apodosis as χρηστέον αὐτῇ τῇ ἀμφιβολίᾳ.

part of a juror but only to exonerate him from a charge of perjury, if he should fail to perceive the meaning of the law. [1]Or that nobody desires that which is absolutely good, but everybody that which is good relatively to himself. Or that the law might as well not have been enacted, if it is not to be obeyed. Again, we may appeal to the other arts arguing that *in Medicine e.g.* it does not pay to be cleverer than the doctor, as there is less danger in the mistakes of the doctor than in the gradually acquired habit of disobeying authority. And *finally* we may urge that it is this effort to be wiser than the laws which is prohibited in all admirable codes.

The foregoing discussion of *the mode of appealing to* the laws must be regarded as sufficient for our purpose. Coming now to witnesses, we say that they are of two kinds, viz. ancient and contemporary, and that the latter may be either involved in the risk *of the action at law* or independent of it. I mean by ancient witnesses the poets and any other authorities who have pronounced notorious judgments. Thus the Athenians appealed to the testimony of Homer in the matter of [2]Salamis, and the inhabitants of Tenedos not long ago to that

(2) wit-nesses

(a) ancient

---

[1] The point of this argument for abiding by the letter of the law seems to be that the law is in its nature rigidly impartial, but the judgment of individuals is warped by personal considerations. Schrader however gives a different explanation, viz. that the laws of a particular state, as being adapted to its necessities, are better and therefore to be more resolutely guarded than laws of a kind abstractedly higher and more ideal.

[2] It was commonly alleged that the famous lines (*Iliad* ii.

of Periander of Corinth in their controversy with
the ¹Sigeans. Thus too Cleophon quoted against
Critias the elegiac verses of Solon in evidence of the
inveterate licentiousness of his family, as Solon—*so
he argued*—could have had no other reason for
writing

"Bid Critias the ruddy-haired go listen to his sire."

While then it is the poets and others who are witnesses
to facts of the past, as to the future the interpreters
of oracles are also witnesses. It was thus that
Themistocles insisted upon the wisdom of naval war-
fare, quoting the expression *of the oracle* "²the wooden
wall." Proverbs too, as has been said³, are forms of
testimony. If one is giving evidence e.g. against
courting the friendship of an old man, one can appeal
to the testimony of the proverb "Never befriend a
dotard"; or *if one is advocating* the slaughter of

557—8) in which the ships of Ajax are represented as stationed
beside the Athenian forces in the war of Troy, had been inter-
polated in the text by Solon, to serve as arguments for the claim
of Athens to the possession of Salamis.

¹ The allusion is really uncertain although Mr Grote (*History
of Greece*, Part ii. ch. 14) thinks the "testimony of Periander"
was his decision on the controversy between the Athenians and
the Mitylenaeans regarding Sigeum.

² See Herod. vii. ch. 141.

³ Not by Aristotle himself; hence Spengel proposes to omit
εἴρηται. Perhaps there is a reference to other writers upon
Rhetoric; perhaps, as is likely enough, the words are due to a
slip of memory. Mr Cope's explanation of them is possible, but
less natural; "proverbs are evidence in the way that has been
stated," i.e. evidence of the future.

the children whose parents have been already slain, *one can appeal to that of another proverb*

"[1]Fool he who slays the sire and spares the son."

Contemporary witnesses on the other hand are all such authorities as have pronounced judgment on a particular point; for the judgments of such authorities are serviceable, whenever the same questions are at issue. Thus Eubulus quoted in court against Chares the remark of Plato in reference to Archibius, that the avowal of rascality had made great strides in the state. Another class of contemporary witnesses consists of people who, if suspected of perjury, are involved in the peril *of the person whom they support by their testimony.* All such witnesses testify simply to the fact that a thing has or has not occurred or does or does not exist, not to its character i.e. to its justice or injustice, expediency or inexpediency; but the credibility of witnesses at a distance extends to character. None however are such credible witnesses as the ancients ; for these it is impossible to corrupt. If we have no witnesses to call, we may employ confirmations of our testimony *by arguing* that judgment should be based upon the probabilities of the case, that this is the meaning of the words "according to the best of my judgment," that probabilities cannot be bribed to deceive and are never convicted of perjury. If on the other hand we have witnesses to call, and our adversary has not, we may urge that probabilities are not responsible agents *like witnesses,* and that testimony would be superfluous,

---

[1] A line of the Κύπρια of the cyclic poet Stasinus.

if it were enough to review the case by the light of arguments. Also as testimony may relate either to ourselves or to our adversary and either to facts or to character, it is clear that we can never be at a loss for useful testimony; for if we cannot *adduce any testimony* in support of our own case or against our adversary's, yet *it may still be possible to produce testimony* to character such as tends to establish either our own respectability or the low morality of our adversary. All such other arguments as tend to prove a witness friendly, hostile or indifferent, estimable, disreputable or neither absolutely the one nor the other or to establish any other similar characteristic must be derived from the same topics as form the materials of our enthymemes.

(3) contracts.

As to contracts; the value of Rhetoric amounts to this, that it is competent to magnify or disparage their importance, to establish their credibility and authority, if they are on our own side, and to invalidate it, if they tell in favour of our adversary. The means of confirming or overthrowing their credibility are precisely the same as in the procedure in the case of witnesses; for their credit is entirely dependent upon the character of the persons who have endorsed them or who have them in their keeping. The existence of a contract being granted, it is necessary to magnify its importance, if it is on our own side. It may be urged that a contract is a law of a special and partial kind, that it is not contracts which impart validity to the law but the laws which impart validity to legal contracts [1] and in general that, as the law

---

[1] Placing only a comma after συνθήκας.

itself is a species of contract, to violate or annul a
contract is *virtually* to annul the laws. It may be
further urged that, as the ordinary dealings of one
man with another and all voluntary transactions are
regulated by contracts, to invalidate contracts is to
destroy the ordinary intercourse of social life. *These
are some of the arguments appropriate to the point*,
and there are others which are ready to hand and
easily found. If however the contract is one which is
adverse *to ourselves* and favourable to our opponents,
it is to be remembered in the first place *that* all such
arguments as might be used in opposition to an
adverse law are appropriate here. It is a strange
thing, *we may urge*, that, while we refuse to acknowledge the duty of obedience to the laws, if they have
been enacted wrongly and under a mistake on the
part of their authors, we still acknowledge the necessity of obedience to contracts. We may urge too
that the juror is an umpire of justice and that therefore the point to be considered is not the particular
document before us but the principle of higher justice.
Justice again, being an ordinance of Nature, cannot
be perverted either by fraud or by force ; contracts on
the other hand may be made under the influence
of cajolery or constraint. Yet again, *it is proper*
to consider whether the particular contract is inconsistent *first* with any law either written or universal
and, if written, either domestic or extraneous, and
secondly with other contracts subsequent or antecedent; for *it may be pleaded* either *that*, if the later
contracts are valid, then the earlier are invalidated, or
that, if the earlier are right, the later are fraudulent,

according as it may serve our purpose at the time. Finally, it is proper to have an eye to the personal interests of the judges, with which the contract may perhaps be inconsistent, and to various other similar points, *which need not be stated*, as they are equally easy to perceive.

(4) tortures.   Tortures constitute a species of testimony and are regarded as possessing credibility, inasmuch as a certain form of compulsion is implied in them. This again is a case in which it is not difficult to define the possible means of exaggeration, showing, if the tortures are favourable to ourselves, that this is the only genuine sort of testimony. If on the other hand they are unfavourable to ourselves and favourable to our adversary, it is possible to dissipate their force by using arguments, which are perfectly true, against tortures generally; for witnesses are fully as likely to give false testimony as true under the compulsion of torture, whether by resolutely persisting in their concealment of the truth or by readily making false accusations in the hope of getting off the rack the sooner. *Lastly*, one should be in a position to refer to parallel instances which have come within the cognizance of the judges.

(5) oaths.   Oaths admit of a fourfold division. A person may either tender and accept the oath, or may do neither, or may do one and not the other, i.e. may either tender the oath without accepting it or accept the oath without tendering it. And the case may be still further complicated, if the oath has been already taken by one of the parties.

If you refuse to tender the oath, *you may plead*

that perjury is easy and that, while [1] your adversary, if he takes the oath, will not *be compelled to* restore *the stolen property*, if he has no opportunity of taking it, you believe the court will pronounce sentence of condemnation against him; or that you prefer the risk of leaving the matter to the jury, as you have confidence in them but not in your adversary.

If you refuse to take the oath when tendered to you, *you may plead* that to take it is to [2]set a pecuniary value upon it; or that, if you had no conscience, you would have bound yourself by the oath, as, if one has not a conscience, one may as well gain something by having none, and that thus, while you would have recovered the property, if you had sworn, by not swearing you are likely to lose it. The consequence will be that *your refusal of the oath* will appear to spring not from the dread of perjury but from a virtuous motive[3]. It will be appropriate too to quote the saying of Xenophanes, that the offer of the oath is not a fair challenge, if the parties are a conscientious and an unconscientious person but is the same as if a strong man were to challenge a weak one to give or take a blow.

If you accept the oath, *you may say* that you have confidence in yourself but not in your adversary, or you may reverse the saying of Xenophanes and urge

---

[1] i.e. if he is not allowed to take the oath, the case will be tried on its merits, and he will be condemned; but if he takes it, the jury are more likely to pronounce a verdict in his favour.

[2] Or in other words, to take it in order to gain a certain pecuniary advantage.

[3] Putting a full stop, as Mr Cope suggests, after τὸ μή.

that the conditions will not be equal, unless it is the unconscientious person who tenders the oath and the conscientious person who accepts it, and that it is monstrous to refuse to take the oath oneself in a case where one expects the jurors to do so before they hear it.

If you tender the oath to your adversary, you may say that it is a pious act to commit the issue to Heaven, and that it is not for your adversary to require any judge but himself, as you are willing to leave the judgment in his hands. Or you may say that it is monstrous to refuse to swear in a case where one expects others to do so.

Having seen then the proper way of dealing with each case separately, we see at once how to deal with them in combination, as e.g. if you are willing to accept the oath yourself but not to tender it, or if you tender it but are not willing to accept it, or if you are willing both to accept and to tender it or to do neither; for as these are necessarily combinations of the cases which have been already described, it follows that the arguments used must be similarly combined.

If you have already taken an oath and it is prejudicial to you, *you may urge* that yours is not a case of perjury; for criminal action is always voluntary, and perjury is a crime, but such actions as are due to force or fraud are involuntary. In this instance then it is right to draw the conclusion that it is not the language but the intention which constitutes perjury.

If on the other hand it is your adversary who has

taken the oath, *you may urge* that not to abide by an oath once taken is to upset everything.　It is because of the sanctity of the oath, *you may assert*, that jurors are sworn before they administer the laws; and, *addressing the jury*, you may exclaim "You we expect to abide by the oaths, which you took before hearing the case, and are we ourselves not to abide by our oaths?"　And so through all the possible means of exaggeration.

This then may be regarded as a sufficient discussion of the inartistic proofs.

BOOK II.

THESE then are the proper materials of exhortation, dissuasion, eulogy, censure, accusation and defence, and the popular opinions and *rhetorical* premisses which are serviceable as supplying proofs in each ; for it is these which are in a special sense, as we may say, the subjects and materials of enthymemes, in each of the *three* kinds of speeches.

The audiences of oratory judicial.

As Rhetoric is intended to be judged—for *in deliberative oratory*[1] we pass judgment on the counsel given, and every legal decision is a judgment—it must necessarily be our object not only to render our speech demonstrative and credible, but also to produce a particular impression of ourselves and a particular disposition in our judges[2]. For in de-

Indirect means of proof.

[1] Epideictic oratory is for the moment left out of sight, whether as being less important than the other kinds or because the audience of epideictic speeches would not in Aristotle's view be strictly described as "judges" (κριταί). See ch. 18 *in init.*

[2] There is then a departure from the principle laid down at the beginning of Book I. But Aristotle's position is that, although the art of Rhetoric properly disregards everything but actual proof, yet practically in forensic and political matters such is the power of the emotions, such the influence of the impressions

liberative and, although to a less extent, even in forensic oratory, it is a highly important element of proof that the speaker should enjoy the credit of a certain character and should be supposed by his audience to stand in a certain relation to themselves, and further that the audience in their turn should, if possible, have a particular disposition to the speaker. The impression of the speaker's character is especially serviceable in deliberative, and the disposition of the audience in forensic, matters ; for our estimate *of a speech* is not the same, but either wholly different or different in degree, according as we regard a person with feelings of affection or dislike, and are angrily or charitably disposed towards him. If we are friendly to the person upon whom we have to form a judgment, we regard him as either innocent or guilty of a very slight offence ; if we are inimical to him, the contrary is the case.

Similarly, when we are in an eager and sanguine mood, the result *which is promised us* is probable and advantageous in our eyes ; when we are dispirited and out of humour, it is the reverse.

The sources of personal credibility in orators are three ; or in other words there are three things, apart from demonstrative proofs, which inspire belief, viz. sagacity, high character and good will. It is *the want*

Sources of personal credibility.

entertained by the audience as to make some discussion of theory indispensable in a rhetorical treatise. δίκαιον γὰρ αὐτοῖς ἀγωνίζεσθαι τοῖς πράγμασιν, ὥστε τἆλλα ἔξω τοῦ ἀποδεῖξαι περίεργα ἐστίν· ἀλλ' ὅμως μέγα δύναται, καθάπερ εἴρηται διὰ τὴν τοῦ ἀκροατοῦ μοχθηρίαν. He justifies in the same way his treatment of style.

of all these qualities or of one of them that occasions great errors in matters of discussion or deliberation ; for either people are so foolish that they entertain erroneous opinions, or, although their opinions are right, they are so corrupt that they do not express their true sentiments, or, although they are persons of sagacity and high character, they are not well-disposed to their audience, and perhaps in consequence do not recommend the best policy, although they understand it. These are the three sources of credibility, and there is no other. The necessary inference is that, if a person is supposed to command them all, he will be deserving of credit in the eyes of his audience.

This being so, the means of getting credit for sagacity and high character must be ascertained from pp. 61 sqq. our analysis of the virtues, as it is by the same means that we shall succeed in establishing our own character and the character of others ; goodwill or a friendly disposition on the other hand must be discussed now under the head of the emotions. And by the emotions I mean all such states as are attended by pain and pleasure and produce a change or difference in our attitude as judges, e.g. anger, compassion, fear and the like and their opposites.

Definition of emotion.

The emotions to be considered under three heads. It is proper to consider each emotion under three heads ; if we take e.g. anger, to consider (1) the conditions under which people are irascible, (2) the usual objects, and (3) the usual causes of anger ; for the knowledge of one or two of these points without the third will not enable us to excite the passion of anger, and the same is true of any other emotion.

Let us follow then our original plan of giving a

detailed account of the proper rhetorical premisses, and let us make an analysis *of the emotions* in the manner already described.

We may define anger as an impulse attended with pain to a conspicuous[1] revenge on account of a conspicuous slight shown in some offence against oneself or one of one's friends without any natural reason for the slight.

Chap. II.
The
emotions.
(1) Anger.
Definition
of anger.

This being the definition of anger, it follows that anger is always directed against an individual, let us say against Cleon, but not against *the genus* man, and is provoked by something done or intended to be done to oneself or one's friend, and that it is invariably attended by a certain pleasure arising from the expectation of revenge. For while there is something pleasant in the thought of attaining our aim, nobody aims at such things as are clearly beyond his power, and *accordingly* an angry man *always* aims at something which is within his power. Hence it is a good description of passion

Conse-
quences
of the
definition.

> "Far sweeter than the flowing stream of honey
> It wells within the heart[2]";

for there is a certain concomitant pleasure which is

---

[1] It is proposed by Spengel and others to omit the word "conspicuous" (φαινομένης), as it goes beyond the definitions of anger given in Τοπικά (viii. p. 152 A$_{32}$ and περὶ Ψυχῆς i. p. 403 A$_{30}$). But, whatever may be his view elsewhere, in the *Rhetoric* Aristotle clearly regards the notoriety of the revenge as being an element of the pleasure attending it. Cp. p. 61, ll. 10—15.

[2] *Iliad* xviii. 109, a passage which has been already quoted in part p. 39, l. 6.

due partly to this *anticipation of revenge* and partly
to the dwelling upon revenge in imagination[1], so that
the impression created at the time, like the impression
of a dream, produces pleasure.

Slight.

[2]A slight is an active manifestation of opinion in
reference to something which appears to be wholly
unimportant; for all such things as are good or evil,
or as conduce to good or evil, we consider to deserve
serious attention; but if a thing has no such tendency
or hardly any, we regard it as wholly unimportant.

Three
species of
slight:
(a) con-
tempt,

(b) spite-
fulness,

There are three species of slight, viz. contempt,
spite and insolence. Contempt is a form of slight;
for if we regard a thing as wholly unimportant, we
feel a contempt for it, and if we feel a contempt for
it, we slight it[3]. A second form of slight is spitefulness, spite being an impediment offered to the wishes
of others not for the benefit of the person who spites
but for the detriment of the person who is spited.
It is the fact that the motive of the spiteful action is
not the benefit of the agent himself which constitutes
the slight; for it is clear that he does not suppose the
person whom he spites will do him any considerable

---

[1] The two elements of pleasure, as here regarded, seem to be
(1) the thought that at some *future* time we shall have our revenge, (2) the *present* picturing to ourselves this revenge.

[2] There is no true apodosis; hence I have disregarded the ἐπεί
in translating. The thread of the sentence is broken by the
parenthesis καὶ γὰρ τὰ κακὰ κ.τ.λ.

[3] The whole sentence will be clearer and more logical, if it is
read thus: ὅ τε γὰρ καταφρονῶν ὀλιγωρεῖ, ὅσα γὰρ οἴονται μηδενὸς
ἄξια τούτων καταφρονοῦσιν, τῶν δὲ καταφρονουμένων ὀλιγωροῦσιν·
καὶ ὁ ἐπηρεάζων, ἔστι γὰρ ὁ ἐπηρεασμὸς κ.τ.λ. The words φαίνεται
καταφρονεῖν are better omitted.

injury or service, as in the former case he would stand in awe of him and would cast no slight upon him, and in the latter he would pay court to him to secure his friendship. Insolence is another form of slight, as being an act of injury or annoyance involving the disgrace of the sufferer, not for the sake of any benefit to the agent beyond the mere fact of its having been done, but only for his personal gratification ; for the requital of injuries is not insolence but revenge. The source of the pleasure found in insolent action is the feeling that in injuring others we are claiming an exceptional superiority to them. This is the reason of the insolence of the young and the wealthy ; they look upon it as a mark of superiority. One species of insolent action is disrespect, and this again involves a slight; for if a thing is wholly unimportant, it is not[1] respected as having any value either for good or for evil. Hence Achilles in his anger says

> [2]"Dishonoured am I ; he hath ta'en my prize
> And doth maintain it."

and again

> " Like some dishonoured vagabond."

implying that this is the cause of his anger. Now we suppose that we have a natural right to a high degree

(o) insolence.

---

[1] It is difficult in English to preserve the two meanings of τιμή (1) "honour" or "respect," which connects it with ἀτιμία, (2) "value" which is suited to the words οὔτ᾽ ἀγαθοῦ οὔτε κακοῦ.

[2] The passages referred to are taken as instances of the slight implied in disrespectful or dishonourable treatment. *Iliad* I. 356; IX. 644.

of consideration at the hands of persons who are our inferiors in birth, power or virtue, and indeed in anything common both to us and to them in which we have a great superiority, as e.g. in wealth a man of large property to a poor man, in oratory a good speaker to a bad one, and *in political affairs* a ruler to a subject, or one who fancies himself born to rule to one who is only born to serve. Hence the [1]lines

"Great pride is there of kings the sons of Gods,"

and

"Yet afterward he beareth still a grudge";

for the indignation *expressed in these lines* is due to the sense of superiority. Again, *we expect especial consideration* from persons who are bound under an obligation, as we suppose, to treat us well, i.e. persons upon whom benefits have been or are being conferred or are or were intended to be conferred either by ourselves or by somebody at our instigation or by one of our friends.

Conditions of anger. We see clearly then from this statement of the case the conditions under which people become angry, the persons with whom they are angry and the grounds of anger. We become angry under a sense of annoyance ; for if a person is annoyed, there is something at which he aims. Whether it is di-

---

[1] The quotations, as their contexts show, illustrate the principle that "one who fancies himself born to rule" expects a high consideration or respect from "one who is only born to serve." In the first (*Iliad* II. 196) it is Odysseus who addresses the chieftains after the speech in which Agamemnon counsels flight ; in the second (*Iliad* I. 82) it is Calchas who deprecates the revengeful anger of Agamemnon.

rectly then that somebody thwarts us in any respect, as e. g. in preventing us from drinking when we are thirsty, or only indirectly, the effect appears to be the same in both cases ; and whether a person opposes us or refuses to co-operate with us or occasions us any other trouble when we are in this condition, we invariably become angry with him. Accordingly it is in sickness, in poverty, [1] in war, in love, when we are thirsty or have any kind of unsatisfied desire that we are irascible and readily excited to anger not only, although in an especial degree, against such persons as show a slighting indifference to our present condition, whether it be our malady, if we are ill, or our poverty, if we are poor, or the war in which we are engaged, if we are at war, or our love, if we are lovers, but similarly against other people as well, according as we are individually predisposed by our present emotion *or condition* to be angry in each particular case. Another *occasion of anger* is when what takes place is the contrary of our anticipations ; for the greatness of the surprise is an intensification of the annoyance, as it is of the pleasure too, if our wishes are gratified.

It is clear then from these considerations what sorts of seasons, times, dispositions and periods of life are easily excited to anger and what are the usual places and occasions of anger ; it is clear too that, the more these conditions are realized, the more excitable to anger we are.

---

[1] Probably Bekker is right in inserting πολεμοῦντες, as without it the sentence given below, πολεμῶν δὲ τοῖς πρὸς τὸν πόλεμον, is out of place.

Persons
against
whom anger
is felt.

Such then being the conditions under which we
are readily excited to anger, the persons against
whom our anger is directed are those who mock and
sneer and gibe at us, as they are insolent to us, or
who do us injury of such a kind as betokens insolence, i.e. such of course as is neither retaliatory
in its nature nor beneficial to the authors of it; for,
if it is neither, it necessarily appears to be due to
insolence. We are angry too with persons who disparage and despise the things to which we ourselves
attach most importance, e.g. our philosophy, if it
is philosophy upon which we pride ourselves, our
personal appearance, if it is our appearance and so
on. And this is particularly the case, if we entertain
a suspicion that we do not possess the said advantages at all, or do not possess them in a high degree,
or are not believed to possess them ; for if it is our
firm persuasion [1] that we possess the advantages in
respect of which, *i.e. for the absence of which*, we are
satirized, we treat the satire with contempt. Again,
we are more disposed *to be angry with* our own
friends than with strangers, *if they treat us badly*,
as we suppose ourselves to have a natural claim to
good treatment rather than the reverse at their
hands. *We are soon angry* too with persons who
have usually treated us with honour or respect, if
they turn round and treat us in a different spirit ;
for we imagine they have come to feel a contempt
for us, as otherwise they would continue to act as
they always have acted. Or with persons who fail

---

[1] Omitting ἐν τούτοις; but it is a question if ἐν οἷς should not
be altered to ἐφ' οἷς.

to requite our services or who fail to make an adequate return for them, or with persons who act against our interests, if they are our inferiors ; [1]for both these classes show a certain apparent contempt for us, the former *by treating us* as inferiors, and the latter *by treating our services* as if they had been rendered by inferiors. *We are* especially *angry* with persons of no consideration, if they pass a slight upon us ; for it is assumed *in accordance with the definition* that the anger provoked by the slight is directed against such persons as have no natural right to treat us in this manner, and it is the natural duty of our inferiors not to slight us. Or with our friends, if they do not speak well of us or treat us well, and still more, if they do the reverse ; or if they fail to perceive what we want, [2]as Plexippus in the play of Antiphon was angry with Meleager ; for the fact of their not perceiving it is an evidence of slight, as, if we respect a person, we do not ignore his wants. Or with persons who rejoice at our misfortunes or show any kind of cheerfulness in the course of them, as such conduct is an indication either of enmity or of slight. Or with those who do not reflect upon the possibility of giving us pain ;

---

[1] Bekker's text does not show, as it should, that the reason alleged applies to both the preceding sentences. It would be better to put a comma only, or at most a colon, after ἀνταποδιδοῦσιν.

[2] This very doubtful allusion is explained, so far as explanation is possible, in Mr Cope's note. Plexippus was uncle of Meleager, and it is supposed that Meleager's insensibility to his wants consisted in not making him a present of the skin, which was the prize of the Caledonian boarhunt.

this is the explanation of the anger felt against the messengers who bring us bad news. Or with those who either listen to the tale of our weaknesses or look on at any exhibition of them *with indifference,* as such behaviour is akin to a slight, if not indeed to actual enmity ; for a man's friends sympathize with the pain he suffers, and [1] everybody is pained at the spectacle of his own weaknesses. Again, *we are angry* with persons who put a slight upon us in the presence of any of the following five classes of people, viz. our rivals, those who are the objects of our admiration, those whose admiration we are desirous to gain, those whom we reverence or those who reverence us. Or with persons who put a slight upon objects which we are bound in honour to defend, such as our parents, children, wives or subjects. Or with persons who make no return for favours conferred upon them, as such a slight is a violation of natural duty. Or who treat us ironically when we are in earnest, as there is something contemptuous in irony. Or who confer benefits upon others, unless they are also benefactors of ourselves ; as it is one sign of contempt not to treat us with the same esteem as everybody else. [2]Another provocative of anger is forgetfulness, e.g. forgetfulness of names, although it is shown only in so trifling a matter ; for forgetfulness too is apparently a sign

---

[1] It is necessary to remember that a friend in the Aristotelian view is " a second self " (ἕτερος αὐτός).

[2] Aristotle passes in this sentence from the objects to the motives or at least to one motive of anger ; but the two heads (p. 55, ll. 22—25) are so closely related as to be inseparable.

of slight, as arising from indifference which is itself a slight.

The persons with whom we are apt to be angry and the conditions and causes of anger having thus been all treated together, it is evident that the task which lies before us is by our speech to bring the audience to a condition of irascibility, and to represent our adversaries as being guilty of the feelings and actions which provoke men to anger and as possessing a character against which anger is felt.

As to become angry is the opposite of becoming placable, and anger of placability, we have to ascertain the conditions of placability, the persons towards whom we are placably disposed and the means by which we become placable. Chap. III. (2) Placability.

The process of becoming placable may be defined as a settling down or quieting of anger. If then it is persons who slight us that are the objects of anger, and a slight is a voluntary action, it is clear that we are placably disposed to such persons as do not treat us with any sort of slight or do so, or appear to do so, unintentionally. Also to persons whose intention is contrary to their action. Or to persons who behave to themselves in the same way as to us; for it is assumed that nobody will put a slight on himself. Or to persons who acknowledge and repent their fault; for then we cease to be angry under the impression that in the pain which they feel at their own past conduct we have received a certain satisfaction. This we may infer from the punishment of domestic slaves; for while, if they contradict us and deny the deed, we increase the punishment, if they admit the justice Definition of placability. Persons towards whom it is natural to be placable.

of the punishment, our anger ceases. The reason
is that the denial of notorious facts is an act of
¹effrontery *or gross disrespect,* and effrontery is a form
of slight or contempt; at all events, if we feel a
thorough contempt for a person, we do not respect
him. Again, we are placably disposed to such persons
as humble themselves before us and offer no contradiction to us; for their attitude looks like a confession of inferiority, and inferiority implies awe, and
nobody who is in a state of awe offers a slight. That
anger subsides when the objects of it humble themselves is evident even from the ²conduct of dogs in not
biting anybody who sits down *when they attack him.*
We are placable too to those who take us seriously
when we are serious, as such seriousness appears to
exclude contempt. Or to those who have laid us
under obligations greater than we can return. Or
to those who entreat us and deprecate our anger,
as so far they humiliate themselves. Or to those who
are never guilty of insolence or mockery or slight
against anybody or against virtuous people or against
people like ourselves. ³(It is indeed a general rule
that the means of producing placability are to be
ascertained by a consideration of their opposites.) Or

---

¹ The etymological connexion of ἀναισχυντία and αἰσχυνό-
μεθα contributes something to the argument and should be noted,
although it can hardly be preserved in translation.

² Mr Cope refers to Homer *Odyssey* xiv. 29—31. It is well
known that sitting was in the Greek view a posture of supplication.

³ There is something strangely abrupt in the introduction of
this sentence ; it is a kind of afterthought or footnote.

to persons who are the objects of our awe or respect; for so long as we are in this state of mind, we do not feel angry with them, as it is impossible to be awed and angry at the same time. Again, if persons have acted on an impulse of passion, we either do not feel angry with them at all or feel less angry, as their action does not appear to be the result of slight; for anger and slight are incompatible, the former being attended with pain and the latter not. [1]And the same is the case, if they are persons who feel a respect for us.

Coming now to the second point, it is clear that we are placable when we are in such a condition as is opposed to angry feeling, e.g. at a time of sport or laughter or festivity or in the enjoyment of prosperity or success or gratification or generally of freedom from pain, of pleasure apart from insolence and of virtuous hope. Also we are placable after a certain interval of time, and when our anger is no longer fresh; for the mere lapse of time appeases anger. Again, anger—even more violent anger—against one person is appeased by punishment already exacted from another. Accordingly it was a clever answer of Philocrates, when he was asked in a time of popular fury, "Why do you not defend yourself?" "Not yet" he replied. "When then?" "As soon as I see somebody else in disgrace." The fact is that we become placable when we have spent our anger upon some-

(margin note: Conditions of placability.)

---

[1] The contradiction between this passage and p. 58, ll. 18—20 is only a seeming one; for Aristotle is there thinking of people who have lost their old respect for us, and here of people who have not lost it but have done something apparently inconsistent with it.

body else, as happened in the case of [1]Ergophilus; for although the Athenians were more indignant with him than with Callisthenes, yet they acquitted him, because on the previous day they had sentenced Callisthenes to death. The same is the case, if we feel pity for a person, or if he has suffered a heavier penalty than we in our anger would have inflicted upon him; for then we feel that we have in a way got our revenge. Or if we consider ourselves to be in the wrong and to deserve no better treatment than we receive; for what is just is not provocative of anger, as we cease in such a case to regard our treatment as a violation of our natural rights, which is essential, as we have seen, to the idea of anger. This is the reason why *actual punishment* should be preceded by expostulation (which is itself a sort of punishment), as it takes the sting out of punishment even in the case of slaves. We are placable again, if we think the victims of punishment will not perceive that it is we who inflict it and that it is inflicted in retaliation for injuries done to us; for anger is always directed against individuals, as is clear from the definition of it. Hence there is a trait of nature in the words

p. 115.

p. 115.

[2]"Say twas Odysseus, pillager of cities,"

[1] It was in 362 B.C. that Ergophilus was in command at the Chersonese against the Thracian king Cotys, and Callisthenes against the Amphipolitans and Perdiccas. See Mr Grote's *History of Greece*, ch. lxxx. vol. x. pp. 129 sqq. Ergophilus was generally unsuccessful, but Callisthenes seems to have suspended operations at the moment when there was a possibility of capturing Amphipolis.

[2] *Odyssey* ix. 504. Odysseus, having blinded the Cyclops, tells

as if the revenge were not complete, unless *the Cyclops* were aware of the author and the motive. It follows that we never grow angry with unconscious beings, nor again do we pursue the dead with our anger, as we believe that their tale of suffering is complete and that they are no more susceptible of pain or any such feeling as it is our effort, when we are angry, to produce. Thus in the case of Hector there is a propriety in the poet's language, [1] when seeking to divert Achilles from his anger against the dead

> [2] "Tis but dull dust his fury violates"—

It is clear then that an orator, if he wishes to produce placability, must choose these topics as the materials of his speech, bringing [3] his audience to a suitable frame of mind and representing the objects of their anger as either formidable or worthy of

him that the author of the deed was "Odysseus son of Laertes, who hath his dwelling in Ithaca."

[1] The idiom by which a writer is represented as actually doing what he describes as being done, or as using the language which he puts into the mouths of his characters, is common enough in Greek as well as in other languages. See Mr Cope's note.

[2] *Iliad* xxiv. 54.

[3] Reading αὐτοὺς i.e. τοὺς κριτάς. Cp. p. 66, l. 17; p. 76, l. 16. It is not the orator who is supposed to be the object of anger in the clause αὐτοὺς μὲν παρασκευάζουσι τοιούτους, nor again is it the orator who is supposed to feel anger in the clause οἷς δ' ὀργίζονται κ.τ.λ. The judges are angry with someone for whom the orator pleads; and it is his effort to appease their anger (1) by producing in them a temper of placability, (2) by showing that the person against whom their anger is directed possesses such qualities or recommendations as should avert it.

respect or as having been former benefactors or involuntary agents or as exceedingly distressed at their own deeds.

CHAP. IV.
(3) Love.
(4) Hatred.
[1]The persons who are the objects of love and hatred and the causes which produce these feelings are now to be described ; but first let us define love and the act of loving.

Definition of love.
We may say that to love a person *or to be his friend* is to wish him all such things as you suppose to be good, not for your own sake but for his, and to

Definition of a friend.
be ready so far as in you lies to effect them. A friend is one who loves and is beloved in return ; people who regard themselves as standing in this relation to each other call themselves friends.

Consequences of the definitions.
From these assumed definitions it follows that a friend is one who shares the pleasure of another in his prosperity and his pain in adversity, not for any secondary motive but solely for that other's sake. For as we all feel pleasure in the realization of our wishes and pain in opposite circumstances, it follows that our pains and pleasures are themselves an indication of our wishes. Again, people are friends, [2]if they have learnt to agree in their conception of things good and evil, or if they have the same friends or the same enemies; for such persons will necessarily agree in their wishes, and therefore, if your wishes for another are the same as for yourself, you show

---

[1] There is a difficulty throughout this chapter in hitting the precise sense of φιλεῖν, which varies between "loving" and "liking," and in preserving the connexion of φιλεῖν with φίλος and φιλία.

[2] Reading ἤδη instead of δή.

yourself thereby to be his friend. Again, we love Persons who are the objects of love.
people, *or are their friends,* if they have rendered
services either to ourselves or to those in whom we
feel an interest, or if they have rendered us important services or have rendered them *con amore* or
on critical occasions or from disinterested motives, or
if we believe that it is their wish to render us
services. We love them too, if they are friends of
our friends and if they love the same people as we
ourselves love; or if they are loved by persons who
are the objects of our own love; or if they have the
same enemies as we have and hate the same people
as we ourselves hate; or if they are hated by the
objects of our own hate. For all these classes of
people consider the same things to be good as we do
ourselves and therefore wish such things as are good
for ourselves, which is the definition, as we have
seen, of a friend. Again, we are fond of persons who
are ready to assist us pecuniarily or in defence against
personal injury; hence the respect paid to generosity
and valour. [1]Or of just persons, and we regard as just
all who do not live by preying upon their neighbours,
i.e. all who work for their living and chief among
these the agriculturalists and chief among agriculturalists *the small farmers* who labour with their own
hands. Or again of temperate *or orderly* persons, because they refrain from crime. Or of persons who
mind their own business, for the same reason. Or
of persons with whom we wish to be friends, if they
show the same inclination, I mean persons of virtuous

---

[1] It is better to put a full stop after τιμῶσι and only a colon
after τοὺς δικαίους.

character and high renown either universally or in
the society of the most virtuous people or of those
who are admired by us or who themselves admire us.
Again, we are fond of such persons as are pleasant
companions for a day or a lifetime, e. g. of good-
natured people who will not be always bringing up
our faults against us and who are not contentious or
crossgrained, as all such people manifest a pugnacious
spirit, which implies that their wishes are contrary to
ours ; [1]or again of people who have a certain amount
of tact in giving and receiving *badinage*, as whether
they are good-humoured butts or graceful jesters, they
have the same object in view as the opposite parties
in the combat of wit, viz. mutual amusement. We
are fond too of people who laud such accomplishments as we possess, especially if we are doubtful
about possessing them. Or of those who are neat in
person, dress and general manner of life. Or who
are not fond of casting our faults or their own services in our teeth, as, if they do either one or the
other, they are censorious. Or who do not bear
malice or nurse their grievances but are always ready
to make friends again ; for as we suppose them to
behave in their dealings with others, so we imagine
they will behave in their dealings with us. Or who
are not backbiters and do not notice the bad points
in our neighbours or ourselves but only the good ; for
such is the conduct of a good man. Or who do not
try to thwart people when they are angry or in earnest,
as a person who will so act is of a pugnacious character.

---

[1] Changing the full stop after βούλεσθαι to a colon, so as to
mark the construction of the sentence.

Or who have a certain good feeling towards us, e.g. who respect us and have a good opinion of us and are fond of our society, especially if the grounds of their respect or fondness are qualities for which we are ourselves particularly anxious either to be respected or thought well of or liked. Or who resemble us and have the same pursuits, so long as they do not interfere with us or get their living in the same way; for then it is a case of "two of a trade." Or who desire what we ourselves desire, provided that it is something which admits of being shared in common; otherwise, the case is the same as before. We are fond too of people with whom we stand upon such terms that in their presence we feel no shame about appearances, provided that this feeling is not due to contempt. Or of people in whose presence we are ashamed of our own real faults. Again, if a person is our rival or one by whom we wish to be emulated, not envied, we either love him or wish to be his friends. The same is the case, if we cooperate with a person for his advantage, provided that *in helping him* we are not likely to incur a greater loss ourselves. Or if he is as true to his friends in their absence as when they are present; hence the kindly feeling we entertain towards those who show themselves the friends of the dead. It is in fact a general rule that we are fond of people who are very true to their own friends and never desert them; for there are no good men who are so much liked as good friends. Or of people who are not artificial in their dealing with us, such as people who speak *frankly* of their own weaknesses. For it has been already said that in the presence of our friends we feel no shame about appearances, and from this it follows that, if such shame is incompatible with friendship, the absence of it is a probable mark of a friend. Or of people who are not formidable to us and [1]in whose presence we feel confidence ; for it is impossible to be fond of anyone whom we fear.

The species of friendship. Its causes.

The various species of friendship are companionship, intimacy, relationship and the like. The causes which produce it are favours conferred and conferred without solicitation and never made public by the benefactor himself, as in such case it is plain that they are conferred from love of the recipient and not from any secondary motive.

Enmity or hatred.

Its causes.

The distinction between anger and hatred.

As to enmity and the feeling of hatred, it is clear that they must be studied by a consideration of their opposites. The causes which produce enmity are anger, spite and prejudice. The difference between anger and enmity is that, while the former is always occasioned by personal wrongs, the latter exists equally without such wrongs ; for if we suppose that a person has a character of a certain kind, we hate him. Again, while anger is always concerned with individual cases, while we feel angry e.g. with *an individual like* Callias or Socrates, hatred is directed equally against whole classes of persons ; for a thief or an informer is an object of universal hatred. In the third place, anger is curable by time, but hatred is not. Also while anger is a longing to inflict pain, hatred on the other hand is a longing to inflict evil ; for an angry

[1] Not οἷς; Mr Shilleto is undoubtedly right in preferring οὓς. For the construction cp. p. 67, l. 6.

man wishes to perceive *the effect of his anger*, but if a man hates another, it is not important to him *that he should perceive the effect of his hatred*. Now although painful things are always objects of perception, the worst evils, such as injustice and foolishness, are the hardest to perceive, for there is nothing painful in the presence of vice. Again, pain is a concomitant of anger but not of hatred ; you cannot feel anger, as you can hatred, without pain. Lastly while there are many things which in anger may produce a sentiment of compassion, it is not so in hatred ; for the aim of the former is to inflict suffering, as a retaliation, upon its object, but that of the latter is to compass his destruction.

From all this it is evident that there is a possibility of demonstrating the fact of enmity or friendship, where they exist, and of creating them, where they do not exist, and, where they are alleged, of refuting the allegation and, if it is disputed *whether a particular action* is due to anger or enmity, of referring it to either the one or the other, as we may choose.

The objects which inspire fear, whether they be persons or things, and the conditions under which we are liable to it, will be evident, if we look at them as follows. CHAP. V.
(5) Fear.

Fear may be defined as a species of pain or disturbance arising from an impression of impending evil which is destructive or painful in its nature. *It is necessary that the evil should be destructive or painful ;* for it is not every kind of evil that we fear—we do not fear e.g. the prospect of being unjust or stupid—but such evil only as amounts to Definition
of fear.

great pain or destruction, and even this only if it is evidently not remote but near at hand and in consequence imminent. For such evils as are exceedingly remote we do not fear; we are all aware e.g. that we shall die, but, inasmuch as death is not near, we do not think about it.

Objects of fear.

Such then being the nature of fear, it is evident that all such things are formidable as appear to have a great power of destroying or of inflicting injury which tends to grievous pain. Accordingly the signs of all such things are formidable, as the sign implies the nearness of the formidable object; for it is just this approach of something formidable which constitutes danger. The enmity and anger of persons who have the power of doing us mischief are examples; for as their mischievous desire is unmistakeable, it is clear that the mischief will not be long postponed. Another example is criminality armed with power; *for the purpose to commit crime may be assumed*, as it is the purpose which constitutes the criminality of a criminal. A third is outraged virtue armed with power; for it is clear that virtue, whenever it is outraged, purposes vengeance, and in the case supposed has the power to execute it. A fourth is fear on the part of persons who have the power of doing us mischief, as such persons too will necessarily be in a state of preparation. But as the majority of men are disposed to vice and are slaves to the love of gain and cowards in the face of dangers, it is for the most part a formidable thing to be dependent upon anybody else; and therefore if a person has committed a deed of horror, his accomplices inspire him with the fear that they will either denounce him or leave him in the lurch. Also persons who are in a position to commit crime are formidable to persons who are in a position to be the victims of it; for it is a general rule that people commit crimes, whenever they can. People who have been or, as they imagine, are still the victims of crime are formidable, as they are always on the watch for an opportunity *of revenge.* People who have already committed crime, if they have the power *of inflicting injury,* are formidable from their fear of retaliation; for it was laid down before that such a condition of fear is p. 134 formidable. So too people who are competitors for the same objects as ourselves, if they are such as cannot be enjoyed simultaneously by both; for we are always at war with people of this kind. Or people who are formidable to our superiors; for if they can actually injure our superiors, *a fortiori* they will be able to injure us. Or who inspire our superiors with fear, for the same reason. Or who have destroyed our superiors, ¹or are making an attack upon our inferiors; for the former are formidable already, and the latter *will be formidable,* when their power has been increased. Among people who have been injured by us and among our enemies or rivals it is not the quick-tempered and outspoken who are formidable, but the undemonstrative and hypocritical and unscrupulous, as we never know whether their attack is imminent and consequently are never sure that it is remote. Again, 'any formidable thing is

¹ There should be only a colon after ἀνῃρηκότες; the reason alleged below applies to both the preceding clauses.

still more formidable, if it is one in which a mistake, once made, cannot be repaired, whether indeed it is absolutely irreparable or reparable only at the pleasure of our adversaries and not at our own. Or if it is one in which remedial action is impossible or very difficult. Generally speaking too, a thing is formidable to us, if it [1]excites compassion when it happens or threatens to happen to others.

Such then being practically the principal things which are formidable and objects of fear, let us proceed to describe the mental conditions under which we ourselves experience fear.

Conditions of fear.

Assuming that fear is attended by an expectation of suffering something of a destructive kind, we see at once that nobody is subject to fear who regards himself as incapable of suffering; nor does anybody feel fear of things which he thinks he will be unlikely to suffer or of people from whom or at times during which he thinks he will be unlikely to suffer them. It is a necessary condition therefore of fear that a person should regard himself as capable of suffering *in the abstract* and of suffering at the hands of particular people and in particular ways and at particular times. Now people who do not believe in their own capability of suffering are those who are or think they are in great prosperity and who are consequently insolent, contemptuous, and audacious, being made so by wealth or bodily strength or the number of their *clientèle* or their power; or again, those who think they have already drained the cup of woes and who have grown

---

[1] ἐλλεεινά is a mere misprint for ἐλεεινά.

callous in regard to the future, like persons at the point of being bastinadoed to death ; *they have no fear, for they have lost all hope,* whereas *in order that fear may be possible* there must be still some under-lying hope of preservation from the evil which causes their agony. One evidence of this truth is that fear inclines people to deliberation, whereas nobody deliberates about a case which is hopeless. Whenever it is our interest then to inspire our audience with fear, it is proper to produce upon their minds the impression that they are capable of suffering, inasmuch as others who were greater than they suffered before them, and to give instances of their peers suffering or having suffered, and that from unexpected quarters and in unexpected ways and at unexpected times.

Having ascertained now the nature of fear and of formidable things and the conditions under which particular classes of people are afraid, we see at once as a corollary the nature of confidence, the sort of things which inspire confidence and the mental con-ditions under which we are confident. For as con-fidence is opposed to fear, and what is a source of confidence to a source of fear, it follows that the hope *which is the characteristic of confidence* is accompanied by an impression of salutary things as near at hand and of formidable things as non-existent or remote. The sources of confidence are the remoteness of dangers and the nearness of [1]en-couragements. *We feel confidence too, if there are*

(6) Confi-dence.

Its nature.

Sources of confidence.

[1] The use of the adjective θαρραλέος in the definition of τὰ θαρραλέα is a singular carelessness.

means of rectification or remedy, whether numerous
or effectual or both, and if we have been neither the
victims nor the perpetrators of crime, and if we have
no competitors at all or such as are powerless or,
if powerful, such as are friendly to us or have rendered us services or received services from us, or
if the persons whose interests coincide with our own
are in a superiority of numbers or power or both.

Conditions
of confi-
dence.

The conditions under which we feel confidence
are when we suppose we have often succeeded and
not come to harm, or when we have often encoun-
tered dangers and survived them ; for there are
two ways in which people are rendered ¹insensible
to fear, viz. either by having had no previous experience *of the danger* or by possessing resources
against it, as in times of peril at sea it is people
who have never seen a storm on the one hand and
people whose experience furnishes them with resources on the other that face the future with confidence.   Another *condition which inspires confidence* is when the danger is not formidable to our
peers or inferiors or to those to whom we consider
ourselves superior, as is the case, if we have con-
quered either them or their superiors or peers.   Or
when we consider ourselves to have the advantage
in the number and degree of those points of superiority which make people formidable, i.e. in wealth,
bodily strength, or strength of connexions, of territory and of all or the most important sinews of

¹ ἀπαθεῖς has here the sense of freedom, not, as usually, from
the πάθη in general but from the πάθος which is especially under
consideration, i.e. fear.

war. Or when we have not committed any crime against anyone or against many people or against such people as are the objects of our fear ; [1] or again in general if our relations to the gods, especially as shown by omens and oracles, are satisfactory ; for there is a certain amount of confidence in anger, and it is a sense of crime committed against us rather than by us which is provocative of anger, and Heaven is assumed to be on the side of the injured. Or *lastly* when we suppose we are likely or certain to take no harm or to be successful in our undertaking.

So much then for the objects which inspire either fear or confidence. I proceed to explain the characteristics of such objects as excite sentiments of shame or shamelessness, the persons in whose presence they are experienced and the conditions under which we experience them.

CHAP. VI.
(7) Shame.
(8) Shamelessness.

Shame may be defined as a species of pain or disturbance in regard to evil things, either past, present or future, which have an appearance of tending to ignominy ; and shamelessness as a species of slight or indifference in regard to these same things.

Definition of shame

and of shamelessness.

Such then being the definition we give of shame, it necessarily follows that we feel shame at all such evil things as appear to be shameful either to ourselves or to the objects of our care, such e.g. as actions which are the results of vice, like the throwing away a shield *in battle* or running away ; for these actions

Consequences of the definition of shame.
Shameful actions.

---

[1] Changing the full stop after φοβοῦνται, as Mr Cope himself suggests, to a colon, in order to mark that the clauses θαρραλέον γὰρ ἡ ὀργή κ.τ.λ. are explanatory of both preceding sentences.

both result from cowardice. Another instance is the refusal to restore a deposit, such an action being a result of criminality. Or sexual intercourse with improper persons or in improper places or at improper times, as it proceeds from a licentious disposition. Or again to make money from mean or shameful sources or from those who cannot help themselves as e.g. the poor or the dead, (whence the proverb "to rob even a corpse *of its shroud* "), for such conduct springs from illiberality and a sordid love of gain. Or to refuse pecuniary assistance, when it is in one's power to give it, or to give it in an inadequate measure. Or to receive such assistance from persons who are not so wealthy as oneself. [1]Or borrowing when it will look like begging, or begging when it will look like asking a return, or asking a return when it will look like begging, or flattering with the view of being taken to beg, and this persistently in spite of previous failure; for all such conduct is a mark of illiberality. [2]*It is shameful* too to praise a person to his face, to praise his good points up to the sky and gloss over his weaknesses, or to display in his presence an exaggerated sympathy with his griefs, and so on, all these being marks of flattery. Or again to be unequal to the endurance

---

[1] The four cases mentioned may perhaps be illustrated as follows: (1) to ask for a loan of money when you have often borrowed money before and never repaid it, (2) to ask for it from one to whom you have recently rendered some service, (3) to ask for the repayment of a loan when it is not the time or place to ask for it, (4) to praise a person's liberality until it is clear that what you want is some pecuniary help from him.

[2] Omitting κολακείας.

of such labours as have been borne by persons who are our seniors or who live luxurious lives or who are higher in authority or in general who are less robust; for all this is a sign of effeminacy. Or to receive services from a neighbour and to receive them often and then to cast one's own services to him in his teeth, these being so many signs of a mean and grovelling temper. Or to employ large and boastful language about oneself and to take credit for the good deeds of other people; for this again is a sign of arrogant assumption. And the same is true of the results of every other vice of character, and of the signs of it and resemblances to it; they are shameful and provoke a feeling of shame. I may add that it is shameful not to participate in the advantages in which all people or all one's own peers or most of them participate, meaning by 'peers' one's co-nationalists, fellow-citizens, contemporaries or kinsfolk and generally all who stand on an equality with us; for *if they are one's equals*, it is at once shameful not to participate in the same advantages with them, as e.g. not to receive equal educational advantages, and so on. And in all these instances the shame is the greater, if the defect is due apparently to oneself; for it necessarily appears to be the result of vice rather than of any other cause, if one has oneself alone to thank for one's defects past, present or to come. [1]Again, we are ashamed of being or having been or being likely to be subjected to such things as tend to bring upon us dishonour and reproach, i.e. to actions which imply a subservience

---

[1] Putting a full stop after μελλόντων.

of the person or a subservience in respect of shameful
deeds, among which I include wanton outrage. In
cases of incontinency this subservience *is shameful*,
whether it be voluntary or not [1](involuntary subservience being subservience under compulsion) as such
passive endurance and non-resistance is itself a result
of effeminacy or cowardice.

Such and similar to these are the things of which
we feel ashamed. But as shame is an impression
in regard to the loss of reputation, and this on its
own account without reference to its consequences,
and as nobody values reputation or good opinion
except for the sake of those who entertain it, it
follows that the persons before whom we feel shame
are those whom we hold in some esteem. This is the
case with people who admire us, or whom we admire,
or whose admiration we desire to win, or whose
rivals we are, or whose good opinion we do not
despise. Now we desire the admiration of people,
and ourselves admire them, if they are in possession
of some good which confers distinction, or if we have
a strong desire of something of which they are masters,
as e.g. in the case of lovers. Again, the people whose
rivals we are are our peers, and the people whom we
esteem as authorities *upon any question* are persons
of practical wisdom i.e. persons advanced in life or
highly cultured. *The shame we feel too is* the greater
in proportion to the patency and notoriety of the

Persons who inspire a feeling of shame.

---

[1] Mr Cope's reading of the passage is an improvement: καὶ
τὰ μὲν εἰς ἀκολασίαν καὶ ἑκόντα καὶ ἄκοντα (τὰ δ' εἰς βίαν ἄκοντα) ἀπὸ
ἀνανδρίας κ.τ.λ.

facts; whence the proverb which says that [1] the eye is the seat of modesty. It is for this reason that we feel a greater shame before such persons as will continually be near us or as watch us closely; for in both cases there are eyes upon us. Or before persons who are not liable to the same imputations as we are; for it is clear that their sentiments are opposed to our own. Or who are not inclined to be indulgent to apparent failings; for as a man is supposed not to be indignant with his neighbours for doing what he does himself, it is evident *conversely* that he is indignant, if they do what he does not do himself. Or who are fond of spreading reports; for a fault may as well not be suspected as *suspected and* not spread abroad. The people who are likely to spread reports are those who have been injured by us, as they are always on the watch for their opportunity, and slanderers, who will speak evil of the innocent and therefore *a fortiori* of the guilty. Also *we have a feeling of shame before persons* who devote themselves to the study of their neighbours' faults, as e.g. satirists and comic poets; for these too are in a certain sense slanderers and telltales. Or before persons in whose presence we have never met with a failure, as to them we may be said to be objects of admiration. This is the reason why we have a feeling of shame in refusing persons who ask a favour of us for the first time, from the idea that we have never yet lost credit

---

[1] It may be doubted whether Aristotle applies this proverbial saying rightly, when he takes it to mean that, the more public or visible a shameful deed is, the greater is the shame attaching to it.

in their eyes. It is the same with those who have recently conceived a wish to be our friends; for it is the best points only *in our character* that they have observed, and hence the appropriateness of the [1]answer which Euripides made to the Syracusans. It is the same too with old acquaintances who have no knowledge of anything against us. Nor is it only of the actual shameful things which have been mentioned that we are ashamed, but of anything that is indicative of them, as e.g. of the indications of illicit love no less than of the illicit love itself. Nor is it only of shameful deeds that we are ashamed but of shameful words. Similarly it is not only the persons above described of whom we feel shame, but those too who will give them information, let us say e.g. servants or their friends. Generally speaking however, we do not feel shame before persons for whose accuracy of judgment we entertain a great contempt—nobody e.g. feels shame before children or animals—nor again is it about the same things that we feel shame before our own intimate acquaintances and before strangers, but before the former it is about

---

[1] The answer, as it is given by the Scholiast, has certainly the air of an invention. Euripides (he says), being sent on an embassy to Syracuse and finding that his efforts on behalf of peace and friendship were unsuccessful, said "You ought, O Syracusans, to respect our prayer and the homage we seem thus to pay you, if for no other reason, yet because we have so recently begun to ask favours of you." It is not however in itself improbable that Euripides, who, as Plutarch relates, was a favourite poet in Sicily, may have been sent to treat with the Syracusans for the ransom of the captives after the disastrous expedition described in the Seventh Book of Thucydides.

such things as are considered to be really and truly
shameful and before the latter about things which are
shameful only conventionally.

The conditions under which we are likely to feel
shame are the following : Firstly, if there are certain
persons actually standing to us in the relation of
those before whom, as we said, we feel shame, i.e.
persons who are admired by us, or who admire us,
or whose admiration we wish to win, or at whose
hands we require a certain service which we shall
not obtain, if we lose credit in their eyes, and these
either actual spectators *of our conduct* (as in the
example of the harangue delivered by Cydias respecting the [1]colonization of Samos, when he begged
the Athenians to imagine that all Greece was standing
around them as eyewitnesses of their votes and not
as mere hearers only after the event), or again if the
persons described are near at hand or are sure to
perceive what we do. This is the reason why in the
hour of our misfortune we do not wish to be seen by
those who were once our emulators, emulation being a
form of admiration. Another *condition in which we
feel shame* is when we are conscious of achievements
and actions upon which we shall bring dishonour,
whether they be our own or those of our ancestors
or of others to whom we are intimately related, [2]or
in general of those on whose behalf we ourselves

---

[1] There were several occasions on which colonists (κληροῦχοι)
were sent to Samos; but nothing is known of Cydias or his speech.
As to the nature of κληρουχία see Mr Grote's *History of Greece*,
ch. xxxi. vol. IV. pp. 97—8.

[2] Changing the full stop after ἀγχιστεία τις to a comma.

have feelings of shame, i. e. not only the persons already described, but all who guide themselves by the standard of our lives, whose teachers and counsellors we have been, or other people, if such there be, like ourselves, whose rivals we are; for it is from a consideration for them that a feeling of shame often leads us to act or to abstain from acting. And again we are liable to shame in a higher degree when we are likely to be seen by the witnesses of our disgrace and to associate with them publicly. This was the point of the remark made by the poet Antiphon when he had been sentenced by Dionysius to be bastinadoed to death and saw his fellow-victims covering their faces on their way through the gates: "What is the good of covering your faces?" he said, "are you afraid of somebody here seeing you tomorrow?"

So much then may be said respecting shame. In regard to shamelessness on the other hand it is evident that, if we choose the topics opposite to these, we shall be at no loss for arguments.

CHAP. VII. · The objects of [1]benevolence, the occasions which
(9) Benevolence. prompt it and the conditions under which it is felt will be evident, when we have defined benevolence itself.

Definition of benevolence. It is benevolence, we may say, in virtue of which the person in whom it resides is said to render a

---

[1] It is necessary in this chapter to observe that the single word χάρις is used in three different senses, (1) benevolence, as a disposition or, as Aristotle calls it, an emotion, (2) a benevolent action, (3) the disposition created by benevolent actions, viz. gratitude.

service to anybody in the hour of need, not in return for previous services nor for any personal benefit to him who renders it but for the benefit of the recipient alone. Further, the service is a great one, if the need of it is extreme, or if its results are great and difficult of attainment, or if it is done at a crisis which is great and difficult, or if this is the only or the first or the greatest occasion of its being done.

Means of enhancing benevolence.

All our natural impulses are needs, especially those which are attended with pain, unless gratified, as e.g. ¹our desires, such as love ²and others which are incident to times of physical suffering and peril ; for desire is felt by anyone in danger or in pain. Hence it is that those who stand by us in poverty and exile, although the service which they have rendered us be a trifling one, yet from the magnitude of our need and the critical occasion are our benefactors, like ³the man who lent the mat in the Lyceum. It follows then that the service rendered must have reference, if possible, ⁴to these points, *which enhance its value,* and, if not, to others of equal or greater importance. As it is evident therefore what are the occasions and causes of benevolence

---

¹ οἱ ἐπιθυμίαι should of course be αἱ ἐπιθυμίαι.

² The stop after ἔρως should be changed to a comma.

³ The Scholiast has a story of a man being shut up in a tower and another who passed by throwing him a mat, so that he could let himself down and escape. But it is a story apparently made to suit the text. The allusion cannot now be explained.

⁴ Reading εἰς ταῦτα I agree with Bonitz (*Index Aristotelicus,* s. v. ἔχειν) in taking τὴν ὑπουργίαν as the subject of ἔχειν and εἰς ταῦτα ἔχειν as a single phrase meaning "to be directed to these ends."

and the usual conditions under which we feel it, it
is clear that these are the materials which we must
employ in trying ¹to work upon *the feelings of our
audience;* we must show that the person benefited
either is or has been in such want or pain as has
been described and on the other hand that the benefactor has done or is doing such a service in such

Means of
disparaging
benevo-
lence.

circumstances of need. Nor is it less evident how to
rob a deed of its benevolence and to represent its
authors as anything but benevolent, by urging that
it is for purely selfish motives (which exclude benevolence) that the service is or was rendered, or
that it was the result of accident or strong compulsion, or that it was a repayment of past services and
not a free gift, whether its authors were aware of
this or not; for in either case it was only a return
and consequently still not an act of pure benevolence. And in examining a benevolent action we
must consider it in regard to all the ²categories ; for
it is such, either as being a particular thing or as
having a particular magnitude or character or as
being done at a particular time or in a particular
place. We infer *the absence of a benevolent intention in a kind deed,* if the person has refused to
render us a smaller service or has rendered the same
or an equal or greater service to our enemies ; for
in this case again it is evident that the deed was

¹ I take παρασκευαστέον in the sense of "working upon" or "influencing" an audience. Cp. the use of παρασκευάζειν, p. 61, l. 22,
p. 66, l. 17, p. 76, l. 16. Aristotle uses κατασκευάζειν in the same
sense, e.g. p. 54, l. 23, p. 59, l. 20.

² The ten Categories are enumerated Κατηγορίαι, ch. 4.

not done from disinterested motives. We have the
same feeling, if it was valueless and the author knew
it to be so; for nobody admits that he wants what is
valueless.

Having now described benevolence and its opposite, we may proceed to consider the things which
excite compassion, the objects of compassion and the
conditions under which we feel it.

Chap. VIII.
(10) Com-
passion.

Compassion may be defined as a sort of pain at
an evident evil of a destructive or painful kind in the
case of somebody who does not deserve it, the evil
being one to which we may naturally expect ourselves or some one of our own friends to be liable,
and this at a time when it appears to be near at
hand; for it is plain that a person who is to be
capable of compassion must be so constituted as to
regard himself or some one of his friends as liable to
suffering evil of some kind, and *not only to evil in
the abstract but* to such evil as has been stated in the
definition or such as is similar or comparable to it.
Hence it is that compassion is not felt by those who
are absolutely ruined—for they regard themselves as
incapable of further suffering, their own sufferings
being already past—nor again by those who believe
in their own supreme felicity, and who *are not compassionate but rather* insolent; for if they suppose
themselves to be in the enjoyment of all possible
goods, it is clear that exemption from the possibility
of any evil, as being itself a good, will be among the
number. The people who would naturally regard
themselves as liable to suffering are those who have
already experienced suffering and survived it, or

Definition
of compas-
sion.

Conditions
of compas-
sion.

those who are somewhat advanced in years, as they possess both sagacity and experience, or those who are *physically* weak or who are especially inclined to be timid or who are well-informed and therefore able to calculate probabilities. The same is true of people who have parents or children or wives living, as these are all parts of a man's self and are liable to such sufferings as have been mentioned. It is true too of those who are not in any such emotional state as engenders courage, e.g. anger or confidence (for these are states which are wholly reckless of the future), nor in an insolent disposition of mind (as people who are insolent are equally reckless of future suffering), but who are in an intermediate condition ; [1] and who on the other hand are not in a state of vehement fear; for there is no feeling of compassion in people who are terror-stricken, as they think of nothing but their own emotion. Again, *it is necessary to the feeling of compassion* that we should believe in the existence of human virtue; for he who does not believe in anybody's virtue will consider that everybody is deserving of evil. It is in a word a general rule *that a person is liable to compassion,* whenever he is in condition to recall similar events as having happened either to himself or to any of his friends or to anticipate the possibility of their happening either to himself or to any of his friends.

Causes of compassion. Such then being the conditions under which we feel compassion, the objects of compassion are evident from the definition. They are all such painful and

---

[1] Placing only a comma after τούτων, as the grammatical construction, like the sense, is unbroken.

distressing things as are destructive and ruinous, and all such evils as are produced by Fortune, if they are serious. By things painful and destructive I mean death in its various forms, bodily injuries and afflictions, old age, disease and want of food ; by the evils of Fortune the absolute lack or the scarcity of friends (and it follows that the separation from friends and intimate acquaintances excites compassion), physical deformity, constitutional weakness and bodily mutilation. Another thing which excites compassion is the occurrence, and *still more* the frequent recurrence, of an evil result from something which naturally might have been expected to lead to good. Another is the attainment of some good, when all is over with the person to whom it comes, [1]as e.g. the present sent from the Great King to Diopeithes at the time when he was already lying dead. Another is the utter failure either to attain anything good or, when it is attained, to enjoy it.

Such then and similar to these being the causes which excite compassion, the persons who are the objects of compassionate feeling are our familiar friends, unless indeed they are very closely related to us, for then our feeling for them is much the same as it would be for ourselves in imminent peril. It was thus that [2]Amasis, while he shed no tears, as the

Objects of compassion.

---

[1] The incident is unknown; for the story which the Scholiast tells is clearly unfounded.

[2] The story is told by Herodotus Bk. iii. ch. 14, but the person of whom he tells it is not Amasis but his successor Psammenitus. It is possible that Aristotle in the words ὡς φασίν is not referring specially to Herodotus. It is more likely however that he has made a slip of memory.

story goes, when his son was led away to execution,
wept when his friend asked an alms of him, the reason
being that, while the latter spectacle moved him to
compassion, the former moved him only to terror; for
the motive cause of terror is not only distinct from
that of compassion but is calculated to expel compassionate feelings and *even* serves in many cases to
arouse its opposites. [1]Again, we experience a feeling
of compassion, when the danger *which threatens others*
approaches ourselves. We compassionate those who
are like ourselves in age, character, habit of mind,
reputation or family, as in all these cases there appears to be a greater probability of the same misfortune happening to ourselves *as to them;* for in
regard to compassion again it is a general principle
to be observed that whatever moves us to fear, when it
affects ourselves, moves us to compassion, when it
affects other people. And as sufferings are objects of
compassion if they are apparently close at hand,
whereas, if they occurred ten thousand years ago or
will occur ten thousand years hence, the anticipation
or remembrance of them, as the case may be, either
excites no compassion at all in us or excites it in a
much smaller degree, it necessarily follows that orators
are more successful in arousing compassion, if they

Means of
exciting
compassion.

---

[1] Such must apparently be the meaning, if the text is right;
cp. p. 72, l. 4. But Vahlen has some reason for suggesting that it
should be οὐ γὰρ ἔτι ἐλεοῦσιν ἐγγὺς αὐτοῖς τοῦ δεινοῦ ὄντος. Cp. p. 73,
l. 8. Aristotle's view is that evil is apt to excite compassion,
when it comes near us; but if it comes too near, if it attacks our
intimate friends or kinsfolk, the compassion is changed into
terror.

aid the effect of their words by their gestures, tones, habiliments and dramatic action of any kind ; for by setting an evil before our very eyes, whether as future or as past, they give it an appearance of proximity. Events of the recent past or of the near future excite a higher degree of compassion for the same reason. Again, *among the elements of compassion it is right to mention* the visible signs *of a tragic event* or ¹*the vivid representation of a person's* actions, as e.g. the clothes and other such relics of the sufferers or the expressions and other such characteristics of people in the hour of their suffering, as e.g. in the very hour of death. But the most powerful of all such elements is a noble demeanour of the sufferer in these critical moments. For all these circumstances increase the compassionate feeling from the apparent proximity of the evil to ourselves, from the impression that it was undeserved by the sufferer and from the vivid representation of it before our eyes.

The proper correlative of compassion is what is called virtuous indignation. For the feeling of pain at unmerited prosperity is in some sense opposed to the feeling of pain at unmerited misfortune, and it proceeds from the same character. Also both these emotions are proper to a virtuous character; for it is right not only to be sympathetic and compassionate in cases of undeserved misfortune but to be virtuously indignant in cases of undeserved prosperity, as any violation of the principle of desert is

Chap. IX. (11) Virtuous indignation.

¹ Probably the words καὶ τὰς πράξεις should be placed before καὶ λόγους l. 29.

an injustice. [1]Accordingly we attribute a feeling of

virtuous indignation even to the Gods. It may be supposed that envy too is in the same sense opposite to compassionate feeling, as being closely connected and indeed identical with virtuous indignation; but really it is different, as although envy, no less than virtuous indignation, is a pain which causes perturbation and is felt in reference to *another's* prosperity, yet it is not now the prosperity of someone who is undeserving but of someone equal and similar to ourselves. [2]That the feeling is wholly disinterested and arises solely from the circumstances of our neighbour is a necessary and equally essential feature of both these emotions; for the one will cease to be virtuous indignation and the other to be envy, and, *instead of being such*, each of them will be *merely* fear, if the ground of the actual pain and perturbation is the expectation that some evil consequence to ourselves will result from the prosperity of the other. It is clear too that these emotions will be attended by their opposites. A person who feels pain at unmerited misfortune will feel pleasure or *at least* will not feel any pain at misfortune when it has been merited; thus no virtuous person will feel any pain when punishment falls upon parricides or murderers, as it is our duty to rejoice at such cases, and similarly at cases of merited prosperity; for both are agreeable to justice and fill the heart of a good man with

[1] There should be a full stop or a colon after γιγνόμενον.

[2] The sentence, if fully expressed, would run, τὸ δὲ μὴ λυπεῖσθαι ὅτι αὐτῷ τι συμβήσεται ἕτερον κ.τ.λ., i.e. literally "the not being grieved because of some evil that will happen to oneself."

joy in the hope, which he naturally feels, that what
has happened to one who resembles him may equally
happen to himself. Further, 'all these feelings are
proper to the same character, and the opposite
feelings to the opposite character ; for a person who
is envious will also be malicious as, if he feels pain Malice.
at the acquisition or possession of a thing *by another*,
he will by a necessary consequence feel pleasure
at the denial or destruction of it. Accordingly these
feelings, *viz. virtuous indignation, envy and malice*,
while they have all a tendency to prevent compassion,
are different for the reasons already assigned and
in consequence may all alike be serviceable as means
of destroying the compassionable aspect of things.

Let us then consider first the feeling of virtuous
indignation, the persons against whom it is directed,
the occasions which excite it and the conditions
under which we are subject to it, and proceed afterwards to the other emotions.

But the truth is evident from what has been Definition
already said ; for if virtuous indignation is a feeling of virtuous
indignation.
of pain at such prosperity as is apparently unmerited,
it is clear in the first place that it is impossible to Objects of
feel such indignation at goods of every kind *indis-* virtuous
indignation.
criminately. It is not for being just or courageous
or for acquiring virtue that one will feel a righteous
indignation against a person, as neither are compassionate feelings excited by the opposites of justice,
courage and virtue, but on account of wealth, power

---

[1] "All these feelings," i.e. pleasure at (1) merited good fortune,
(2) merited ill fortune, and vexation at (1) unmerited good fortune,
(2) unmerited ill fortune.

and the like, and indeed in general terms of all such
things as are properly due to those who are *morally*
good and who are in possession of the goods of
nature, i.e. of nobility, beauty and the like. And
as antiquity *of possession* seems to approximate to
natural right, it follows that, where two persons
are in possession of the same good, the indignation
felt is the greater in the case of one who has recently
acquired it and who is prosperous in consequence
of the acquisition ; for greater annoyance is caused
to us by the *nouveaux riches* than by persons of
ancient and hereditary wealth. The same may be
said too of official status, power, a numerous *clientèle*,
a good and beautiful family and the like. Nor is
it otherwise with any other good which may accrue
to persons in consequence of these ; for here again
it is the *nouveaux riches* in the enjoyment of an
official position which they owe to their wealth who are
a greater source of annoyance to us than members of
the old substantial families. It is the same again in
all other cases. The reason is that the old proprietors
seem to possess what is theirs *by right*, and the others
do not ; for the appearance of perpetuity has an air
of reality, so that the *nouveaux riches* look as though
they were usurpers. Again, each particular kind
of good is not appropriate to all persons indiscriminately, but there is a certain correspondence and
propriety, fine armour e.g. being appropriate not to
the just man but rather to the brave, and grand
alliances not so much to the *nouveaux riches* as to
members of the *genuine* aristocracy. [1]Accordingly

[1] Mr Cope is clearly right in regarding the protasis, which has

it is a cause of virtuous indignation that a person, if his character stands high, should fail of his appropriate reward, or that an inferior should compete with one who is superior to him, [1]especially when the comparison is made on ground common to both; whence the saying of Homer *that Cebriones*

> [2]" Shunned the good sword of Telamonian Aias;
> For Zeus was wroth with whoso combated
> Against a braver hero,"

but in a less degree whatever be the point of inferiority, as e.g. if a musician enters into competition with a just man, inasmuch as justice is a better thing than music.

The persons against whom we feel righteous indignation and the causes of it are now evident; for they are such as have been described or very similar.

Passing to the conditions, we are disposed to this indignation, if it is the case that we deserve the greatest goods and actually possess them, as there is something unjust in the promotion of persons who are unlike ourselves *and inferior to us* to the like advantages. [3]A second condition is when we are

Conditions of virtuous indignation.

been broken by the intervening examples, as resumed in the words ἐὰν οὖν ἀγαθὸς ὢν κ.τ.λ. But it seems better to break up the sentence in translating.

[1] A bad musician competing with a good one would be an instance of a comparison made "on ground common to both" (ἐν τῷ αὐτῷ); a musician competing with a just man would be a comparison of another kind.

[2] *Iliad* xi. 542. The second line does not occur in the received text of Homer.

[3] It is not quite easy to distinguish the second case from the first; hence Muretus proposed to insert μὴ before τυγχάνωσιν. But

good and virtuous persons ; for then we are good judges and haters of injustice. A third, when we are ambitious and eagerly desirous of particular functions, and especially if our ambition directs itself to certain objects of which others, who attain them, are unworthy. It is indeed a general rule that, if we consider ourselves to be worthy of particular things and others to be unworthy of them, we are liable to feel a virtuous indignation against them and to feel it on account of these things. And from this it follows that slavish, mean and unambitious natures are not subject to virtuous indignation, as there is nothing of which they consider themselves to be worthy.

From all this it is evident what are the cases of misfortune, disaster or failure in which it is proper to rejoice or at least to feel no pain ; for from the conditions which have been described the opposite conditions are manifest, and the result is that, if the speech which is delivered produces a proper frame of mind in the judges who hear it and proves that those who claim compassion on certain specified grounds do not deserve to obtain it or even deserve not to obtain it, in such case the feeling of compassion becomes impossible.

CHAP. X. (12) Envy. Definition of envy.

Nor is it difficult to see what are the occasions and objects of envy and the conditions under which we feel envious, envy being defined as a species of

in the first case the ground of indignation is, I think, that others, who are less deserving than we are, are promoted to an equality with us; in the second it is that others are promoted to advantages which they do not deserve, whether we ourselves enjoy them or not.

pain felt at conspicuous prosperity on the part of persons like ourselves in respect of such goods as have been already described, and this not with any view to our own personal advantage but *solely* because they are prosperous.

For people will be envious, if there are or if they think there are persons like themselves, like, I mean, in race, family, age, habit of mind, reputation or possessions. Or if they only just fall short of having everything *which men can desire;* hence the envious disposition of persons who are engaged in important affairs or who are highly prosperous, as they fancy all the world is robbing them of their due. Or again if they have a permanent reputation for something, and especially for wisdom or happiness. Ambitious persons too are more liable to envy than the unambitious. Pretenders to wisdom are envious, as being ambitious of the credit of wisdom; and in general persons who are eager for reputation in a particular subject are envious in regard to it. Lastly, mean-minded persons are envious; for everything appears important to them.

Conditions of envy.

As regards the occasions of envy, the goods which provoke it have been already stated; for all achievements or possessions of which we covet the reputation or are ambitious, all things which arouse in us a longing for reputation, as well as all the various gifts of Fortune are practically without exception natural objects of envy, and of these such especially as we ourselves either desire or imagine we have a right to possess, or as by their acquisition confer a slight superiority or inferiority.

Causes of envy.

It is clear too who are the natural objects of envy, as they are implied in the statement which has just been made ; they are persons who are near to us in time, place, age or reputation. Hence the saying

> [1] "For to be kin is to be envious."

We are envious too of people whom we are ambitious of rivalling, i.e. of such people as have been mentioned, but not of those who lived many ages ago or who are yet unborn or dead or [2]at the ends of the world. Nor again, where there are people to whom we think we are far inferior or far superior, whether we depend upon our own opinion only or upon that of the world at large, have we the same feeling of rivalry in regard to them and in cases like theirs. But as this rivalry extends to those who are our antagonists in any competition or in love and indeed to all who aspire to the same things as ourselves, these will necessarily be the principal objects of envy ; whence the proverb "Two of a trade never agree." Again, we are envious of people who have attained a rapid success, if we have succeeded with difficulty or have not succeeded at all. Or of people whose possession of a thing or whose success is a reproach to us, such people again being near and similar to ourselves ; for as it is evidently [3]our own fault that we fail to obtain the good *which they obtain*, it is the annoyance of this fact which

---

[1] A line attributed by the Scholiast to Æschylus.

[2] The pillars of Hercules were in the Greek view the bounds of the known world.

[3] Reading παρ' αὑτούς.

produces in us the feeling of envy. Or again of people who either naturally or by acquisition possess anything which naturally belonged to us or had been acquired by us; this is the reason why seniors are envious of their juniors. Lastly, people who have spent a large sum upon a particular thing are envious of those who have spent little upon it *with an equal result.*

We see now clearly [1]the occasions upon which envious people experience a feeling of pleasure, the persons whose cases give rise to such a feeling and the conditions under which people experience it; [2]for, whatever be the conditions the absence of which produces pain *at certain things,* their presence will produce pleasure at the opposite things. Hence if the audience has been brought to an envious condition of mind and the persons on whose behalf a claim to compassion or to good of any kind is advanced are such as have been described, *i.e. proper objects of envy,* it is evident that they will not meet with compassion at the hands of those who are masters of the position.

The conditions of emulation, its causes and the persons who are the objects of it are evident from the following considerations.

CHAP. XI.
(13) Emula-
tion.

---

[1] Reading ἐφ᾽ οἷς, the οἷς being neuter.

[2] Upon the whole, although not without a good deal of uncertainty, I have retained the οὐκ before ἔχοντες. Aristotle's meaning seems to be this: that, if there are certain conditions which excite pain in the bosom of the envious man, then the opposite conditions will excite pleasure in it, and that, while the cause of the pain is the good fortune of people like himself, the cause of

Emulation is a species of pain at the manifest presence of such goods as are valued highly and also attainable by ourselves in persons who have a natural resemblance to us, and this not because somebody else is in possession of them but because we are not equally in possession of them ourselves. [1](Accordingly emulation is a virtuous emotion, and its subjects are virtuous, whereas envy is vicious, and its subjects vicious; for while the emulous man is induced by his emulation to contrive that he himself should acquire these goods, the envious man is induced by his envy to contrive that his neighbour should not enjoy them.) It follows at once then that people are inclined to emulation, if they consider themselves entitled to goods which they do not actually enjoy, *provided of course that these goods are attainable by them*, for nobody supposes himself to be entitled to such goods as are evidently impossible. This is the ground of emulation in the young and the highminded. It is the same in persons who possess such goods as are appropriate to people who are held in honour, i. e. wealth, a large circle of friends, official positions and so on; for it is from the feeling that they have a natural claim to goodness, as possessing the things which, as we have seen, naturally belong to the good, that they emulously claim such goods as are the marks of honour. It is the same too in

the pleasure will be the opposite of it, viz. the ill-fortune of people like himself.

[1] The sentence enclosed in brackets is parenthetical. The apodosis begins at the words ἀνάγκη δὴ ζηλωτικοὺς μὲν εἶναι.

persons who are regarded by the world at large as
entitled to these goods. Again, if there is any particular thing for which our ancestors or kinsmen or
friends or race or nation have been held in honour, it
is a subject upon which we are disposed to emulation, thinking that it is proper to ourselves and that
we have a title to it.

If then it is such goods as are held in honour Causes of
emulation.
which are the objects of emulation, it follows that
this is true of the virtues and of all things which
are serviceable and beneficial to the world at large,
as we hold our benefactors and good men generally
in honour, ¹and also of all goods from which our
neighbours derive enjoyment, such as wealth and
personal beauty rather than health.

It is evident also who are the objects of emula- Objects of
emulation.
tion. They are persons who are in possession of
these or similar advantages, e.g. valour, wisdom, and
official power ; for a great opportunity of beneficence
is open to persons in power, such as generals, orators
and all who have influential positions of a similar
kind. Or again they are persons who are widely
looked upon as models or as desirable acquaintances
and friends or who are objects of admiration to the
world at large or to ourselves or whose eulogies and
panegyrics are pronounced by poets and orators.

The objects of contempt are the opposites of (14) Contempt.
these, contempt being the antithesis of emulation,
and a contemptuous mood of an emulous one. It Conditions
of con-
follows that those who are in a condition to emulate tempt.
others or to be themselves the objects of emulation,

---

¹ Reading only a colon after ἀγαθούς.

will be so far inclined to contemn those who are
subject to such evils as are contrary to the goods
which provoke emulation. And hence we often contemn fortunate people, when their Fortune is unattended by such goods as are held in honour.

So much then for the means of creating and dissipating the emotions, these means being the sources
of argumentative proofs respecting them.

CHAP. XII.   It remains for us to describe the varieties of cha-
Varieties of racter dependent upon the emotions, habits of mind,
character. times of life and accidents of Fortune, meaning by
"emotions" anger, desire and the like, which have
been already discussed, and by "habits of mind" vir-
pp. 60, 61. tues and vices; these too have been already discussed
as well as the objects of individual choice and action.
The "times of life" are youth, the prime of life and
age. And by "Fortune" I mean nobility, wealth,
power in any of its forms and the opposites of these
and indeed any kind of prosperity or adversity.

The cha-   The young are in character prone to desire and
racter of ready to carry any desire they may have formed into
youth. action. Of bodily desires it is the sexual to which
they are most disposed to give way, and in regard to
sexual desire they exercise no self-restraint. They
are changeful too and fickle in their desires, which
are as transitory as they are vehement; for their
wishes are keen without being permanent, like a sick
man's fits of hunger and thirst. They are passionate,
irascible and apt to be carried away by their impulses.
They are the slaves too of their passion, as their ambition prevents their ever brooking a slight and renders them indignant at the mere idea of enduring an

injury. And while they are fond of honour, they are fonder still of victory; for superiority is the object of youthful desire, and victory is a species of superiority. Again, they are fonder both of honour and of victory than of money, the reason why they care so little for money being that they have never yet had experience of want, as [1] the saying of Pittacus about Amphiaraus puts it. They are charitable rather than the reverse, as they have never yet been witnesses of many villainies; and they are trustful, as they have not yet been often deceived. They are sanguine too; for the young are heated by Nature as drunken men *by wine*, not to say that they have not yet experienced frequent failures. Their lives are lived principally in hope, as hope is of the future and memory of the past, and while the future of youth is long, its past is short; for on the first day of life it is impossible to remember anything, but all things must be matters of hope. For the same reason they are easily deceived, as being quick to hope. They are inclined to be valorous; for they are full of passion, which excludes fear, and of hope, which inspires confidence, as anger is incompatible with fear, and the hope of something good is itself a source of confidence. They are bashful too, having as yet no independent standard of honour and having lived entirely in the school of conventional law. They have high aspirations; for they have never yet been humiliated by the experience of life, but are unacquainted with the limiting force of circumstances; and a great idea of one's own deserts, such as is characteristic of a sanguine disposition, is itself a form of high aspiration.

[1] The saying is unknown.

Again, in their actions they prefer honour to expediency, as it is habit rather than calculation which is the rule of their lives, and, while calculation pays regard to expediency, virtue pays regard *exclusively* to honour. Youth is the age when people are most devoted to their friends or relations or companions, as they are then extremely fond of social intercourse and have not yet learnt to judge their friends or indeed anything else by the rule of expediency. If the young commit a fault, it is always on the side of excess and exaggeration in defiance of [1] Chilon's maxim; for they carry everything too far, whether it be their love or hatred or anything else. They regard themselves as omniscient and are positive in their assertions; this is in fact the reason of their carrying everything too far. Also their offences take the line of insolence and not of meanness. They are compassionate from supposing all people to be virtuous or *at least* better *than they really are;* for as they estimate their neighbours by their own guilelessness, they regard the evils which befall them as undeserved. Finally, they are fond of laughter and consequently facetious, facetiousness being disciplined insolence.

CHAP. XIII.
The character of age.

Such being the character of the young, it may be said generally that elder men who have passed their prime have characters mostly composed of the qualities opposite to these. For as they have lived many years and have been often the victims of deception and error, and as vice is the rule rather than the exception in human affairs, they are never positive about

[1] The maxim of Chilon is the famous rule μηδὲν ἄγαν.

anything and always err on the side of too[1] little excess. They "suppose," they never "know" anything; and in discussion they always add "perhaps" or "possibly," expressing themselves invariably in this guarded manner, but never positively. They are uncharitable too, i.e. they are ready to put the worst construction upon everything. Again, they are suspicious of evil from not trusting anybody, and they do not trust anybody from having had experience of human wickedness. Hence too they have no strong loves or hatreds; but according to the [2]precept of Bias their love is such as may some day be converted into hatred and their hatred such as may some day be converted into love. Their temper of mind is neither grand nor generous; not the former, for they have been so much humiliated by the experience of life as to have no desire of any great or striking object or of anything but the mere appliances of life; nor the latter, for property is a necessity of life, and they have learnt by experience the difficulty of acquiring it and the facility with which it may be lost. They are cowards and perpetual alarmists, their disposition being exactly contrary to that of the young; for as they are not fervent like the young, but have cooled down, their old age has in consequence paved the way for cowardice, fear

---

[1] The curious phrase ἧττον ἄγαν is an oxymoron; but it is coined to be a negative of ἄγαν.

[2] The precept of Bias, which is again quoted in ch. 21, is best known from the lines of Sophocles, *Ajax*, 678—683. It may be remarked that Ajax was eminently one who had been brought to his cautious or distrustful mood by his sad experience of human life.

itself being a sort of cooling process. ' They are fond of life, and never so fond of it as on their last day; for it is the absent which is the object of all desire, and that which we *most* lack we are most desirous to possess. They are selfish to a fault, selfishness again being a species of mean-mindedness. And from their selfishness it follows that their standard of life is too apt to be expediency rather than honour; for expediency is what is good to the individual, and honour what is good in an absolute sense. They are apt to be shameless rather than the contrary; for as they pay less regard to honour than to expediency, they are able to disregard appearances. They are despondent too partly from their experience of life—for the generality of things which occur in the world are bad or at least do not turn out so well as they might—and partly from their cowardly disposition. Again, they live by memory rather than by hope; for while the remainder of their life is *necessarily* short, its past is long, and the future is the sphere of hope, the past the sphere of memory. This too is the explanation of their garrulity; they are perpetually talking over what has happened in the past because of the pleasure they feel in recollection. Their fits of passion, although violent, are feeble; their sensual desires have either died away or become enfeebled, so that they are not prone either to desire or to action regulated by their desires but are rather guided in their actions by self-interest. The consequence is that people at this time of life are capable of self-control, as the strength of their desires has abated and self-interest is their mastering passion. Again, it is calculation rather

than character which regulates their lives; for while
calculation is directed to expediency, morality is
directed to virtue *as its end*. The offences which
they commit take the line of petty meanness rather
than of insolence. The old are compassionate as well
as the young, not however for the same reason; for
in the one case the reason is humanity, and in the
other infirmity, as the old suppose all manner of suffering to be at their door, and this is a state of mind
which, as we have said, excites compassion. Hence p. 152.
they are querulous, not facetious nor fond of laughter;
for querulousness is opposed to the love of laughter.
Such then are the characteristics of youth and age.
And as everybody approves such speeches as are
framed according to his own character or reflect it, it
is easy to see the proper way of treating our speeches
in order that we and the speeches we make may assume the requisite character.

　　As to persons who are in the prime of life, it is Chap. XIV.
evident that in character they will occupy a position The cha-
intermediate between the young and the old. They racter of the
will be exempt from the excess of either; they will prime of
be neither excessively confident, as excess of confi- life.
dence is foolhardiness, nor excessively fearful, but
will preserve a proper balance of confidence and
fear; they will be neither universally trustful nor
universally distrustful, but will rather form their
judgment in accordance with the facts; their rule
of life will be neither honour only nor expediency
only but both, and neither parsimony nor extravagance but a proper mean. The same will be true
in regard to passion and desire. They will combine

temperance with valour and valour with temperance, these being qualities which are distributed separately among the young and the old; for the young are brave and licentious and the old are temperate and cowardly. It may indeed be said generally that, wherever there are advantages distributed between youth and age, persons in the prime of life enjoy both, and that, wherever there are excesses or defects inherent in youth and age, they observe moderation and propriety in respect to them. The body, I may say, is at its prime from 30 to 35, and the soul about 49.

CHAP. XV.   So much for the several characters of youth, old age and the prime of life. We have next to consider the various gifts of Fortune by which the characters of men are shaped and influenced.

The character of nobility.   Now it is one characteristic of nobility that the possessor of it is distinguished by his ambition; for everybody who has anything to start with generally makes it a basis of his accumulations, and nobility is inherited distinction. Another is that such people are apt to despise even those who are on an equality with their own ancestors; for the same things confer more distinction and form a better subject of boasting, when they happen at a remote distance than when they happen near at hand. [1]The word "nobility" has reference to family virtue, the word

---

[1] The distinction here made between the words εὐγενής and γενναῖος occurs again περὶ τὰ ζῷα ἱστορίαι, p. 488 B$_{18-20}$ εὐγενὲς μὲν γάρ ἐστι τὸ ἐξ ἀγαθοῦ γένους, γενναῖον δὲ τὸ μὴ ἐξιστάμενον ἐκ τῆς αὑτοῦ φύσεως. For the meaning of φύσις see note on p. 82 of this translation.

"nobleness" to the non-degeneracy from the *proper*
nature *of the individual,* although this is generally
not the case with nobles, who are usually insignificant persons ; for there is a sort of succession
of crops in families as well as in the fruits of the
ground, and sometimes, if the family is a good one,
there arise distinguished men in it during a certain
period of time, and then on the contrary it fails. *It
may be remarked that,* while clever families degenerate
into the characteristics of insanity, as happened to the
descendants of Alcibiades and the elder Dionysius,
staid families like those of Cimon, Pericles and
Socrates degenerate into insipidity and dullness.

The characteristics which accompany wealth lie
on the surface and are easily seen. The wealthy
become insolent and overweening, being affected in
some degree by their acquisition of wealth. This
disposition originates in the idea that they are in
possession of every kind of good ; for as wealth is
in a way a standard of the value of everything else, it
seems as if everything else were purchasable by wealth.
Again, *the wealthy are* voluptuous and ostentatious,
voluptuous from their luxury and the display of
their prosperity, ostentatious and ill-mannered from
the habit which is common to us all of devoting our
time and thought to the objects of our love and admiration and from the idea that everybody else is emulous of the same things as they are themselves. Nor
indeed is this state of mind unreasonable ; for there
are many people who require the services of the rich.
It was this which gave rise to the saying of Simonides
about wisdom and wealth, when he was asked by

CHAP. XVI.
The cha-
racter of
wealth.

the wife of Hiero whether it were preferable to become a man of property or a philosopher. "A man of property," he said, "for I see the philosophers hanging about the doorsteps of the men of property." Another *characteristic of the wealthy* is a belief in their own title to authority, arising from a belief that they are in possession of the things which make authority worth having. In a word, the character of wealth is prosperity without good sense. There is a difference of character however between people who have only lately acquired wealth and people who have long enjoyed possession of it, in that the defects of wealth are found in a larger measure and in an aggravated form in the *nouveaux riches*, as they have not yet, so to say, been educated to their wealth. The offences which they commit are not of a petty fraudulent character but are offences either of insolence or of licentiousness, such e.g. as assault and battery or adultery.

CHAP. XVII
The character of power.

Similarly, the characteristics of power may be said to be generally evident, being in some cases identical with those of wealth and in others superior to them. Thus the powerful are more ambitious and heroic in their characters than the wealthy, as they aspire to all such actions as they have authority to perform in virtue of their power. They are more energetic, as being always on the alert from the necessity of looking to the conditions of their power. Their air is one of dignity rather than of offensive importance, as their high position by rendering them more conspicuous renders them moderate, and dignity is a soft and graceful air of importance. And their offences, if they commit any, are never petty but always on a large scale.

The characteristics of good Fortune are determined by [1]its shares of the advantages we have described. For the greatest elements of good Fortune, as they are called, follow these lines; and it may be added that good Fortune ensures superiority in respect of family blessings or of personal gifts. Thus while good Fortune inclines people to be somewhat arrogant and unreasonable, there is one excellent characteristic which it evokes, viz. the godfearing disposition of the fortunate and their general attitude towards religion, as the goods of which Fortune is the mother inspire a feeling of trustfulness in the Gods.

The characters produced by age or Fortune have now been described; for the opposites of those which have been described, i.e. the characters of the poor, the unfortunate and the powerless, are evident from a consideration of their opposites.

We are now in a position to sum up the results obtained. [2]Speeches of which persuasion is the

Chap.
XVIII.
Recapitula-
tion.

---

[1] Reading κατὰ τὰ μόρια.

[2] The long sentence with which the chapter begins stands in need of some little explanation. Rhetoric, whether deliberative or forensic, is always, says Aristotle, addressed to a judge. In the case of a deliberative speech the judge may be either an individual, as when you try to persuade or dissuade a friend in private life, or a number of persons, as when you address the Public Assembly. But nothing is said in the text about addressing a number of persons, the clause corresponding to ἄν τε πρὸς ἕνα κ.τ.λ. is not expressed. Further, a forensic speech may be either an argument against a real antagonist, as in a court of law, or an

The judicial character of an audience. object are invariably intended to be judged; for if we know a thing and have passed judgment upon it, there is no longer occasion for a speech. And this is true, even if it is only an individual whom it is the speaker's aim to encourage or dissuade, as happens *often* in admonition or persuasion; for the individual is as truly a judge as a large audience, inasmuch as anybody who is to be persuaded may be said in general terms to be a judge. It is equally true, whether the speech is directed against a real antagonist or an imaginary case; for *in the latter instance* the orator must employ his speech in upsetting an opposite hypothesis, and against this he argues as against a real antagonist. The case is the same in regard to epideictic oratory, where the composition of the speech has in view the audience as a judge. But as a general rule it is only the person who passes judgment upon questions in political contests that is strictly and properly a judge; for *in political cases (which include judicial)* there is a question either as to the truth of the points in dispute or as to the subject of the deliberation. The characters congenial to the different pp. 57 sqq. polities have been already discussed under the head of deliberative oratory, so that the means and

argument against some theory or abstract case, as in School or College declamations. See Prof. Mayor's note on Juvenal i. 16.

As to the construction of the sentence, it is more than probable that Aristotle has forgotten the need of a regular apodosis. At all events the clause ὥστε διωρισμένον ἂν εἴη κ.τ.λ. p. 85, l. 13, is an inference only from the preceding clause, not from all the clauses of the protasis.

methods of investing our speeches with [1] an ethical
character may be said to be pretty well determined.

We have seen that the ends are different in the p. 23.
several kinds of Rhetoric; we have ascertained the
opinions and premisses in each from which proofs pp. 25 sqq.
are derived in deliberative and epideictic or forensic
oratory; and we have determined the means by
which it is possible to invest our speeches with· an
ethical character. It remains for us then to discuss
the common topics, *as they may be called;* for *apart
from the special topics which have been described*
it is always necessary to employ the topic of possibility or impossibility in our speeches and to try to
prove either that a thing will be or that it has already occurred. Also the topic of degree is common
to all kinds of Rhetoric; for all orators use depreciation or exaggeration, whether in deliberative
Rhetoric or in eulogy or censure or in accusation
or defence. After determining the common topics,
it will be proper to say what we can in general
terms about enthymemes and examples, so as to
supply the deficiency which still remains and in this
way fulfil the original plan of our treatise. Among p. 70.
the common topics exaggeration, as has been said,
is especially adapted to epideictic oratory, fact past
to forensic oratory, as it is upon facts of the past that

---

[1] It should be borne in mind that a speech may be called
"ethical" either, as here, because it is adapted to the character of
the audience to whom it is addressed or because it displays
certain ethical qualities in the speaker himself. (Cp. ch. i.)
Still it is very strange that Aristotle makes no reference here
either to ἦθος in its more usual sense or to the πάθη.

the judicial decision turns, and the possible or future to deliberative oratory.

Let us take first the topic of possibility and impossibility.

Chap. XIX.
The common topics.
(1) Possibility. If there are two opposites, and the existence or production of one of them is possible, so presumably is the existence or production of the other. For instance, if a human being can be cured, he can also fall ill, inasmuch as the potentiality of opposites, [1]*qua* opposites, is identical. Again, if there are two similar things, and one of them is possible, so is the other. Or if the more difficult of two things is possible, so is the easier. Or if the production of a thing in an excellent and noble form is possible, its production generally is possible, as the making of a fine house is harder than the making of a house. Again, if the beginning of a thing is possible, so is the completion of it, as no impossibility ever comes or begins to come into being; the commensurability e.g. of the diagonal of a square with its side cannot begin to come, nor ever does come, into being. Or if the completion of a thing is possible, so is its beginning; for whatever comes into being originates from a beginning. Or if the [2]posterior in essence or in gene-

---

[1] It is necessary to insert this limiting clause; for although health and sickness, in so far as they are opposites, are equally possible to a human being, yet he may constitutionally be inclined to one rather than to the other. But throughout the chapter it must be remembered that the arguments suggested are only rhetorically useful, not necessarily or presumably valid in logic.

[2] Aristotle lays down in the *Metaphysics* (xiii. ch. 2, p. 1077 A 第) the principle that τὸ τῇ γενέσει ὕστερον τῇ οὐσίᾳ πρότερον.

ration is capable of coming into being, so is the prior; thus if a man can come into being, so can a boy, the boy being prior in generation, and if a boy can come into being, so can a man, the man being *essentially* a beginning. Again, the objects of natural love or desire are possible, as in general nobody is enamoured or desirous of impossibilities. Again, the existence of any science or art implies the possibility of the existence or production of the objects with which it deals. The same is true of anything, if the origin of its production depends upon things which we can influence by force or persuasion, i. e. upon persons whose superiors or masters or friends we are. Again, if the parts of a thing are possible, so is the whole, and if the whole is possible, so in general are the parts; thus if it is possible to produce an instep, toe-cap and body of a shoe, it is possible also to produce shoes, and if it is possible to produce shoes, it is possible also to produce an instep, toe-cap and body. Again, the possibility of producing the genus as a whole implies the possibility of producing the species, and *vice versa;* the possibility e.g. of producing a vessel implies the possibility of producing a trireme, and the possibility of producing a trireme implies the possibility of producing a vessel. And of two things which are naturally inter-dependent if one is possible, so is the other; if double e.g. is possible, so is half, and if half, so is double. Again, if a thing can be produced without art and preparation, it can *a fortiori* be produced by means of art and careful pains; whence the lines of Agathon

[1]"Of some must art be mother, some accrues
To us of fortune or necessity."

Lastly, if a thing is possible to inferior, weaker and less intelligent people, it is possible *a fortiori* to their opposites, according to the [2]saying of Isocrates that it was strange, if he should himself be unable to discover what a person like Euthynus had learnt.

On the subject of the impossible, it is evident that *the orator* has a stock *of topics* ready to hand in the opposites of those which have been mentioned.

(2) Fact past.

The fact of a thing having occurred or not in the past is to be examined by the light of the following considerations. In the first place, if that which is less likely to have occurred has occurred, it would appear that that which is more likely has also occurred. Or if that which is usually subsequent has occurred, *it may be argued that* that which is usually antecedent has occurred, as e.g., if a person has forgotten something, that he had once learnt it. Or if a person had at once the power and the will to do a certain act, *it may be argued that* he has done it; for everybody acts, when he has the power to do what he wishes, as there is then no impediment to

---

[1] The point of the lines, which are taken from an unknown play, is that things may be brought about either by art or by fortune, and that, if they are brought about by fortune, they are easier.

[2] There is no passage in the speech of Isocrates πρὸς Εὐθύνουν, if indeed it be genuine, or in any other of his extant speeches which suits this allusion. Mr Sandys has suggested that Aristotle may be referring by a slip of memory to an expression in the speech πρὸς Καλλίμαχον.

his action. The same is true, if he had the wish
and there was no external obstacle, or if he had the
power and was in an angry mood, or if he had the
power and with it the desire; for it is a general
rule that people, when they are eager to do a thing,
actually do it, as soon as they have the power, if they
are bad people from the lack of self-control, and if
they are good, because the objects of their desire
are honourable. Again, if it was a person's intention[1] to do a thing, *it may be argued that he did
it*, as there is always a probability that the intention
was carried out. Or if all the natural preliminaries
or means to a thing have occurred, *it may be argued
that the thing itself occurred*, as e.g., if it lightened
that it thundered too, and if a thing was attempted,
that it was done. Similarly, if the natural sequel or
end of anything has occurred, *it may be argued that*
the preliminaries and means to it have occurred also,
as e.g., if it thundered, that it lightened, and if a thing
was done, that it was attempted. In all these cases
the rule is sometimes one of necessity, and sometimes
one of only general validity.

Arguments against the occurrence of an event in
the past may evidently be derived from the topics
opposite to these.

As to arguments in regard to the future, it is (3) **Fact
future.**
clear *that they may be derived* from the same
sources. *It may be argued* that a thing will be
done, if there is both the power and the wish to do
it or if there is desire, anger and calculation combined with power. Accordingly it will be done, if

.[1] Omitting γίγνεσθαι, καί.

12—2

one has an immediate impulse or an intention to do it; for what is intended is generally more likely to happen than what is not; or if it has been preceded by all its former natural antecedents; if e.g. the sky is clouded, there is a probability of rain. Finally, if the means to an end have happened, there is a probability of the end itself happening; thus the foundation of a house implies the house itself.

(4) Degree. The topic of the greatness and smallness of things, in themselves and in comparison with each other and of great and small things generally is evident from the remarks we have already made, for in our pp. 46 sqq. chapters upon deliberative Rhetoric we have discussed the greatness of goods and comparative greatness or smallness in the abstract. Hence as in each of the three kinds of Rhetoric the end proposed is a good, whether expediency, honour or justice, it is evident that these must be the means of supplying the materials of amplification in each case. It is idle to look for anything more than this in regard to abstract greatness and superiority, particular facts being more important than general truths to the purpose *which we have now in hand.*

So much then for the possible and impossible, for the proof or disproof of facts past or future and also for the greatness and smallness of things[1].

Chap. XX. It remains then to speak of the proofs which are
The common proofs. common to the three kinds of Rhetoric, as the special

---

[1] There are then four κοινοὶ τόποι, as appears from this chapter, not three, as Mr Cope states in his note on § 26, nor yet the same four as he enumerates in his Introduction, p. 129, but (1) Possibility, (2) Fact past, (3) Fact future, (4) Degree.

proofs have already been discussed. These are two
in kind, viz. example and enthymeme ; for the maxim
is part of an enthymeme. It will be proper to begin
with example, as example corresponds to induction,
and [1]induction is a beginning *or principle of knowledge.*

Examples are of two kinds, one consisting in the (1) The example. allegation of historical facts and the other in the
invention of facts for oneself. Also invention com-
prises illustration on the one hand and fables, such
as those of Æsop and the [2]Libyan, on the other.

An instance of the allegation of historical facts (a) His-torical parallels. would be the case (let me say) of a person urging
the policy of arming against the Persian King and
preventing him from subjugating Egypt on the
ground that Darius did not cross *the Ægœan sea*
until he had made himself master of Egypt, although
no sooner was he master of it than he did so, and
Xerxes again did not invade *Grecian territory* until
he had made himself master of Egypt, although no
sooner was he master of it than he crossed the sea,
the inference being that the[3] present king will cross,

---

[1] Aristotle explains his own meaning in other passages, e.g.
Nicom. Eth. vi. ch. 3; *Analyt. Post.* ii. ch. 19.

[2] It would appear that, besides the fables attributed to Æsop,
there was a collection of fables called generally Libyan. They are
recognized by Quintilian (*Instit. Orat.* v. 11, 20) among others;
and a line is quoted by Hermogenes from the *Myrmidons* of
Æschylus

ὡς δ' ἐστὶ μύθων τῶν Λιβυστικῶν λόγος.

[3] It has been thought that Aristotle has in mind the occasion,
—it was in the year 350 B.C.—when Artaxerxes III. surnamed
Ochus sent ambassadors to the different Greek states to ask for

if he makes himself master of Egypt, and that consequently this must not be allowed.

(b) illustra-
tions.

As an instance of illustration I may cite the Socratic method. Suppose e.g. one were to insist upon
the absurdity of entrusting official power to a body
of men selected by lot, by urging that we might as
well select as our athletes, not the ablest combatants,
but any chance people upon whom the lot has fallen,
or might as well employ the lot in selecting the pilot
from among the crew, on the principle that the right
man is the one upon whom the lot has fallen rather
than the one who possesses the requisite knowledge.

(c) fables.

The fable may be exemplified by the fables of
Stesichorus respecting Phalaris and of Æsop in defence of the demagogue. At the time when the
people of Himera had elected Phalaris general, had
invested him with absolute powers and were on the
point of allowing him a body-guard, Stesichorus at
the close of a long argument told them the following
fable. There was a horse (he said) which was the
sole occupant of a meadow, when a stag came and
wasted his pasture ; so wishing to wreak his vengeance on the stag, he asked the man whether it
would be possible for him with his help to inflict
chastisement on the stag. "Oh ! yes" said the man,
"if you will be bridled and let me mount upon your
back, spear in hand." The horse consented, the man
mounted, and instead of taking vengeance upon the
stag, the horse found himself from that moment the
man's slave. "So do you too take care" said Stesi-

auxiliaries in his projected invasion of Egypt. Grote's *History of
Greece*, ch. xc. vol. xi. pp. 243—4.

chorus, "lest in your desire to avenge yourselves upon your enemies you experience the same fate as the horse. The bridle is already in your mouth, since you elected a general with absolute powers; give him a body-guard, let him mount upon your back, and from that moment you will be the slaves of Phalaris." Æsop again at Samos, as counsel for a demagogue who was being tried for a capital offence, said that a fox in crossing a river was swept down into a cleft of the rock and, being unable to get out, was for a long time in a sorry plight, and a number of dog-ticks fastened upon her body. A hedgehog strolling about happened to catch sight of her, and was moved by compassionate feeling to inquire if he should remove the dog-ticks from her. The fox however would not allow him to do so, and being asked the reason replied, "Because these have already taken their fill of me and do not now suck much blood; but if you take these away, others will come and in their hunger will drain up all the blood that is left." "Yes and in your case, men of Samos," said Æsop, "my client will not do much further mischief—he has already made his fortune—but, if you put him to death, there will come others who are poor and who will consume all the revenues of the State by their embezzlements."

Fables are suited to popular oratory and have this advantage that, while historical parallels are hard to find, it is comparatively easy to find fables. For fables have to be invented, like illustrations, if one has a faculty of seeing analogies; and the discovery is facilitated by culture. It may be added that, while it is less difficult to furnish illustrations in the shape of fables, historical illustrations have a higher value in deliberation, inasmuch as history tends to repeat itself.

The use of examples.
It is proper in default of enthymemes to make use of examples as logical proofs, these being the natural means of producing conviction, but otherwise to make use of them as testimonies by way of a supplement to our enthymemes. For if we put them first, they resemble an induction, and induction is something inappropriate to Rhetoric unless in exceptional cases ; but if we put them last, they resemble testimonies, and testimony is invariably persuasive. And from this it follows that, if we put them first, it is necessary to employ a considerable number of them, but if last, a single one is sufficient, as even a single credible witness is of service.

The discussion of the different species of examples and of the methods and occasions of using them is now complete.

Chap. XXI.
Maxims.
In regard to the art of maxim-making it will be easiest to see the proper subjects of maxims, the proper occasions of using them and the persons to whom they are appropriate, if we first define the nature of a maxim.

Definition of a maxim.
A maxim is a declaration, not however relating to particulars, as e.g. to the character of Iphicrates, but to universals ; nor yet again to all universals indiscriminately, as e.g. that straight is the opposite of crooked, but to all such as are the objects of human action and are to be chosen or eschewed in

The maxim that regard. Enthymemes then being, as we may

say, the form of syllogism appropriate to these a part of the enthymeme. matters, if the syllogistic form is done away, the conclusion of an enthymeme or its major premiss is a maxim. For instance, the lines

> [1] "No man of common sense
> Should have his children taught to be too clever,"

are a maxim, but add the motive or reason, i.e.

> "For they are idle sluggards and besides
> Gain envious hatred from the citizens,"

and the whole is an enthymeme. Again,

> [2] "No man that lives is altogether happy,"

or,

> [3] "There is no man that is or can be free,"

is a maxim; but it becomes an enthymeme by the addition of the next line

> "For money is his master or else Fortune."

Such then being the definition of a maxim, it Four kinds of maxims. follows at once that there are four kinds of maxims, as they may either have or not have a logical supplement. Demonstrative proof is requisite in all such maxims as contain a statement which is paradoxical or disputable; but where there is nothing paradoxical, a supplement is unnecessary. It is unnecessary in this case either because the maxims are already familiar, as when it is said :

---

[1] Euripides *Medea*, 295, sqq.

[2] A fragment of Euripides, said to be the first line of the *Sthenobœa*.

[3] Euripides *Hecuba*, 864—5.

[1] "For a man, methinks, there is no such wealth
In the world we live in as excellent health,"

this being a pretty general opinion, or because they are intelligible at a glance, as in the saying

[2] "True love is love for evermore."

On the other hand, such maxims as have a logical supplement are either parts of an enthymeme like *the lines beginning* "No man of common sense" or, although enthymematic in their form, are not *actually* parts of an enthymeme ; and it is these last which are most generally popular. There are maxims in which the reason of the statement made is virtually expressed in the maxim itself as in the line

[3] "Nurse not immortal anger, being mortal."

For while the prohibition of nursing one's anger for ever is a maxim, the addition of the words "being mortal" conveys the reason. The saying

[4] "A mortal should think mortal thoughts
Not thoughts immortal,"

is an instance of the same thing.

[1] The history of the Greek line quoted is unknown, but it closely resembles the beginning of a σκόλιον or drinking-song which Athenæus (*Deipnosoph*. xv. p. 694 E), attributes to Simonides. See Mr Cope's note.

[2] Euripides *Troades*, 1051.

[3] An unknown line ; but it exactly corresponds in sentiment with a fragment of the *Philoctetes* of Euripides (Fragment 796 in Dindorf's *Poetae Scenici Græci*). Whoever may have been the author of it, it was borrowed or imitated by Menander.

[4] A line which Bentley in his *Dissertation on Phalaris* attributes, not without some cause, to Epicharmus.

From what has been said then it is evident how
many various kinds of maxims there are, and what
is the kind of subject to which each is appropriate.
Where the statement is disputable or paradoxical,
it is never proper to omit the supplement; we must
either put it first and make a maxim of the conclusion, as e.g. in the words, "For my own part
then, as one is bound not to incur envy and not
to waste one's time, I deny the duty of having children educated"; or we must state the conclusion
first and append the supplement. But where the
statement is obscure although not paradoxical, we
must add the reason in as terse a form as possible.
In such cases there is a certain appropriateness in
Laconic utterances and enigmatical sayings, such
as [1] that of Stesichorus at Locri, that "they had better
not be insolent, or perhaps the cicalas would chirp
upon the ground."

The use of maxims is appropriate when the speaker *The use of
maxims.*
is a person of some age and the subject one of which
he has experience; for it is as unbecoming as story-
telling in the mouths of the young, and in the absence
of experience is a mark of folly and lack of culture, as
indeed is sufficiently evident in the case of rustics who
are always fond of coining maxims and ready to air
them. The practice of unwarranted generalization is
most appropriate in bitter complaint and indignation,
whether at the beginning of a speech or after the

---

[1] The point of this saying is explained in Mr Cope's note. As
the cicalas, when they chirp, sit in the trees, they would not
chirp upon the ground, unless the trees were all cut down, i.e. unless
the land had utterly been ravaged.

demonstration. Nor is it right to neglect even trite and commonplace maxims, if they are useful; for their very commonness and general acceptance imparts to them an air of truth, as e.g. if *a general* exhorts *his troops* to face the enemy, although they have not first offered sacrifice, *by quoting the language of Homer :*

[1]" The best of omens is our country's cause,"

or to do so against odds *by reminding them of*

[2]"The even chance of war,"

or to destroy the children of their enemies, although they may not have committed any offence, *by quoting the proverb*

"Fool he who slays the sire and spares the son."

Again, there are some proverbs which are also maxims, e.g. the proverb [3] "An Attic neighbour."

Maxims may be cited too in contradiction of sayings which have become the public property of the world, such e.g. as "Know thyself" and "Avoid excess", when there is a chance of our presenting our character in a more favourable light *by citing them* as they are uttered by us in an emotional state of mind. It would be a case of a maxim uttered under emotion, if one should say in a moment of anger "It is not true that we ought to know ourselves ; at least, if this man

---

[1] *Iliad* xii. 243 ; and the line is especially appropriate, as being spoken by Hector, when Polydamas has been urging the force of an adverse omen.

[2] *Iliad,* xviii. 309.

[3] "An Attic neighbour" is clearly a neighbour of a restless, troublesome, unscrupulous kind. See e.g. Thucydides i. ch. 70 ; iv. ch. 92.

knew himself, he would never have had the presumption to be general". And our character would appear in a more favourable light, *if we should say* "It is not right, as we are told, to love as if our love might be converted into hatred; we ought rather to hate as if our hatred might some day be converted into love". We should incidentally exhibit our moral purpose in our language or, if not, should subjoin the reason, saying e.g. either "It is right to love, not as we are told to love *in the proverb*, but as if our love would last for evermore; for there is something insidious in the other kind of love," or else "The adage does not satisfy me, for a true friend should love as though his love would last for evermore;" or again "Neither does the maxim 'Avoid excess' satisfy me, for we ought to have an excessive hatred of evil."

One great service which maxims render to our speeches is owing to the vulgarity of our audience, as they are delighted when a general statement of the speaker hits the opinions of which they have a partial grasp. My meaning, and with it the true method of discovering maxims, will be evident from the following rules. The maxim, as has been said, is a general statement, and people are pleased by a general statement of anything of which they already entertain a partial conviction; thus anybody who has been unfortunate in his neighbours or his children will be glad to hear it said that there is nothing which is so troublesome as a pack of neighbours or nothing so foolish as the procreation of children. It is proper, therefore, to conjecture what are the manner and character of their prepossessions, and, having done so, to put forward a general statement in regard to them. This is one advantage in the use of maxims ; but there is another which is more important, as they impart an ethical character to our speeches. A speech is ethical, if its moral purpose is apparent. But this is the invariable effect of maxims ; for a speaker who gives utterance to a maxim makes a statement in general terms about the object of his moral predilection, and hence, if the maxims are virtuous, they give the appearance of a virtuous character to the speaker.

So much then in regard to maxims, their nature, and their various kinds, the manner of using them and the benefit they confer.

CHAP.
XXII.
(2) The en-
thymeme.
Coming now to enthymemes, we will discuss in general terms *first* the true method of looking for them and secondly their topics ; for these two parts of the subject are generically distinct.

Definition
of an en-
thymeme.
pp. 13, 16.
We have already stated that the enthymeme is a species of syllogism, and in what sense it is so, and how it differs from the syllogisms of dialectic, in that its conclusions may not be drawn from remote premisses— for this would be so long a process as to be obscure— nor by the introduction of each particular step *in the argument,* as the statement of self-evident facts would lead us into prolixity. This is in truth the reason why the uneducated have more persuasive power among the masses than the educated ; they are the more accomplished speakers, as [1]the poets say, in a mob, for while the educated deal in universal or general statements, such statements as are made by un-

[1] No doubt there is a special reference to Euripides' *Hippoly-
tas,* 988—9.

educated persons are not far-fetched but based upon facts within the experience of their audience. It fol- The mate-
lows that the proper materials of enthymemes must rials of en- thymemes.
be not all opinions indiscriminately, but certain definite opinions, defined, I mean, either by our audience or by persons in whom they believe, and *in the latter case* the fact of such an opinion being entertained ¹must be well known to all or the great majority of our audience. Again, the premisses from which our conclusions are drawn must be not only such as are necessary, but such also as are only generally true.

It is proper to begin by apprehending the necessity of knowing all or some of the special facts of the case upon which we are to speak or reason, whether the subject of the reasoning be political or any other, as in the absence of such knowledge there will be no materials from which our conclusions may be drawn. How e.g. should we offer counsel to the Athenians as to the policy of declaring war or not, unless we know what is the nature of their forces, whether they are naval or military or both, and what is their strength, what are the revenues of the State and its friends or foes, or again what wars it has been engaged in and with what success and so on? how eulogize them, if we had no knowledge of the seafight at Salamis or the battle of Marathon or the services rendered by them to the Heracleidae or anything else of the same kind, seeing that eulogy must always be based upon honourable deeds either actual or supposed? Similarly it is from facts of an oppo-

---

¹ The infinitive, as Mr Shilleto says, is intelligible, if it is remembered that λεκτέον is equivalent to δεῖ λέγειν.

site kind that we derive our topics of censure, by considering what there is or seems to be that is censurable in them, as e. g. that they [1]reduced the Greeks to subjection and enslaved the [2]Æginetans and [3]Potidaeans who had been the bravest of their allies against the Persians and so on, or any other similar offence which is found in them. And so again it is from a consideration of the facts of the case that we derive our topics of accusation or defence. It makes no difference in this respect whether our subject be the Athenians or the Lacedaemonians or man or God; for whether we are advising Achilles or eulogizing or censuring or accusing or defending him, it is the facts actual or supposed which we have to ascertain, so as to base upon these our statement of what is honourable or shameful, in a speech of eulogy or censure, of what is just or unjust in accusation or defence, and of what is expedient or injurious in deliberation. Similarly as regards any subject, let us say, justice, in considering whether it is or is not a good, we must start with the characteristics of justice or of good. This method of demonstration then is found to be universal, whether in the more exact or in the looser species of reasoning, as it is not from all facts indiscriminately that we derive our premisses but from the characteristic facts of each particular subject, and this is the sole method of proof which is possible by means of the speech. Hence we clearly

---

[1] Cp. the speech of the Mitylenaean envoys at Olympia, Thuc. iii. ch. 9 seq.

[2] See Thuc. ii. ch. 27; iv. ch. 57.

[3] See Thuc. ii. ch. 70.

see the necessity in Rhetoric as well as in the ¹Topics of Dialectic of having first of all a selection of arguments respecting the possibilities and the most opportune circumstances of each subject and, as to circumstances which arise on the spur of the moment, of possessing the same method of investigation, fixing our eyes not upon vague generalities but upon the special facts of the subject of our speech, and bringing into the sphere of our argument the greatest possible number of facts and of facts as closely connected as possible with the subject; for the more facts we have in our possession, the easier is the proof, and the more nearly they touch the case, the more germane and the less general they are. And when I speak of "general facts," I am referring e. g. to a eulogy of Achilles for being a man or one of the demi-gods or for having taken part in the expedition against Ilium, which facts are all true of many other people, so that to use such language is to eulogize Diomedes as much as Achilles; by "special facts" I mean those which are true of Achilles alone, as e. g. that he slew Hector the bravest of the Trojans and Cycnus the invulnerable who prevented the disembarkation of all the host, or that he was the youngest of those who went to the war, or that he went without being bound by oath, and so on.

This being then one primary principle of selection, viz. the topical *or selection by topics*, let us proceed to the elements of enthymemes, and by an element of

---

¹ The reference is perhaps to the first book of the *Topics* in general.

enthymeme I mean the same thing as a topic. Let us begin however with the necessary preliminaries.

Two species of enthymemes : There are two species of enthymemes, viz. demonstrative enthymemes which prove that a thing is or is not so and so, and refutative enthymemes, the difference between the two being the same as between a refutation and a syllogism in dialectics. The (a) demonstrative.
(b) refutative. demonstrative enthymeme consists in drawing conclusions from admitted propositions, the refutative in drawing conclusions which are inconsistent *with the conclusions of one's adversary.*

It may now be said that we have ascertained the topics relating to the several special subjects of a useful and necessary kind ; for as the propositions suitable to each have been selected, the topics from which to derive enthymemes regarding what is good or evil, noble or shameful, just or unjust, and similarly the topics of the characters, emotions and habits of mind are known to us by the process of selection already made. We will proceed then in another way to ascertain some general topics applicable to all subjects alike and to indicate side by side the refutative and demonstrative topics and the topics of enthymemes which are apparent but not real, as neither are apparent syllogisms real ones. And having cleared up these points, we will determine the proper sources from which to bring refutations and objections to bear upon our enthymemes.

CHAP. XXIII.
Topics of enthymemes. One topic of demonstrative enthymemes may be derived from a consideration of opposites. *If we take any two things, of which one is said to be predicable of the other,* we have to consider whether the

opposite of the one is predicable of the opposite of
the other, upsetting *the original proposition*, if it is
not predicable, and confirming *the original proposition*, if it is, as e.g. arguing that self-restraint is expedient on the ground that licentiousness is injurious.
There is an example of this topic in [1]the Messenian
oration of Alcidamas. "If the war (he says) is the
cause of our present troubles, then it is by means of
the peace that we must remedy them."
　　Another example is afforded by the lines

> "If Justice suffers not to rage against
> The involuntary authors of our harm,
> So, whoso is constrained to do us good,
> No thanks are due for services to him[2]."

or by these

> "If falsehood is persuasive i' the world,
> The contrary too must hold, that many things
> I' the world are true, yet unbelievable[3]."

A second topic is derived from the 'inflexions of
the same stem, as that which is or is not predicable of
one is or is not predicable of another. Thus *we
may argue* that justice is not always good ; else
the word "justly" would always have a good sense,
whereas to be justly put to death is the reverse of
desirable.

---

[1] The Messenian oration has been already mentioned, but in
a passage where the text is defective, p. 45, l. 34.

[2] The lines are variously ascribed to Agathon or to Theodectes.

[3] A fragment of the *Thyestes* of Euripides.

[4] This passage should be compared with p. 26, ll. 9—13; p. 30,
ll. 25—28.

There is another arising from relative terms. *It may be argued that*, if "honourably" and "justly" are terms which are predicable of the action of the agent, they are predicable also of the suffering of the patient, and that if they are predicable of the command, they are predicable of its execution. It was in this sense that the tax-gatherer Diomedon said of his taxes "If there is no disgrace in your selling them, there is none in my purchasing them." Again, *it may be argued that* if "honourably" or "justly" may be predicated of the patient, they may be predicated also of the agent and *vice versa*."[1] (But there is a possibility of fallacious argument here. A person, let us say, deserved to suffer so and so ;[2] but possibly not at your hands. Accordingly what we have to do is to consider separately the appropriateness of the suffering to the patient and of the action to the agent and then apply the result in either way that suits best ; for it sometimes happens that there is a discrepancy, and *the justice of the suffering* does not at all prove *that the action is not a wrong one*. It is so in the [3]Alcmaeon of Theodectes.

"Did no man loath thy mother?"

says Alphesiboea. Alcmaeon's answer is

"We must distinguish ere we judge."

---

[1] This sentence seems to me nothing better than a διττογρα-φία.

[2] Omitting δικαίως πέπονθεν.

[3] Alphesiboea is the wife of Alcmaeon; and she charges him with the murder of his mother Eriphyle for her guilt in betraying Amphiaraus to death.

"How so?" she says, and he replies

"Her they doomed
To death, not me to be her murderer")[1].

There is a parallel instance in the case [2] of Demosthenes and of the murderers of Nicanor; for as they were judged to have a right to kill him, it was held that he had been rightly killed. It was the same in the case of [3]the man who was put to death at Thebes; *the counsel for the defendants* exhorted the judges merely to consider whether the murdered man had deserved to die, assuming that the murder of one who deserved to die could not be unjust.

Another topic is the argument from degree. Thus *it may be argued that*, if the Gods themselves are not omniscient, much less are men, meaning that if a condition is not realized, where it would be more natural, it will evidently not be realized, where it would be less so. But the argument that a person is capable of striking his neighbours because he actually strikes his father depends upon the principle that, if [4]the rarer fact is true, the commoner fact is

[1] Mr Cope rightly urges that the foregoing clauses should be regarded as parenthetical. The argument proceeds consecutively, when they are so treated.

[2] The incident is not known from other sources.

[3] I cannot feel sure that Buhle, although Mr Cope follows him, has proved his point in connecting this allusion with the story told by Xenophon *Hellen*. vii. ch. 3.

[4] This must clearly be the meaning of τὸ ἧττον and τὸ μᾶλλον, if the reading of the passage is correct. Perhaps however it should be εἰ τὸ ἧττον εἰκὸς ὑπάρχει, καὶ τὸ μᾶλλον ὑπάρχει, as Τοπικά ii. ch. 10 would suggest.

true also. ¹*The argument therefore is one that may be employed,* whether the conclusion which we wish to establish be positive or negative. Again, the topic is applicable to a case of parity, as in the lines

> "Thy sire
> Is pitiable having lost his sons,
> And Œneus, of his noble child bereft,
> Is he not pitiable²?"

Similarly we may argue that, if Theseus was innocent, so was Alexander (Paris) or, if the sons of Tyndareus were innocent, so was Alexander, or that, if Hector had a right to slay Patroclus, so had Paris a right to slay Achilles, or again that, if other artisans are not contemptible, neither are philosophers, or that, if generals should not be condemned for being often defeated, neither should sophists, or again, ²"If each individual is bound to study your reputation, you are bound in your turn to study the reputation of all the Greeks."

There is another topic depending upon a consideration of the time. Thus ⁴Iphicrates in defending

---

¹ I cannot help thinking that the clause καθ᾽ ὁπότερον ἂν δέῃ δεῖξαι κ.τ.λ., belongs to both preceding sentences. It would be well then to change the full stops after ἄνθρωπος, l. 18, and ἧττον l. 20 to colons or commas.

² A quotation supposed to be taken from the *Meleager* of Antiphon. Œneus was the father of Meleager.

³ A supposed appeal of an Athenian orator to the Public Assembly for a chivalrous devotion to the interests of Greece.

⁴ Harmodius opposed the motion to erect a statue of Iphicrates in commemoration of his victory over the Lacedaemonians, B.C. 392. (Grote's *History of Greece*, ch. 75, vol. IX. pp. 173, sqq.)

himself against Harmodius said "Suppose that before the action I had demanded the statue in case
of doing it, you would have granted it; now that
the action has been done, will you refuse it? Do
not then make a promise in anticipation, and de-
fraud me of it, when you have received the benefit." Again, if the object is to induce the Thebans
to [1] afford Philip a passage into Attica, it may
be argued that, "if he had preferred the request
before giving them assistance against the Phocians,
they would have consented; it is a monstrous shame
that they should not afford him the passage, because he threw away his opportunity and trusted
their honour."

Another topic consists in applying to our adversary's case anything that he has said about ourselves.
[2] It is a topic of singular force as may be seen in the
[3] *Teucer*. It was employed by Iphicrates in his reply
to Aristophon, when he asked him if he would take
a bribe to betray the fleet. "No" said Aristophon.
"Well, then" he replied "if you an Aristophon would
refuse the bribe, shall I an Iphicrates accept it?" It
is assumed of course that our adversary is one who
would be thought more likely to have been guilty
of the crime; otherwise, there would clearly be
something ridiculous in such a retort, if it were used
as a means of meeting the attack of an Aristeides.

---

[1] It was a short while only before the battle of Chæronea that
Philip applied to the Thebans for a free passage.

[2] Reading ὁ τόπος.

[3] No doubt the *Teucer* of Sophocles; but the precise point of
the reference is unknown.

[1] *It is meant on the contrary* to create distrust of the prosecutor, as he generally affects a higher virtue than the defendant, and it is this which [2] requires to be disproved. But the topic is always an absurd one, when a person censures others for doing what he himself does or is capable of doing, or exhorts them to do what he himself does not or is incapable of doing.

There is another topic arising from definition, as e.g. [3] *the argument* that the supernatural must be either God or the work of God ; but anybody who believes in the existence of a work of God necessarily believes also in the existence of Gods. Another instance is 'Iphicrates's argument that the most virtuous person is the noblest, because there was nothing noble in Harmodius and Aristogeiton until they had performed a noble deed ; or his argument that he was himself a nearer relation of theirs than *their own descendant,* "at all events my actions are more nearly related to those of Harmodius and Aristogeiton than yours are." Similarly, in the [5]*Alexander*

---

[1] It is difficult to believe that Gaisford is right in taking the whole passage from οἶον ἐν τῷ Τεύκρῳ l. 8, to τοῦτό τις εἴπειεν l. 14 to be parenthetical. The construction is simpler, if some such words as τοῦτο χρὴ λέγειν are mentally supplied with πρὸς ἀπιστίαν τοῦ κατηγόρου.

[2] Reading δεῖ instead of ἀεί.

[3] The reference is plainly to the argument used by Socrates at his trial. See Plato *Apology*, pp. 26, 27.

[4] It may well be supposed that in the speech πρὸς 'Αρμόδιον, which is alluded to p. 97, l. 34, Iphicrates had made use of this argument as an answer to the taunts levelled at his humble origin. (Cp. p. 27, l. 8: p. 32, l. 21.)

[5] Some eulogy of Alexander or Paris by an unknown author;

it is said "Everyone will admit that licentious people are not content with the enjoyment of a single love." Socrates's reason for not going to the court of Archelaus is also a case in point; he said it was as ignominious to be without the power of returning a benefit as to be without the power of returning an injury. In all these cases the speaker first defines a term and ascertains its nature and then proceeds to reason from it on the point at issue.

Another topic springs from the various senses of a word; I may refer to the discussion of the right use of words in the [1] *Topics.*

Another from division, as e.g. if there are three possible causes of a crime, and while two of these are out of the question, the third is not alleged even by the prosecution.

Another topic depends upon induction; and of this the [2]Peparethian case supplies an example. It was argued in it that the decision of women about their children is everywhere correct; for in one instance at Athens, in the dispute between Mantias the rhetorician and his son, the declaration of the mother *was regarded as final,* and in another at Thebes, in the dispute between Ismenias and Stilbon, Dodonis *the mother* affirmed that Ismenias was the father of the child, and accordingly *the child* Thettaliscus was always considered to be his son. Or again, to quote

it is apparently quoted several times in this and the next chapter.

[1] Τοπικά i. ch. 15; ii. ch. 3.

[2] This was a *cause célèbre* relating to the parentage of a child.

the [1]"law" of Theodectes, "If we do not entrust our own horses to those who have mismanaged other people's, or our ships to those who have wrecked other people's, it follows that, if this rule is of universal application, we should be wrong in entrusting our own safety to those who have proved themselves inefficient guardians of the safety of others." Such a case too is the statement of Alcidamas that all the world pays honour to the wise, "at least the Parians have honoured Archilochus, reviler as he was, the Chians Homer, although he was not their fellow-countryman, and the Mitylenaeans Sappho despite her sex, the Lacedaemonians, the least literary of all people, bestowed a seat in their senate upon Chilon, as did also the Italian Greeks upon Pythagoras, and the Lampsacenes gave Anaxagoras a public burial, although he was an alien, and continue to the present day to pay him honour." [2]*Again, it may be argued that states are always prosperous under the laws of philosophers,* because the Athenians prospered under the laws of Solon and the Lacedæmonians under those of Lycurgus, and at Thebes no sooner did [3]the leading men become philosophers than the state entered upon a career of prosperity.

There is another topic derivable from a judgment already pronounced upon the same or a similar or an

[1] Apparently a speech delivered by Theodoctes—it is quoted again p. 101, l. 9—upon a law proposed by himself or somebody else in reference to the position of mercenaries.

[2] It is clear that something has fallen out of the text and must be supplied to make the instances quoted apposite.

[3] "The leading men" are Pelopidas and Epaminondas.

opposite question, especially if it is the judgment of all men and all times, or, failing that, of a large majority or of all or nearly all the wise or good or again of the judges themselves or of those whose authority they admit or whose judgment admits of no contradiction, as e.g. if they are those who are masters of the situation or who cannot be opposed without impropriety, such as the Gods or a parent or one's teachers. This was the point of [1]Autocles's remark against Mixidemides, "The idea of the awful Goddesses (the Eumenides) submitting to be tried before the Court of Areopagus and Mixidemides refusing"; or Sappho's that "it is an ill thing to die, for so have the Gods decided; else would they die themselves"; or Aristippus's reply to Plato who had, he thought, rather assumed an air of dogmatism, "Well, anyhow that was not our friend's way," meaning Socrates. Agesipolis again, after consulting the oracle at Olympia, went on to ask the God at Delphi whether he was of the same mind as his father, implying that it would be disgraceful to contradict him. Again [2]in the case of Helen Isocrates contended that she must be virtuous, inasmuch as she was approved by Theseus, and in that of [3]Alexander, *that he must be virtuous*, as he had been the favourite of the Goddesses; [4]Evagoras also (says Isocrates) was virtuous, at all events when Conon found himself in difficulties, he left everybody else and went to Evagoras.

---

[1] It may be inferred that Mixidemides had denied the authority of the Court of Areopagus in a case concerning himself.

[2] The passage is in the *Helen*, §§ 23—25.

[3] Probably in the *Helen*, § 46.   [4] *Evag.* § 61.

¹Another topic consists in *taking separately* the parts *of a subject, in considering* e.g., as is done in the ²*Topics*, what sort of motion the soul is, as it must be this or that. The ³*Socrates* of Theodectes will supply an illustration, *where he says* "What temple has he profaned? where is the God, among all the Gods recognized by the State, to whom he has not paid due honour?"

Also, as it happens in the great majority of cases that the same thing has consequences partly good and partly bad, another topic consists in using the attendant circumstances as means of exhortation or dissuasion, accusation or defence, eulogy or censure. Thus education is attended by envy, which is an evil, and by wisdom, which is a good; hence it is possible to argue against education on the ground that envy is a thing to be avoided, and in its favour on the ground that wisdom is a thing to be desired. This is the topic which constitutes the entire rhetorical system of Callippus, if we add to it the topic of possibility and the other topics, ⁴as has been said.

There is another topic when in reference to two opposite things it is necessary to employ exhortation or dissuasion and to apply to both the method already

---

¹ It is not easy to distinguish this topic from the one described p. 98, l. 34, except that the latter is specially forensic in its bearing.

² Τοπικά ii. ch. 4, p. 111, B₄₋₁₁.

³ An ἀπολογία Σωκράτους or imaginary speech of Socrates in his own defence.

⁴ There has been no reference to the τέχνη of Callippus; but perhaps Aristotle means the other "common topics" which have been discussed in ch. 19.

described, the difference being that, whereas in the last case it was any two things, it is here two opposites that are contrasted. Thus there was a certain priestess who forbade her son to go into politics; "for if what you say is just" she said "you will be hated by men, and if it is unjust, by the Gods." But a plea might equally well be advanced for political life, for "if what you say is just, you will be a favourite with the Gods, and if it is unjust, with men." This is the same thing as the proverb "to take the fat with the lean"; [1] "divarication," as it is called, is simply the case of two opposites having each a good and an evil consequence, which are respectively opposite to each other.

Again, as there is a difference between the objects which people praise in public and in secrecy, and, while they make a show of lauding justice and honour above everything else, they prefer expediency in their hearts, another topic consists in trying to use *an adversary's premisses, whichever mode of sentiment he adopts*, to infer the opposite *of his conclusion;* for there is no topic of paradoxes so entirely effective as this [2].

[1] Although it is impossible, I think, to represent the rhetorical βλαίσωσις by any equivalent existing English word, it is comparatively easy to infer its meaning from the example. Honesty and dishonesty (it may be said) are the opposites. Each has a good and an evil attached to it, to honesty the favour of Heaven and the hatred of the world, to dishonesty the favour of the world and the hatred of Heaven, and these goods and evils are "respectively opposite to each other". A metaphor derived from legs irregularly diverging would express as nearly as possible this relation.

[2] The meaning seems to be that, if an adversary takes a high

Another topic is derived from analogy of results. Iphicrates, for instance, resisted an effort to impose a public burden upon his son because of his size, although he was under the legal age, by saying "If you reckon tall boys men, you will have to vote short men boys." Theodectes again in his [1] "law" said "If you enfranchise mercenaries like Strabax and Charidemus in consideration of their respectability, will you not expatriate those of the mercenaries who have been guilty of irreparable crimes?"

Another topic consists in arguing identity of cause from identity of effect. Xenophanes, for instance, contended that it was as impious to affirm the birth of the Gods as to affirm their death; for in either case it follows that there is a time when they do not exist. And under this topic falls the general rule of assuming the result of either of two things to be invariably the same as that of the other, *as in the words* "It is not about Isocrates but about a study that you have to decide *in deciding* whether it is right to practise philosophy." Similarly *it may be argued* that the giving of earth and water is equivalent to slavery and that participation in the [2] general peace is equivalent to allegiance to Alexander. However we may adopt whichever view suits us best.

moral line in his argument, we must prove the facts on which he depends to be consistent with selfish expediency; if on the other hand he argues from the view of expediency, we must contend for the higher morality.

[1] See note on p. 99, l. 10.

[2] "The general peace" was the treaty which the Greek states, except the Lacedaemonians, made with Alexander after the death of Philip in 336 B.C.

There is another topic depending upon the fact that people do not always make the same choice at a later as at an earlier time, but often reverse it. Take e.g. the following enthymeme, [1] " It will be monstrous if during our expatriation we fought for our restoration and, now that we are restored, shall be expatriated rather than fight"; the choice being in the one case to remain at the cost of fighting and in the other to avoid fighting at the cost of exile.

Another topic consists in treating the conceivable as the actual reason of a thing existing or [2]having come into existence, as in the supposition that a person would make a present in order to inflict the pain of taking it away.   This is the spirit of the [3]lines

> "On some men Heaven in no favouring mood
> Bestows large blessings that the after-ills
> They shall sustain may be more palpable,"

or the passage in the *Meleager* of Antiphon.

> "Not for the slaughter of the boar
> *The heroes came*, but to be witnesses
> Of Meleager's bravery to Hellas,"

or the argument in the *Ajax* of Theodectes that Diomedes [4]gave the preference to Odysseus not as honouring him but in order that his companion might

---

[1] The words which follow are quoted, although incorrectly, from a speech of Lysias in which the Athenians, who had been restored after the expulsion of the Thirty in 403 B.C., are exhorted not to submit to the dictation of the Lacedaemonians.   It is entitled περὶ τοῦ μὴ καταλῦσαι τὴν πάτριον πολιτείαν Ἀθήνησι.   See Mr Cope's note.

[2] Changing εἰ μὴ γένοιτο to ἢ γένοιτο.

[3] The source of the quotation is unknown.

[4] In the episode known as the Δολωνεία.   See *Iliad* x. 218, seq.

be inferior to himself, this being a possible explanation of his conduct.

There is another topic common to forensic and deliberative oratory, viz. to consider the inducements and discouragements and the motives of acting or abstaining from action ; for these are the conditions, the presence or the absence of which renders action desirable or the reverse. It is to be considered e.g. whether a thing is possible, easy and advantageous either to oneself or to one's friends or wasteful and detrimental to one's enemies or if the penalty is not adequate to the deed. These are the materials of exhortation, and their opposites of dissuasion. [1] They are also the materials of accusation and defence, the inducements of the former and the discouragements of the latter. In fact it is this topic which constitutes the whole rhetorical systems of Pamphilus and Callippus.

There is yet another topic in the case of things which are supposed to happen but are difficult to believe. *It may be urged* that people would not have [2]supposed these, had they not been true or nearly true ; nay, that they are especially *likely to be true,* as everything believed is either actual or probable, and therefore, if a thing is hard to believe and is not probable, it must be true, as at all events it is not the probability or plausibility of it which is the

No doubt in the *Ajax* of Theodectes, there was a passage in which the prowess of Odysseus was rudely handled. Cp. p. 103, ll. 5—7.

[1] The meaning is that an advocate may seek to prove guilt or innocence by pointing to the causes which would naturally tend to induce or to prevent criminality.

[2] Perhaps ἴδοξεν would be better than ἴδοξαν.

reason of its being so supposed.   There is an instance
of this in the remark of Androcles of Pitthus in his
declaration against the law.   Being interrupted by
expressions of dissent at the words "The laws require
a law to set them right," he said "Yes, and so do fish
require salt, although it is neither likely nor plausible
that they should require it, as their life is spent in
the brine, and oil-cakes require oil, incredible as it is
that the things which supply oil should require it."

Another topic, which is proper to refutation, consists in examining whether there is any contradiction
in the series of dates, actions or words, and this under
three separate heads, viz. firstly in reference to your
adversary, as e.g. *if you can say*, "Although he pre-
tends to be your friend, he took part in the conspiracy of the Thirty," secondly in reference to yourself, as "Although he calls me litigious, it is beyond
his power to prove that I have ever been party to a
suit," thirdly in reference to yourself and your adversary, as "While he has never lent you a farthing,
there are actually many of you whom I have ran-
somed."

Another topic, where there is or appears to be a
prejudice against particular persons or things, is to
state the explanation of the circumstance which is un-
accountable, as there is always something which accounts for the appearance. . . .   Thus in the *Ajax*
of Theodectes Odysseus explains to Ajax how it is that
he has not the reputation of being braver than Ajax,
although he is so.

Another topic consists in arguing from the presence
or absence of the cause the existence or non-ex-

istence of the effect ; for cause and effect go always hand in hand, and there is nothing which has not a cause. This was the point of [1]Leodamas's defence, when Thrasybulus had accused him of being one whose name had been posted in the Acropolis and of having erased it under the government of the Thirty. This was impossible (said Leodamas) as the Thirty would have been more disposed to trust him, if there had been this record of his hostility to the people.

Another topic is to consider whether it was or is possible to take a better course than that which the person either recommends or takes or has taken in action ; for if this course has not been taken, it is evident that he has not done the deed, as nobody voluntarily and intentionally chooses what is bad. But in this there is a fallacy ; for it often happens that the better method of action becomes evident subsequently, but in the first instance was unknown.

Again, if an intended action is inconsistent with some action already performed, there is another topic which consists in viewing them side by side. Thus when the inhabitants of Elea inquired of Xenophanes whether they should sacrifice to [2]Leucothea and lament for her, he gave them as his advice, if they regarded her as a goddess, not to lament, if as a mortal, not to offer sacrifice.

[1] The passage shows that before the era of the Thirty the name of Leodamas, as an enemy of the people, had been inscribed on a pillar in the Acropolis. See Mr Cope's note.

[2] Ino the wife of Athamas, in a fit of madness threw herself into the sea and became (as the story went) a sea goddess named Leucothea.

Another topic is to discover a ground of accusation or defence in any mistake that has been made. In the *Medea* of Carcinus for example, Medea is accused of having murdered her children ; at all events (it is urged) they have disappeared, the fact being that Medea made a mistake in sending her children away; and Medea's reply is that it is not her children but Jason whom she would have murdered, as assuming her to have been capable of the other crime, it would have been a mistake in her not to have committed this.　This is the topic or species of enthymeme which constitutes the entire earlier system of Theodorus.

Another topic is derivable from a play on names, as in Sophocles

> [1] "Sidero, ayo and rightly named,"

or as is so common in panegyrics of the Gods or as when Conon called Thrasybulus "rash counsellor" or when Herodicus said to Thrasymachus "You are ever as brave as your name" or to Polus "You are always colt by nature as by name" or of the legislator Draco, that his laws are not the laws of a man but of a dragon, alluding to their severity.　So too Hecuba in Euripides says of Aphrodite

> [2] "Well may her name
> Be first in folly,"

---

[1] A line from the *Tyro* of Sophocles.　Sidero, "iron by name and iron by nature," was Tyro's stepmother.

[2] *Troades* 990.　"'Αφροδίτη and ἀφροσύνη have the first half of the word in common" (Cope).

or Chaeremon *has the line*

[1]" Pentheus, prophetic name of ill to come."

Demonstrative and refutative enthymemes.
The reason why refutative enthymemes are more popular than demonstrative is that a refutative enthymeme is a conclusion of opposites within a small space and that things are rendered clearer to an audience by juxtaposition. But of all refutative or demonstrative syllogisms none are so much applauded as those which are understood at once, not however because they are superficial, as the audience are pleased with themselves for anticipating the conclusion, and those with which we can so nearly keep pace as to understand them as soon as they are stated.

CHAP. XXIV.
True and apparent enthymemes.
As there may be true syllogisms and syllogisms which are apparent but not true, it follows at once that there are true and apparent enthymemes, because the enthymeme is a species of syllogism.

Topics of apparent enthymemes.
Among topics of apparent enthymemes the first is that which arises from the use of language, and of this there are two divisions. [2]The first is when, as in Dialectic, we make a final statement as if it were the conclusion of a syllogism without having gone through the process of reasoning, *saying,* "It follows that this is not so and so," or "It must therefore be so and so"; similarly in enthymemes the use of a

[1] In allusion to the connexion of Πενθεὺς with πένθος. Cp. Euripides *Bacchae*, 508.

[2] Reading, mainly after Vahlen, καὶ τούτου ἐν μὲν μέρος, ὥσπερ ἐν τοῖς διαλεκτικοῖς τὸ μὴ συλλογισάμενον συμπερασματικῶς τὸ τελευταῖον εἰπεῖν, οὐκ ἄρα τὸ καὶ τό, ἀνάγκη ἄρα τὸ καὶ τό, καὶ ἐν τοῖς ἐνθυμήμασι τὸ συνεστραμμένως καὶ ἀντικειμένως εἰπεῖν φαίνεται ἐνθύμημα.

compact and antithetical phrase has the appearance
of an enthymeme ; for language of this kind is the
province of enthymeme.   It is apparently the style of
the language used which is the occasion of such fal-
lacies.   But in order to give our language an air of
syllogistic reasoning it is useful to state the heads of
a large number of syllogisms, as " Some he saved ; the
others he aided ; he was the liberator of Greece" ;
for although the proof of these several assertions was
derived from other premisses, their combination appears to produce some new result.   Secondly, there is
the topic of [1]equivocation, as if one should assert that
the mouse is an estimable creature, [2]because it gives
its name to the most venerable of all religious rites,
viz. the mysteries, or if in a panegyric of a dog one
includes the heavenly dog, *viz. the dogstar*, or Pan,
because [3]Pindar used the words

> " Blessed deity
> Whom the Olympians style the dog,
> The manifold dog of the great Cybele,"

or *argues* that, [4]as it is a great disgrace to have no
dog in the house, it is evident that a dog is honourable.   Another instance is the argument that Hermes
is the most communicative of all the gods, as he is

---

[1] The Aristotelian " homonyms " or " equivocables " are things
which have the same name.   See Κατηγορίαι i. ch. 1 and cp. Quintilian *de Instit. Orat* vii. ch. 9, § 2.

[2] Polycrates wrote a panegyric of mice (p. 106, l. 10) ; and in
it he must have dwelt upon the supposed etymological connexion
between μῦς (a mouse) and μυστήριον (a mystery).

[3] The lines are a fragment of Pindar's lost *Parthenia*.

[4] Schrader is perhaps correct in supposing that there is a play
upon dogs and the dog-philosophers or Cynics.

the only god who is called [1]" Common Hermes"; or the argument that [2]accounts (λόγος) are excellent things, because it is not of money but of account that good men are worthy, the phrase to be of account (λόγου ἄξιον εἶναι) being one that is capable of a double meaning.

Another topic consists in combining what is separate or separating what is combined; for as a thing appears the same *when so treated*, although it is often not the same, we must represent it in whichever way best serves our purpose. This is the *favourite* argument of Enthydemus, e.g. [3]that he knows there is a trireme in the Piraeus because he knows each of two facts. A second instance is that anybody who knows the letters knows the verse, as it is the same thing. A third that, if a double portion of a certain thing is baneful, the single portion too cannot be wholesome, as it cannot be supposed that two good things make one bad thing. While the topic, if put in this way, is refutative, it is demonstrative, if put

---

[1] The connexion of κοινωνικός and κοινός is not easily preserved in English. "Common Hermes" or "Hermes in common" (κοινὸς Ἑρμῆς) was a favourite expression of those who claimed to "go shares" with someone in a treasure-trove (ἕρμαιον).

[2] λόγος has two senses (1) speech, (2) account or esteem; but there is no word which corresponds to it in English.

[3] There is no more difficult passage in the *Rhetoric* than this. If it be compared with *Sophist. Elench.* ch. 20, p. 177 B$_{12}$ and illustrated by *Sophist. Elench.* ch. 4, p. 166 A$_{23-32}$, the inference will, I think, be that the illicit combination lies in combining the clauses "He knows (being) in the Piraeus" and "He knows there is a trireme" into the single clause "He knows there is a trireme in the Piraeus."

as follows, "One good thing cannot be made up of two bad things." The whole topic however is fallacious. [1]Again, we may instance the saying of Polycrates about Thrasybulus that he overthrew thirty tyrants, where he uses combination, or the passage in the *Orestes* of Theodectes, which illustrates division :

" '' 'Tis just that whoso slays her husband die,'

" and it is just that a father's blood should be avenged by his son ; well, this is exactly what has occurred." *But the argument is fallacious*, as, when the two things are combined, it is very likely that the result will no longer be just. This fallacy may also be ascribed to omission, the name of the author of the action being left out.

Another topic is that of indignant asseveration whether in a constructive or destructive sense, as when, without having proved the perpetration of a certain act, we exaggerate the horror of it ; for by so doing we produce the impression either that the act has not been perpetrated, if it is the defendant who employs the exaggeration, or the reverse, if it is the prosecutor who is in a passion. This then is no *true* enthymeme ; for the audience is only betrayed into concluding that an act has or has not been perpetrated without demonstrative proof having been offered.

Another topic is the use of a mere sign *or single*

---

[1] The "combination" consists in representing the Thirty Tyrants as being each the victim of Thrasybulus ; the "division" in treating the murder of Clytaemnestra by Orestes as simply a case of avenging a father's bloodshed or putting the murderer of her husband to death without considering the relationship between the son who slays and the mother who is slain.

instance as an argument, the conclusion here again not being logically complete. Thus it might be argued that lovers are of service to States, as it was the love of [1] Harmodius and Aristogeiton which overthrew the tyrant Hipparchus ; or that [2] Dionysius is a thief, because he is a bad man, such a conclusion again being illogical, as all bad men are not thieves, although all thieves are bad men.

There is another topic, dependent upon accidental circumstances. We may take as an instance of this the remark of Polycrates about the mice, that they gave valuable aid [3] by gnawing the bow-strings. Or it might perhaps be urged that there is no compliment so great as an invitation to dinner, as it was [4] from not receiving an invitation that Achilles got into a passion with the Achaeans at Tenedos; whereas the fact was that his passion was owing to his sense of the dishonour that was done him, and it was only an accident that this took the form of his not being invited to dinner.

There is another topic, [5] which arises from the consequence of an action. In the *Alexander* e. g. it is argued that the hero was a man of elevated mind,

[1] The story of Harmodius and Aristogeiton is told by Thucydides vi. ch. 54 sqq.

[2] The name of Dionysius is taken at random; it is not any individual who is meant.

[3] Cp. Herodotus ii. ch. 141, whether this is or is not the incident which Aristotle had in mind.

[4] The reference is to a scene in a play of Sophocles.

[5] The topic consists in arguing from identity of effect to identity of cause, whereas the same effect may be the result of various causes.

because he disdained the society of numbers and remained on Mount Ida by himself; for as this is conduct natural to persons of elevated minds, he would appear to possess such elevation. Again, *it may be argued that,* because a person dresses well and goes out at night, he is a rake, such being the habits of rakes. Another argument of a similar kind is that beggars sing and dance in the temples and that exiles are allowed to live wherever they choose; for as these are the characteristics of apparent happiness, it may be supposed that anyone who possesses them is happy. There is a difference however in the manner *of doing these things;* and hence the topic falls under the head of omission.

Another topic is to treat that which is not a cause as the cause, because e.g. it has occurred simultaneously or subsequently; for the sequel is here assumed to be the effect, especially in public life, as when Demades pronounced the policy of Demosthenes to be the cause of all the evils, because it was after it that the war occurred.

There is another topic arising from the omission of the time or manner, as *when it is urged* that Alexander had a right to take Helen, because her father allowed her her choice *of a husband.* This is a fallacy; for it was not, we must suppose, perpetually but only at the first that the choice was given her, as after the first choice the authority of her father ceased. It would be a similar case, if one were to say that to strike a free man is a wanton insult; for this is not the case universally, but only when the striker is the aggressor.

Again, it is possible here, as well as in eristical discussions, to derive an apparent syllogism [1]from the interchange of the absolute with that which is not absolute but particular. Such a case in Dialectic is the argument that the non-existent is, on the ground that the non-existent *is* non-existent; or that the unknown is knowable, because the unknown is known to be unknown. Similarly in Rhetoric an apparent enthymeme may be derived from a probability which is not absolute but particular. This *particular probability* however is not universal, as indeed Agathon says in the lines

" It may be one would call it probable
  That many things improbable occur;"

for as what is contrary to probability sometimes occurs, it follows that what is contrary to probability is itself probable. This being so, the improbable will be probable—[2]not, however, probable in an absolute sense. The truth is that, as in eristical discussions it is by omitting the condition, relation and mode that we create the deception, so here it is the probability which is not absolute but particular that is the occasion of the fallacy. It is this topic of which the rhetorical system of Corax is composed. For if the defendant is not liable to the charge brought against him, if e.g. he is a feeble person and is charged with assault and battery, he defends himself by pleading the improbability of the case; or if he is liable to it, if e.g. it is a strong man against whom the charge is

---

[1] The word " is " has two senses, one absolute, the other relative or particular, in the following instances.

[2] Changing the full stop after εἰκός to a comma.

brought, he too pleads the improbability of the case on the ground that it was sure to seem probable. The same rule holds equally in other cases. A person must either be liable to a charge or not; and this being so, while both appear probable, in the one case the probability is absolute, and in the other it is not absolute but *particular*, as has been said. This in fact is the meaning of converting the worse argument into the better. Accordingly people were justified in showing their disapproval of [1]Protagoras's profession, as it is a falsehood and not true but only apparent probability and has no place in any art except Rhetoric and Eristic.

So much then for enthymemes both real and apparent. The next subject to be treated is refutation.

Chap.
XXV.
Refutation.
Methods of
refutation:

There are two ways of refuting an argument, viz. either by a counter-syllogism or by adducing an objection. It is clear that the counter-syllogisms may be constructed out of the same topics as the syllogisms *of which we have spoken;* for it is the common opinions of the world which form the materials of syllogisms, and opinions are often contradictory. Objections on the other hand, [2]as in the *Topics*, may be adduced in four different ways, viz. either from the enthymeme of your adversary himself, or from analogy, or from antithesis, or from a previous decision.

(1) Counter
syllogism;

(2) Objec-
tion.
Four dif-
ferent kinds
of objection.

As an instance of an objection *derived* from *the enthymeme of* an adversary himself, let us suppose

[1] Protagoras is said to have originated the theory that there were two contradictory arguments possible on any subject.

[2] Τοπικά, viii. ch. 10.

that the subject of his enthymeme is the virtue of love;
then it may be objected either generally that *love is
a craving and* that every kind of craving is an evil, or
in particular that there would be no such proverb as
[1]"*Caunian love,*" unless there were evil forms of love
as well as good. *It would be an objection* derived
from antithesis, if the enthymeme were to show that
a good man is the benefactor of all his friends, and
it were objected that a bad man on the other hand
is not the enemy of all his friends. [2]*It would be an
objection* from analogy, if the enthymeme were meant
to show that the victims of crime always cherish a
feeling of hatred, and *it were objected* that the re-
cipients of benefits on the other hand do not always
cherish a feeling of affection. *Lastly,* the decisions
to which I refer are those of eminent persons. Thus
if it were the point of an enthymeme that some
allowance shall be made for intoxicated people, as
they commit their offences in ignorance, it might be
objected that, *if this is so*, Pittacus deserves no
commendation, or he would not have ordained heavier
penalties for offences committed by a person in a
state of intoxication.

Materials of enthy-memes: The materials of enthymemes are four, viz. probabilities, examples, demonstrations and signs. They
are probabilities, when the conclusion is derived
from such facts as either are or are supposed to be
generally true; examples, when it is reached [3]by

[1] The love of Byblis for her brother Caunus was a typical
instance of disastrous love.

[2] This case is not really different from the preceding.

[3] I should be glad to omit δι' ἐπαγωγῆς.

induction from an analogy of one or several instances,
the universal rule being first ascertained and the
particulars afterwards inferred from it ; demonstrations, when it depends upon a rule which is necessary
and absolute ; signs, when upon general or particular
statements which may be either true or false. A
probability then being not an invariable but a general
rule, it is clear that enthymemes which are so constructed may invariably be refuted by an objection,
although the refutation is apparent and not real ;
for it is not the probability but only the necessity
of the opponent's case which is disproved by the
objection alleged. Hence this fallacy always offers an
opportunity of gaining an unfair advantage in defence
rather than in accusation. For the accuser employs
probabilities as his means of proof ; but there is a
difference between disproving the necessity and disproving the probability of a case, and a general rule,
if it is to be only probable and not invariable and
necessary, must always admit of objections. Yet if
once the necessity of a thing has been disproved, the
audience assume either that it is not probable or that
they have no business to decide it ; although, as I
said, their conclusion is wrong, as their decision
ought to rest upon probabilities as well as upon
necessary truths, such being the meaning of the
words " to decide according to the best of our judgment." Hence it is not enough for the defendant
to prove that a thing is not necessary ; he needs to
disprove its probability. But this will be done only
if the objection is more generally true than the fact
objected to ; and it may be more generally true in

margin note: (1) proba-
bilities,

respect either of time or of the circumstances of the case, although it will be most convincing, if it is so in both these respects; for if the majority of cases are in our favour, the balance of probability is on our side.

(2) signs,

pp. 18, 19.

Signs however and the enthymemes which are based upon them admit of refutation, even if true, as I said at the outset; for we saw in the [1]*Analytics* that fallible signs are always inconclusive.

(3) examples.

Enthymemes depending upon examples may be refuted in the same way as probabilities; [2]for a single contrary instance disproves at once the necessity of a thing, even although the majority of cases are on the other side; but if the majority of cases make in favour of our opponent, we must contend that the present case is not similar to them in nature or conditions, or at least presents certain points of difference.

(4) demonstrations.

Demonstrations on the other hand and the corresponding enthymemes cannot be refuted on the ground of inconclusiveness, as we saw in the [3]*Analytics*, and there is no resource left us except to disprove the fact.

If however there is no doubt about the fact or about its being a demonstration, the case is one which does not admit of refutation, as here each step is demonstratively proved.

---

[1] *Analyt. Prior.* ii. ch. 27; cp. *Rhet.* i. ch. 2.

[2] Reading as Mr Cope, ἐάν τε γὰρ ἔχωμέν τι οὐχ οὕτω, λέλυται, ὅτι οὐκ ἀναγκαῖον; εἰ καὶ πλείω ἢ πλεονάκις ἄλλως· ἐάν τε καὶ πλείω καὶ τὰ πλεονάκις οὕτω, μαχετέον ἢ ὅτι κ.τ.λ.

[3] *Analyt. Prior.* ii. ch. 27.

Exaggeration and depreciation is not an element of an enthymeme. An element is in my view the same thing as a topic, being a head under which a number of enthymemes fall. Exaggeration and depreciation are rather enthymemes tending to show that a certain thing is great or small, as there are other enthymemes showing that it is good or bad, just or unjust, and so on. All these being the subjects of syllogisms and enthymemes, it follows that, if none is a topic of an enthymeme, neither is exaggeration and depreciation such a topic. Again, refutative enthymemes do not form a species distinct from constructive. For it is clear that refutation consists either in urging positive proof or in adducing an objection. In the first case we prove the opposite *of our adversary's statement;* I mean that, if he has proved a particular thing to have occurred, we prove the opposite and *vice versa.* The distinction then cannot lie here; for the same means are common to both, as in both enthymemes are advanced either to disprove a fact or to prove it. An objection on the other hand is not an enthymeme but as in the *Topics* the mere statement of an opinion intended to show that the reasoning of our opponent is inconclusive, or that there has been something false in his assumptions.

Now there are three proper subjects of study in regard to speech ; and the remarks we have made may suffice for the means of discovering or refuting examples, maxims, enthymemes and the inventive part of Rhetoric generally. We have still however to consider style and arrangement.

BOOK III.

Chap. I. THERE being three proper subjects of systematic The three subjects of a rhetorical treatise. treatment in Rhetoric, viz. (1) the possible sources of proofs (2) style and (3) the right ordering of the parts of the speech, the first of these has been already discussed. We have ascertained the number of the sources of proofs, which are three, the nature of these sources, and the reason why they are not more numerous, viz. that persuasion is invariably effected either by producing a certain emotion in the audience itself or by inspiring the audience with a certain conception of the character of the speaker or *thirdly* by positive demonstration. The sources from which pp. 101 sqq. enthymemes are to be derived have also been stated; for these are both special and common topics of Style. enthymemes. We have next to discuss the question of style, as it is not enough to know what to say but is necessary also to know how to say it, and *the art of saying things* is largely influential in imparting a certain colour to the speech.

The first point which was naturally the subject of investigation is that which is first in the natural order, viz. the sources from which facts themselves derive their persuasiveness, the second is the disposition *or setting out* of the facts by the style, and the third, which has never yet been attempted, although it has the greatest weight, is the art of [1]declamation. *Nor is* Declama- *it surprising that declamation should have been* tion. *neglected;* for it has only lately been introduced into the tragic art and rhapsody, as poets were themselves originally the declaimers of their own tragedies. It is clear then that there is such a thing as an art of declamation in Rhetoric as well as in Poetry; and indeed it has been systematically treated by Glaucon of Teos among others. [2]The art consists in understanding (1) the proper use of the voice for the expression of the several emotions, i.e. when it should be loud or low or intermediate, (2) the proper use of the accents, [3]i.e. when the tone should be acute or grave or intermediate, and (3) the rhythms suitable to each emotion. For there are three things which are matters of such investigations, viz. magnitude *or volume of sound,* harmony and rhythm. It is people who are careful about these that generally carry off the prizes in the *dramatic*

---

[1] Aristotle uses ὑπόκρισις in a limited sense, confining it, as he says below, to the management of the voice and especially excluding delivery or gesticulation, which is treated as a part of ὑπόκρισις by Longinus and as a part of *actio* by Cicero and Quintilian.

[2] Reading αὕτη.

[3] The "intermediate" or "middle" accent is the circumflex, which may be regarded as a combination of the others. It is clear that each accent marks a particular *tone* of voice, and that the rhetorical harmony (ἁρμονία) consists in a due variation of the tones.

and rhapsodical competitions, and as in such
competitions the influence of the declaimers *or
actors* is greater now-a-days than that of the poets,
so is it also in political competitions owing to the
depraved character of our polities. But up to the
present time no scientific treatise upon declamation
has been composed; for it was not till a late date
that the art of style itself made any progress, and *declamation* is still popularly considered, and indeed is
rightly supposed, to be something vulgar. Still as
the entire study of Rhetoric has regard to appearance, it is necessary to pay due attention to declamation, not that it is right to do so but because it is
inevitable. Strict justice indeed, if applicable to
Rhetoric, would confine itself to seeking such a delivery as would cause neither pain nor pleasure. For
the right condition is that the battle should be fought
out on the facts of the case alone; and therefore
everything outside the *direct* proof is *really* superfluous, although extraneous matters are highly effective, as has been said, owing to the depraved character of the audience. Nevertheless attention to style
is in some slight degree necessary in every kind
of instruction, as the manner of stating a fact has
some effect upon the lucidity of the explanation.
Still the difference is not so great *as is supposed;*
these tricks of style are all merely pretentious and
are assumed for the sake of gratifying the audience,
and accordingly nobody teaches geometry after this
fashion.

pp. 5, 113.

The art of declamation, when it comes into vogue,
will produce the same effects as the histrionic art;

The art of
rhetorical
declama-
tion.

and there are some writers, e.g. Thrasymachus in
his *Rules of Pathos* (ἔλεοι), who have in a slight
measure attempted to treat it. The truth is that
a capacity for *declaiming or* acting is a natural gift,
comparatively free from artistic regulations, although
it may be reduced to an art in its application to
style. Hence it is that people who possess this
faculty, *viz. the faculty of a histrionic style*, are the
winners of prizes in their day, as are also rhetorical
actors; for [1]in written speeches the style is more
effective than the thought.

The origin *of this style* was due, as is natural, to History of
the poets. For not only are all names imitations, but style.
there was the *human* voice, which is the most imitative of all our members, ready to their use. Thus
it was that the various arts, rhapsody, the histrionic
art and others, as I need not say, were composed.
And it was because the poets were thought, despite
the simplicity of their sentiments, to have acquired
their reputation by their style that *prose* style assumed at first a poetical form, as e.g. [2]the style of
Gorgias. Nay even at the present time it is the
opinion of most uneducated people that a poetical
style is the finest. This however is an erroneous idea,
the styles of prose and of poetry being distinct, as
is shown by the fact that the writers of tragedies

---

[1] The reference is to the epideictic style of orators, in which
the speeches were more usually written than delivered.

[2] Dr Thompson has excellently shown the poetical nature of
Gorgias's style in the Appendix to his edition of Plato's *Gorgias*
pp. 175 sqq.

themselves have ceased to use *the poetical style* as
once they did, and that, as they passed from the
tetrameter to the iambic measure as being the metre
which bears the closest resemblance to prose, so too
they have abandoned all such words as depart
from the usage of *ordinary* conversation and were
employed as ornaments by earlier dramatic writers
and are still so employed by the writers of hexameter
verse. It is absurd then to imitate those who themselves no longer employ their old style.

It clearly results from all this that we should
be wrong in entering upon a minute discussion of all
the possible points of style, and that we must confine
ourselves to those of *rhetorical* style, which is now
under our consideration. The other *or poetical* style
has been discussed in my treatise on *Poetry*.

CHAP. II.
Virtues or
graces of
style. We may rest content then with our study of
that question, and may take it as settled that
one virtue of style is perspicuity. There is an evidence of this in the fact that our speech, unless it
makes its meaning clear, will fail to perform its
proper function. [1]Again, style should be neither
mean nor exaggerated, but appropriate; for a poetical
style, although possibly not mean, is still not appropriate to prose. Among nouns and verbs, while
perspicuity is produced by such as are proper *or
usual*, a character which is not mean but ornate is
the result of the various other kinds of nouns enu-

---

[1] The sentence σημεῖον γὰρ ὅτι ὁ λόγος......τὸ ἑαυτοῦ ἔργον is
parenthetical and should be marked off from the context by
colons.

ARISTOTLE. 229

merated in my ¹treatise on *Poetry.* The reason is
that such variation imparts greater dignity to style;
for people have the same feeling about style as about
foreigners in comparison with their fellow-citizens,
i.e. they admire most what they know least. Hence
it is proper to invest the language with a foreign air,
as we all admire anything which is out of the way,
and there is a certain pleasure in the object of
wonder. It is true that in metrical compositions there
are many means of producing this effect, and means
which are suitable in such compositions, as the
subjects of the story, whether persons or things,
are further removed *from common life.* But in prose
these means must be used much more sparingly,
as the theme *of a prose composition* is less elevated.
For in poetry itself there would be a breach of propriety, if the fine language were used by a slave or a
mere infant or on a subject of extremely small importance. It is rather in a *due* contraction and
exaggeration that propriety consists even in poetry.
Hence it is necessary to disguise the means employed,
and to avoid the appearance of speaking not naturally, but artificially. For naturalness is persuasive,
and artificiality the reverse; for people take offence
at an artificial speaker, as if he were practising a
design upon them, in the same way as they take
offence at mixed wines. *The difference is much the
same* as between the voice of ²Theodorus and those

---

¹ *Poetic* ch. 21.
² Theodorus was a famous tragic actor, of whom a story is
told in the *Politics* IV (VII) p. 129 ll. 8 sqq. (p. 220 of my Translation).

of all the other actors ; for, while his appears to be
the speaker's own voice, theirs have the appearance
of being assumed. But the deception *which we have
in view* is successfully effected, if words are chosen
from ordinary parlance and combined, as is the
practice of Euripides and indeed is the practice of
which he was the first to set an example.

Words. Nouns and verbs being the component parts of
the speech and the nouns being of all the various
kinds which have been considered in my ¹treatise on
Poetry, it is only seldom and in few places that we
must make use of ²rare or foreign words, ³compound
words or words *specially* invented *for the occasion*.
The question where they should be used we will
discuss at a later time; the reason for using them
but rarely has been already stated, viz. that they
constitute too wide a departure from propriety. It is
only the ⁴proper and the special name of a thing and
the metaphor that are suited to the style of prose
composition. We may infer this from the fact that
these alone are of universal use, as everyone in conversation uses metaphors and the special or proper

¹ *Poetic* ch. 21.
² Although in the *Poetic*, ch. 21, p. 172, l. 19, Aristotle says
λέγω δὲ κύριον μὲν ᾧ χρῶνται ἕκαστοι γλῶτταν δὲ ᾧ ἕτεροι, it is
clear that in the *Rhetoric* he includes rare and obsolete as well
as foreign words under the general term γλῶτται. See the
instances given p. 116, ll. 13 sqq.
³ That διπλᾶ ὀνόματα are "compound words" is clear from ch. 3
in init. p. 116, ll. 4 sqq. Cp. *Poetic*, ch. 21, p. 172, ll. 11—14.
⁴ There seems to be practically no difference in meaning
between "proper" and "special" names; they are the names employed in ordinary speech.

names of things. It is clear therefore that successful composition will have an air of novelty without betraying its art and a character of lucidity, and these, as we have seen, are the virtues of rhetorical speech. p. 228. Among nouns, while it is [1]homonymous nouns, *i.e. words which have several meanings*, that are serviceable to a sophist, as being the instruments of logical deception, it is synonyms which are serviceable to a poet. As an instance of proper and synonymous words I may mention e.g. "going" and "proceeding;" for these are both proper and also synonymous.

The nature of these several terms, the number of kinds of [2]metaphor, and the extreme importance of metaphor, both in poetry and in prose, are matters which have been discussed, as we said, in the [3]treatise on *Poetry*. But they deserve the [4]more diligent attention in prose in proportion as prose is dependent upon a smaller number of aids than metrical composition. Perspicuity, too, pleasure and an air of strangeness are in an especial sense conveyed by means of metaphor, and for his metaphors a speaker must depend upon his own originality. The epithets and metaphors used must alike be appropriate, and

Metaphors.

---

[1] Aristotle's own definitions of a "homonym" and a "synonym" will explain his meaning here: ὁμώνυμα λέγεται ὧν ὄνομα μόνον κοινόν, ὁ δὲ κατὰ τοὔνομα λόγος τῆς οὐσίας ἕτερος...συνώνυμα δὲ λέγεται ὧν τό τε ὄνομα κοινὸν καὶ ὁ κατὰ τοὔνομα λόγος τῆς οὐσίας ὁ αὐτός. Κατηγορίαι 1.

[2] Retaining μεταφοράς.

[3] There is no discussion of synonyms in the *Poetic*, perhaps, as Schmidt suggests, because the book in its present form is more or less imperfect.

[4] Reading τοσούτῳ.

the appropriateness will arise from [1]proportion *or analogy;* otherwise there will be a glaring impropriety, as the contrariety of contraries is rendered most evident by juxtaposition. It is our business on the contrary to consider, as a scarlet robe is becoming to a young man, what it is that is becoming to an old man; for the same dress is not appropriate to both.

Propriety in the use of metaphors. Again, if it is your wish to adorn a subject, the proper means is to borrow your metaphor from things superior to it which fall under the same genus; if to disparage it, from such things as are inferior. An instance of this, as contraries fall under the same genus, is to describe one who begs as a suppliant and to describe one who prays as a beggar, *praying and begging* being both forms of request. It was thus that Iphicrates called Callias a [2]mendicant priest instead of a torchbearer in the Mysteries, and Callias replied that he could never have been initiated or he would not have made such a mistake. The fact is that both are offices of divine worship, but the one is an honourable office and the other an ignoble one. Again, while somebody calls actors mere [3]parasites of

[1] Proportion or analogy (τὸ ἀνάλογον) in the choice of epithets implies that they agree in meaning with the words to which they belong, and in the choice of metaphors that there is no incongruity or confusion in the transference of ideas. See Mr Cope's note.

[2] The δᾳδουχία was a high hereditary office in the ritual of the Eleusinian Demeter. A μητραγύρτης, on the other hand, was no better than a begging friar who collected alms at the festival of Cybele or some other deity. See Lobeck *Aglaophamus,* p. 629.

[3] "Parasites of Dionysus", i.e. hangers-on of the god who was the presiding deity of the drama. It is to be noticed that the

Dionysus, they call themselves artists; both these terms are metaphorical, but one is defamatory and the other the contrary.　Again, pirates now-a-days style themselves purveyors; and by the same rule one may describe crime as error, error as crime and stealing as either taking or plundering.　Such a phrase as that of Telephus in Euripides

> " Lord of the oar and setting forth to Mysia "

is a breach of propriety, as the word "lording" is too pompous for the subject, and accordingly the [1]deception is unsuccessful.　A mistake may be made too in the mere syllables of a word, if they are not significant of sweetness in a voice.　It is thus that Dionysius the [2]Brazen in his elegies calls poetry "Calliope's screeching," as both *poetry and screeching* are voices *or sounds*; but his metaphor is only a sorry one, as the sounds of screeching, *unlike poetical sounds*, possess no meaning.　Again, the metaphors should not be far-fetched, but derived from cognate and homogeneous subjects, giving a name to something which before was nameless, and manifesting

Aristotelian use of μεταφορά is considerably wider than that of "metaphor" in English.　Any transference of a word from its proper or ordinary application to another would be a μεταφορά, whether it involved a comparison or not.　See the definition given in *Poetic*, ch. 21, p. 172, ll. 22—25, and the illustrations of it which follow; also Mr Cope's *Introduction*, Appendix B to Book iii.

[1] "the deception," i.e. the concealment of art which the speaker or writer has in view.　See p. 113, ll. 11 and 24.

[2] Dionysius, an Athenian rhetorician of the 5th century B.C., is said by Athenaeus (*Deipn.* xv. p. 669 D) to have received the name or nickname of "the Brazen", as having first suggested the use of bronze money.

their cognate character as soon as they are uttered. There is a metaphor of this kind in the popular enigma

[1]"A man on a man gluing bronze by the aid of fire I discovered",

for the particular process was nameless, but, as both processes are kinds of application, *the author of the enigma* described the application of the cupping-glass as gluing. It is generally possible in fact to derive good metaphors from well-constructed enigmas; for as every metaphor conveys an enigma, it is clear that a metaphor *derived from a good enigma* is a good one. Again, a metaphor should be derived from something beautiful, and the beauty of a noun, as Licymnius says, and similarly its ugliness, resides either in the sound or in the sense. There is a third point to be observed in regard to metaphors, which upsets the sophistical theory. For it is not true, as Bryson said, that there is no such thing as the use of foul language, because, whether you say one thing or another, your meaning is the same. For one word is more properly applicable to a thing than another and more closely assimilated to it and more akin to it, as setting the thing itself more vividly before our eyes. Nor again is it [2]under the same conditions that a word signifies this or that, and hence on this ground

---

[1] Athenaeus (*Deipn.* x. p. 452 a.) gives the second line of the enigma or riddle thus :

οὕτω συγκόλλως ὥστε σύναιμα ποιεῖν.

[2] The difference seems to be that, although two words or expressions may have practically the same meaning, yet one may suggest widely different associations from the other.

alone we must regard one word as being fairer
or fouler than another; for although both words
signify the fairness or foulness of a thing, it is not
merely in respect of its fairness or foulness that they
signify it, or, if so, at least they signify it in different
degrees. The sources from which metaphors should
be derived are such things as are beautiful either in
sound or in suggestiveness or in *the vividness with
which they appeal to* the eye or any other sense.
Again, one form of expression is preferable to another
e.g. "rosy-fingered dawn" to "purple-fingered," while
"red-fingered" is worst of all. In regard to [1]epithets
again, the applications of them may be derived from
a low or foul *aspect of things*, as *when Orestes is
called* a matricide, or from the higher aspect, as *when
he is called* the avenger of his father. *There is a
similar instance in the story of* Simonides who, when
the victor in the mule-race offered him only a poor
fee, refused to compose *an ode*, pretending to be
shocked at the idea of composing it on "semi-asses,"
but on receipt of a proper fee wrote *the ode beginning*

"Hail! daughters of storm-footed mares,"

although they were equally daughters of the asses.
The same result may be attained by the use of
diminutives. [2]By a diminutive I mean that which

*Sources of
metaphors.*

Epithets.

---

[1] Aristotle uses ἐπίθετον to denote any word or words
describing or characterizing a "proper noun," not merely a single
adjective, as the English "epithet."

[2] ὑποκορισμός may properly be rendered in this place by the
neutral word "diminutive," but it would not ordinarily include
such diminutives as are of a depreciatory or censorious character.

diminishes either the good or the evil of a word, and
I may cite as instances the banter of Aristophanes in
the *Babylonians* where he substitutes "goldlet" (χρυ-
σιδάριον) for gold, "tunickin" (ἱματιδάριον) for tunic,
"wee little censure" (λοιδορημάτιον) for censure, and
"sickiness" (νοσημάτιον) for *sickness.* But in the
use both of epithets and of diminutives it is necessary
to be cautious and never to lose sight of the mean.

CHAP. III.   Faults of taste occur in four points of style. Firstly,
Faults of
taste   in the use of compound words, such as Lycophron's
(τὰ ψυχρά).   "many-visaged heaven," "vast-crested earth," and
"narrow-passaged strand," or Gorgias's expressions,
"a beggar-witted toady," or " forsworn and [1]forever-
sworn." There are instances too in Alcidamas, e.g.
"his soul with passion teeming and his face fire-
painted seeming," or "he thought their zeal would
prove end-executing," or "his words' persuasiveness
he made end-executing," or "steel-gray the ocean's
basement ;" for all these are terms which, as being
compound, have a certain poetical character. A second
cause of faults of taste is the use of rare words, as
when Lycophron called Xerxes "a vasty man," and
Sciron "a man of bale," or when Alcidamas said
"baubles in poetry," "the retchlessness of his nature,"
and "[2]whetted with his mind's unadulterated ire." A
third fault lies in the misuse of epithets, i.e. in making
them either long or unseasonable or very numerous.

---

[1] It is apparently the compound κατευορκήσαντας which is objectionable, as the simpler form εὐορκήσαντας would express the
meaning.

[2] The γλῶττα here, as Mr Cope says, is the word τεθηγμένον,
which is rare and generally poetical in its usage.

For if in poetry it is proper to speak e.g. of "white milk," such epithets in prose are in any case inappropriate, and, if there are too many of them, they expose *the art of the style* and show it to be *simple* poetry. I do not say that epithets should not be used, as they are means of diversifying the ordinary style and giving the language a certain air of strangeness. But it is important to keep the mean ever in view, as *exaggeration* is worse in its effect than carelessness; for while in the latter there is only the absence of a merit, in the former there is a positive defect. Hence the epithets of Alcidamas appear tasteless, being so numerous and prolix and obtrusive as to be used not like a seasoning of the meat so much as like the meat itself. He says e.g. not "sweat" *simply* but "the damp sweat," not "to the Isthmian games" but "to the general assembly of the Isthmian games," not "laws" but "laws the sovereigns of states," not "by running" but "with the impulse of his soul at a run," not "a museum" but "a museum of all Nature that he had inherited." Again, *he says* "the thought of his soul sullen-visaged," "artificer" not "of favour" but "of universal favour," "steward of the pleasure of his audience," "concealed" not "with boughs" but "with the boughs of the wood," "he clothed" not "his body" but "his body's shame," "his soul's ambition counterfeit" (ἀντίμιμος)—a word which is at the same time a compound and an epithet, so that *the prose* is converted into poetry—and "the excess of his villainy so abnormal." The consequence is that this poetical diction by its impropriety is a source of absurdity and tastelessness as well as of obscurity from its verbiage ; for any speaker who accumulates words, where the audience is already cognizant of the subject on which he is speaking, involves it in an obscurity which is fatal to distinctness. People *for the most part* only use compound words when what they want to express is destitute of a name and the word they use is easily compounded, as e.g. pastime (χρονοτριβεῖν) ; if this is overdone, the effect is wholly poetical. Hence it is that compound words are eminently serviceable to dithyrambic poets, whose style is noisy ; rare words to epic poets, as epic poetry is a stately and austere *style of composition;* and metaphors to iambic writers, for the iambic is now the vehicle *of tragic poetry,* as I have remarked.

p. 228. There is a fourth and last fault of taste which is shown in the use of metaphors ; for metaphors too may be inappropriate, whether from their absurdity— for they are used by comic as well as by tragic poets —or from an excess of dignity and tragic effect, or again they may be obscure, if they are far-fetched. Take e.g. such expressions as Gorgias's, "a business green and raw" (*a case of obscurity*), or "you sowed in shame and reaped in misery," which is too poetical, or Alcidamas's description of philosophy as "an out-post against the laws," and of the *Odyssey* as "a fair mirror of human life," or his *phrase* "importing no such bauble into poetry," all which for the reasons stated fail in persuasiveness. Gorgias's address to the swallow, when she dropped her leavings on his head, is in the best style of tragic diction, "For shame," he said, "Philomela." The point is that it was not a shame to a bird to have behaved so, but it was to a maiden. It was a happy thought then in his censure to speak of her as she was rather than as she is.

The simile too is a metaphor, the difference be- Chap. IV. tween them being only slight. Thus when *Homer* Similes. says of Achilles that[1] "he rushed on like a lion," it is a simile; but when he says that "he rushed on, a very lion," it is a metaphor, for here, as valour is an attribute common to both, he transfers to Achilles the metaphorical appellation of "a lion." The simile is useful in prose as well as in poetry, although it should not be employed except sparingly, as it has a poetical character. The use of similes must be much the same as that of metaphors; for they are metaphors, but with the difference already stated.

An instance of a simile is e.g. that which Androtion applied to Idrieus when he said that he resembled curs which have been just unchained; for they fly at you and bite you, and so Idrieus was vicious when just unchained. Another is Theodamas's comparison of [2]Archidamus to Euxenus *minus* his knowledge of geometry; which is a [3]proportional simile, for *vice versa* Euxenus will be Archidamus *plus* his geometrical knowledge. Another is the expression in the [4]*Republic* of Plato that people who

---

[1] The words quoted are not found in the existing poems of Homer, but for the simile see *Iliad*, xx. 164.

[2] Euxenus and Archidamus are unknown, except from this passage.

[3] The "proportional" or "reciprocal" metaphor is illustrated in the *Poetic*, ch. 21, p. 173, ll. 1 sqq. See *infra* l. 29, p. 132, l. 3.

[4] *Republic*, v. p. 469 D.E.

despoil the dead are like curs that bite the stones thrown at them without touching the thrower. Or [1] Plato's comparison of the commons to a ship's captain who is strong but a little deaf. Or the [2] simile which he applies to poets' verses, that they are like blooming faces without beauty; for such faces, when the bloom has faded from them, and poets' verses, when they are broken up, both entirely lose their former appearance. Or the similes of Pericles about the Samians, that they are like children which take their sop but cry while taking it, or about the Boeotians, that they are like their own holm-oaks, for, as these are cut to pieces by axes made of their own wood, so are the Boeotians cut to pieces by civil war. Again, there is [3] Demosthenes's comparison of the commons to seasick passengers on board ship; or Democrates's of the orators to nurses who swallow the bonbon themselves, while they slobber the children with kisses; or Antisthenes's of Cephisodotus the thin to frankincense, as giving pleasure only by wasting away. For these may all be expressed either as similes or as metaphors, so that such as are popular, when expressed as metaphors, will be always convertible into similes, and the similes, if the explanatory words are omitted, into metaphors. But the proportional metaphor should be always transferable reciprocally and

Similes and metaphors.

---

[1] *Republic*, VI. p. 488 A.

[2] *Republic*, X. p. 601 B.

[3] It is doubtful whether this is the great orator or not; his name has been mentioned, but not any passage of his speeches, p. 106, L 28.

to either of the two congeners; e.g. if the goblet
is the shield of Dionysus, then the shield may be
properly called the goblet of Ares.

Such then being the component elements of the
speech, the basis of style is purity of language. But
purity of language falls under five heads; and of
these the first is *the proper use of* connecting words
or clauses, i.e. when they are made to correspond
in the natural relation of priority or posteriority to
one another, as some of them require, e.g. as μὲν
and ἐγὼ μὲν require δέ and ὁ δέ *as correlatives.* But
the correspondence should take place before the
audience has had time to forget *the first of the* words
or clauses, and the two should not be too widely
separated, nor should another such word or clause
be introduced before the one required as a correlative to the first, as such a construction is generally
inappropriate. *Take e.g. the sentence* " But I, as soon
as he told it me—for Cleon came to me with prayers
and expostulations—set out with them in my com-
pany." In cases like this there are sometimes a
number of connecting words or clauses prematurely
introduced before the one which is required *as a
correlative.* But if the clauses intervening between
the protasis and the *verb* "set out" are numerous, *the
sentence is rendered* unintelligible. A second point
of purity of style consists in calling things by their
own proper names rather than by *general or* class-
names. A third consists in the avoidance of ambiguous terms, but this only if your purpose is not
opposed *to perspicuity.* People use ambiguous terms
when they have nothing to say but make a pretence

CHAP. V.
Style con-
tinued.
Purity of
language.

of saying something, and, if this is their object, they express themselves ambiguously in poetry, as e.g. Empedocles; for the length of their circumlocution imposes upon their audience and affects it as common people are affected in the presence of soothsayers; for they signify their assent to *such* ambiguous phrases *as*

> "If Crœsus pass the Halys, he shall whelm
> A mighty empire."

Again, it is because there is less opportunity of error *in generalities* that soothsayers express themselves in general terms of their subject; for as in the [1]game of "odd and even" you have a better chance of being right if you say simply "odd" or "even" than if you specify the number of things held in the hand, so too *in prophecy you have a better chance if you say* that a thing will be than if you say when it will be, and this is the reason why soothsayers never go so far as to specify the date of an event. All these *circumlocutions, ambiguities and the like* must be classed together *as so many faults*, and must therefore be avoided, unless you have some such object as I have suggested. A fourth point is to observe Protagoras's classification of nouns generically as masculine, feminine and neuter; for it is important that the genders should be properly

---

[1] The Greek game known as ἀρτιασμός is briefly described by Becker *Charicles*, Excursus III. to Scene VI.; *Gallus*, Excursus II. to Scene X. It was played by two persons, of whom one would hold in his hand a number of counters and the other would guess whether the number was odd or even, or more accurately what the number was.

assigned, ¹as e.g. ἡ δ' ἐλθοῦσα καὶ διαλεχθεῖσα ᾤχετο. A fifth is the correct expression *of number*, *i.e.* many, few or unity, as e.g. οἱ δ' ἐλθόντες ἔτυπτόν με.

It is a general rule that the composition should be such as is easy to read and—which is the same thing—easy to deliver. But this will not be the case where there are many connecting words or clauses or where the punctuation is difficult, as in the writings Punctuation. of Heracleitus. It is no easy task to punctuate his writings, from the difficulty of determining to which of two words, the preceding or the following, a particular word *in his sentences* belongs. There is an example of this difficulty at the beginning of his book, where he says, "Although this divine reason exists for ever men are born into the world without understanding"; it is impossible to tell to which of the words "exists" or "are born" the words "for ever" should be joined by punctuation. Again, you are Zeugma. guilty of a solecism, if in writing two words in a single phrase you fail to assign to them a word appropriate to both. Thus *if you take e.g. the word* "sound" or "colour", the participle "seeing" does not apply to both alike, but "perceiving" does. And Parenthesis. you become obscure, if in seeking to introduce a number of details in the middle *of a sentence* you do not complete the sense before you mention them, as

---

¹ The point of the illustration is the agreement of the feminine participles with the preceding feminine relative. But Mr Cope is, I think, right in arguing that the "classes" of Protagoras were not the same as the ordinary genders of classical grammar but composed (1) male agents, (2) female agents, (3) all inanimate or inactive things.

e.g. if you say "I meant, after discussing with him this, that and the other, to proceed" rather than "I meant to proceed after discussing with him, and then this, that and the other occurred."

We will pass now to dignity of style. The following are the causes which contribute to it. *Firstly*, to use a definition instead of the simple name of a thing, *to say* e.g. not "a circle" but "a plane figure which is at all points equidistant from the centre." (If brevity is the object, the contrary should be the rule, viz. the substitution of the simple name for the definition.) *Secondly*, where the subject is one that is foul or indecorous, if the foulness lies in the definition, to use the name, and if in the name, to use the definition. *Thirdly*, to employ metaphors and epithets as means of elucidating the subject, being on your guard at the same time against a poetical style. *Fourthly*, to put the plural for the singular, as the poets do when they say e.g.

"Unto Achaean harbours,"

when there is only one harbour, or

"Lo! here the manifold tablet-leaves,"

meaning a single leaf. *Fifthly*, [1] not to combine *two cases by a single article but* to give each case its own article, as in τῆς γυναικὸς τῆς ἡμετέρας. (But here again for brevity's sake the contrary τῆς ἡμετέρας γυναικός). *Sixthly*, to use connecting particles or, if for brevity's sake you omit the connecting particle, to

---

[1] The instance given shows that Victorius, whom Mr Cope follows, is right in understanding the rule to mean *non copulare vincireque uno articulo duos casus, sed utrique suum assignare.*

preserve the connexion, *saying e.g.* πορευθεὶς καὶ διαλεχθείς or πορευθεὶς διελέχθην, *not* πορευθεὶς διαλεχθείς. Another useful practice is Antimachus's device of describing a thing by attributes it does not possess, as he does in the case of Teumessus *in the* [1] *lines beginning*

"There is a low and wind-swept crest,"

for there is no limit to this method of amplification. This mode of treatment by negation is one that is applicable indifferently to things both good and bad, as occasion may require. It is the source of the epithets which poets use *such as* "stringless, lyreless music"; for they add privative epithets, as these are popular in proportional metaphors[2], as e.g. in calling the trumpet-blast "a lyreless music."

The conditions of propriety in a speech are that the style should be emotional and ethical, and *at the same time* proportionate to the subject-matter. By a proportionate style I mean that the manner of the composition should not be slovenly if the subject is pompous, or dignified if it is humble; and that there should be no ornamental epithets attached to unimportant words; otherwise *the composition* has the air of a comedy, like [3]Cleophon's poetry, which contains

Chap. VII.
Propriety.

---

[1] The quotation is from the *Thebais* of Antimachus, an epic poem on the theme of the ἑπτὰ ἐπὶ Θήβας. Teumessus was a hut or village in Bocotia.

[2] The "proportional" metaphor has been already illustrated; see marginal reference. Here the "proportion" would apparently be this:

Trumpet : trumpet-blast :: lyre : music of lyre (μέλος).

[3] A tragic poet, whose name occurs more than once in the *Poetic*.

some expressions as *ridiculous as* [1]it would be to say
e.g. "a sovereign fig." The means of expressing
emotion, if the matter is an insult, is the language of
anger; if it is impiety or foulness, that of indignation
and of a shrinking from the very mention of such a
thing; if it is something laudable, that of admiration;
if something pitiable, that of depression, and so on.
This appropriateness of language is one means of
giving an air of probability to the case, as the minds
of the audience draw a wrong inference of the speaker's
truthfulness from the similarity of their own feelings
in similar circumstances, and are thus led to suppose
that the facts are as he represents him, [2]even if this
is not really so. It should be added that a listener is
always in sympathy with an emotional speaker, even
though what he says is wholly worthless. This is the
reason why a good many speakers try to overwhelm
the audience by their clamour. This method of proof
depending on *external* signs is ethical, as the appropriate characteristics are assigned to any particular
class or moral state. I understand under "class" the
different periods of life, boyhood, manhood and old
age, *the sexes*, male and female, or nationalities such
as the Lacedaemonian or Thessalian; and under
"moral states" such as determine the character of a
person's life, as it is not every such state which influences the characters of lives. If then the words
which the speaker uses are also appropriate to the
moral state, he will produce this ethical effect; for

---

[1] Omitting ἄν or perhaps better εἰ before εἴπειεν.

[2] There is no good reason for omitting the clause εἰ καὶ
μὴ οὕτως ἔχει, ὡς ὁ λέγων.

there will be a difference both in the language and in
the pronunciation of a clown and an educated person.
Another means of moving an audience is the trick
which is used *ad nauseam* by speech writers, viz. *the
introduction of such phrases as* "Who is not aware?",
"Everybody is aware", where a listener is shamed
into an admission of the fact for the sake of partici-
pating in the knowledge which everybody else *is
said to possess.*

The question of opportuneness or inopportune- Opportuneness in the use of any rhetorical device is one that ness.
belongs equally to all the species of Rhetoric. There
is one remedy for exaggeration of every sort in the
popular rule, that a speaker should [1]anticipate censure by pronouncing it on himself, as *the exaggeration* is then regarded as correct, since the speaker
is aware of what he is doing. Let me add the rule of
not employing simultaneously all the different means
of proportion *or correspondence,* as this is one way to
deceive the audience. What I mean is e.g. if the
words used are harsh in sound, not to carry the
harshness into the voice and countenance and the
other appropriate *means of expression;* for the
result of so doing is that the nature of each becomes
conspicuous, whereas, if you use some and omit
others, although you equally make use of art, you
succeed in escaping detection.

It is a *general* result *of these considerations* that,
if a tender subject is expressed in harsh language or
a harsh subject in tender language, there is a certain
loss of persuasiveness. The multiplication of com-

---

[1] Reading προεπιπλήττειν.

pound words or epithets and the use of strange words are most appropriate to the language of emotion; for a person in a state of passion may be pardoned, if he speaks of an evil as "heaven-high" or "colossal." *The same excuse holds good* when the speaker has mastered his audience and has roused them to enthusiasm by praise or blame or passion or devotion, as [1] Isocrates e.g. does in his panegyrical speech, where he says at the end "sentence and sense" (φήμη καὶ γνώμη), and again "seeing that they brooked it" (οἵτινες ἔτλησαν). For this is the language of enthusiasm and is consequently acceptable to an audience in a state of enthusiasm. It is suitable to poetry for the same reason, as poetry is inspired. It must be used thus or else ironically, as by Gorgias and in the [2] *Phaedrus* of Plato.

CHAP. VIII.
Structure of the style.

The structure of the style should be neither metrical nor wholly unrhythmical. If it is the former, it lacks persuasiveness from its appearance of artificiality, and at the same time diverts the minds of the audience from the subject by fixing their attention upon the return of the similar cadence, so that they anticipate its coming as children anticipate the answer to the herald's summons, "Whom chooses the freedman for his attorney?" *and the answer is*

---

[1] Of the expressions cited from Isocrates, the first is a misquotation; and as the point seems to consist in the jingle of words, the original φήμην δὲ καὶ μνήμην καὶ δόξαν (*Paneg.* § 220) would be more appropriate. In the second (*Paneg.* § 110, not at the end of the speech), it is the poetical word ἔτλησαν which gives it colour, although the MSS. of Isocrates have ἐτόλμησαν.

[2] See e.g. *Phaedrus* pp. 238 D. 241 E.

"¹Cleon." If on the other hand the composition
is wholly unrhythmical, it has no definiteness, whereas
it ought to be definitely limited, although not by
metre, as what is indefinite is disagreeable and incapable of being known. It is ²number which is Rhythm.
the defining *or limiting* principle of all things, and
the number of the structure of style is rhythm, of
which metres are so many sections. Hence a prose
composition should have rhythm but not metre, or
it will be a poem. But the rhythm should not be
elaborately finished, or in other words it should not
be carried too far.

I pass now to the three kinds of rhythm. The Kinds of
heroic rhythm is too dignified, and is deficient in rhythm.
conversational harmony. The iambic rhythm on the
other hand is the very diction of ordinary life, and
is therefore of all metres the most frequent in conversation; but it is deficient in dignity and impressiveness. The trochaic rhythm approximates too
much to broad comedy, as appears in *trochaic*
tetrameters; for the tetrameter is a tripping rhythm
(τροχερὸς ῥυθμός). There remains the paean, which
has been used by prose writers from Thrasymachus

---

¹ It was part of Cleon's policy to pose as the champion of
those who, like freedmen, could not appear for themselves in
Court, and the children, whether in Aristotle's own day or later,
seem to have caught up his invariable name.

² This is the well-known Pythagorean principle; see Ritter and
Preller *Historia Philosophiae Graecae et Romanae* §§ 52 sqq.
Aristotle, in applying it to style, means that words which are
themselves formless and incoherent are reduced to order by
number, i.e. by rhythm. There is a very similar remark relating
to music in Plato *Philebus*, p. 26 A.

downwards, although they did not understand the definition of it. ¹The paean is the third rhythm, and is closely connected with the preceding ones, having in itself the ratio of 3 to 2, while they have the ratios of 1 to 1 and 2 to 1 respectively. The ratio of 3 to 2 is connected with both of these, *and is in fact the mean between them;* and this is the ratio of the paean.

While the other rhythms should be discarded, partly for the reasons which have been already given and partly because of their metrical character, the paean should be adopted *in prose compositions,* as it is the only one of the rhythms named which cannot form a regular metre and is therefore the most likely to escape detection. It is the fashion—a wrong fashion, as I think—at the present time to use the same paean both at the beginning and ² at the end of sentences. There are two opposite kinds of paean, of which one is suitable to the beginning of a sentence and in fact is so employed; it is the one beginning with a long syllable and ending with three short ones, *as in*

Δαλογενὲς εἴτε Λυκίαν,

or   χρυσεοκόμα Ἑκατε παῖ Διός.

---

¹ It is clear, on the principle of a long syllable being equivalent to two short ones, that the parts of the spondee (– –) or the dactyl (– ◡ ◡), which are the admissible feet in hexameter verse, have the ratio of 1 to 1, those of the iambus (◡ –) or the trochee (– ◡) have the ratio of 2 to 1, and those of the paean (– ◡ ◡ ◡ or ◡ ◡ ◡ –) have the ratio of 3 to 2.

² It is very doubtful whether the words καὶ τελευτῶντες need be inserted in the text; Mr Cope justly says Aristotle would be likely to let them be mentally understood.

The other, which is opposite to it, has three short syllables at the beginning and the long syllable at the end, as

μετὰ δὲ γᾶν ὕδατά τ' ὠκεανὸν ἠφάνισε νύξ.

This is the paean which *properly* terminates a sentence; for the short syllable from its incompleteness has a mutilated effect, whereas the sentence should be cut off by the *final* long syllable, and its end be marked not by the scribe nor by the [1] marginal annotation but by the *natural* rhythm.

So much for the proof that the style should be rhythmical and for the nature and structure of the rhythms which make it so.

The style must be either jointed, i.e. united only by its connecting particles, after the manner of *modern* dithyrambic preludes, or compact, like the antistrophes of the ancient poets. The jointed style is the original one, *as in* [2] *Herodotus, e.g.* "The following is a statement of the researches of Herodotus of Thurii"; it was formerly universal but is now confined to a few writers. By a "jointed style" I mean one which has no end in itself except the completion of the subject under discussion. It is disagreeable from its *endlessness or* indefiniteness,

CHAP. IX.
Two kinds of style.

(1) Jointed,

---

[1] The "marginal annotation" (Gk. παραγραφή, Lat. *interductus librarii*) would answer to the modern full-stop.

[2] The opening passage of Herodotus's History, Ἡροδότου Θουρίου ἤδ' ἱστορίης ἀπόδειξις, is cited as a case of writing where there is no attempt to build up a sentence of parts subordinated to each other, but the sentence is a simple clause or consists of clauses which are merely pieced or jointed by connecting particles.

as everybody likes to have the end clearly in view. This is the reason why *people in a race* do not gasp and faint until they reach the goal; for while they have the finishing-point before their eyes, they are insensible of fatigue. The compact style on the other (2) periodic. hand is the periodic; and I mean by a "period" a sentence having a beginning and an end in itself, and a magnitude which admits of being easily comprehended at a glance. Such a style is agreeable and can be easily [1]learnt. It is agreeable, as being the opposite of the indefinite style and because the hearer is constantly imagining himself to have got hold of something from constantly finding a definite conclusion *of the sentence*, whereas *in the other style* there is something disagreeable in having nothing to look forward to or accomplish. It is easily learnt too, as being easily recollected, and this because a periodic style can be numbered, and number is the easiest thing in the world to recollect. It is thus that everybody recollects [2]verses better than irregular *or prose* compositions, as they contain number and are measured by it. But the period should be completed by the sense as well as by the rhythm and not be abruptly broken off like the iambics of [3]Sophocles

"This land is Calydon of Pelops' soil,"

---

[1] It is to be remembered that the Greek and Roman orators were in the habit of getting their speeches by heart; hence the importance of μνήμη or *memoria* in a treatise on rhetoric.

[2] The reason alleged depends in part upon the etymological connexion of μέτρα with μετρεῖσθαι.

[3] The line belongs really to the *Meleager* of Euripides, not to

for a wholly erroneous supposition is rendered possible by such a division, as e.g. in the instance quoted, that Calydon is in Peloponnesus.

A period may be (1) divided into members *or* *clauses*, (2) simple. If it is the former, it should be complete in itself, properly divided and capable of being easily pronounced at a single breath, not so however at the *arbitrary* division *of the speaker* but as a whole. A member *or clause* is one of the two parts of a period. A simple period on the other hand is a period consisting of a single member.

The members *or clauses* and the periods themselves should be neither truncated nor too long. If they are too short, they often make a hearer stumble ; for if, while he is hurrying on to *the completion of* the measure *or rhythm*, of which he has a definite notion in his mind, he is suddenly pulled up by a pause on the part of the speaker, there will necessarily follow a sort of stumble in consequence of the sudden check. If on the other hand they are too long, they produce in the hearer a feeling of being left behind, as when people who are taking a walk do not turn back until they have passed the usual limit ; for they too leave their fellow-walkers behind. Similarly periods of undue length become *actual* speeches and resemble a dithyrambic prelude *in their discursiveness.* The result is what Democritus of Chios

any play of Sophocles. It is objectionable in Aristotle's view, because the rhythmical pause comes after χθονός but the pause in the sense after γαία, the words Πελοπείας χθονός being connected with the next line

ἐν ἀντιπόρθμοις πέδι᾽ ἔχουσ᾽ εὐδαίμονα.

quoted as a taunt against Melanippides for writing dithyrambic preludes instead of regular *stanzas or antistrophes* :

[1] "A man worketh ill to himself in working ill to his neighbour,
And there is nought to its author so ill as a—long-winded
preludo ;"

for a similar taunt may be suitably applied to the patrons of long-winded clauses. Periods in which the clauses are too short are not periods at all ; hence *such a period* drags the audience with it headlong.

The *periodic* style, which is divided into clauses,
The periodic is of two kinds, according as the clauses are simply
style. divided, as in the sentence [2] "I have often wondered at those who convened the public assemblies and
Antithesis. instituted the gymnastic games," or opposed, where in each of the two clauses either one of two contraries is placed beside the other, or the two contraries are connected together by the same word, as [3] "Both parties they helped, those who stayed behind and those who went with them ; for the latter they won a new land larger than that which they possessed at home, and to the former they left sufficient in that which was theirs at home." Here the words " staying behind" and " going with them," the ideas "sufficient" and "larger", are contrasted. *An-*

---

[1] The second line is a parody of Hesiod's,

ἡ δὲ κακὴ βουλὴ τῷ βουλεύσαντι κακίστη.

"Εργα κ. Ἡμέραι, 263.

[2] A quotation from Isocrates *Paneg.* § 1.

[3] *Ibid.* § 37; but the words are not quoted exactly. The connexion (ἐπίζευξις) lies in the verb ὤνησαν, which governs both τοὺς ὑπομείναντας and τοὺς ἀκολουθήσαντας (comp. p. 120, l. 6); the juxtaposition of opposites is explained in the text.

other instance is [1]"to those who wanted money and
to those who desired enjoyment," where *sensual* enjoyment is opposed to the acquisition *of money.* Again,
"It often happens in these cases that the wise are
unfortunate and the fools are successful"; or "They
were immediately presented with the prize of valour
and not long afterwards acquired the empire of the
sea"; or "To sail through the mainland and march
through the ocean, by bridging the Hellespont and
digging through Athos"; or "Citizens by nature
but divested by law of their citizenship"; or "Some
of them had a miserable end, and others a shameful
deliverance"; or "In private life using foreigners as
domestic servants and in public life suffering many
of the allies to be slaves"; or "Either to bring them
alive or to leave them dead." Another instance is,
the remark which somebody made about Pitholaus
and Lycophron in the Court of Law, "These fellows,
who when at home used to sell you, now that
they have come here, have purchased you." All
these are instances of an antithetical style. The
agreeableness of such a style lies in the fact that
contraries are so easily known, especially when they
are set in juxtaposition, and that it *is a style which*
has a resemblance to a syllogism, the refutative syllogism being a bringing together of opposites. Such
then is the explanation of antithesis. [2]Parisosis is Parisosis.

[1] The following quotations are all taken (although sometimes
inexactly) from the same panegyrical oration of Isocrates. Mr
Cope gives the references.

[2] It is, I fear, impossible to help importing Aristotle's own
terms into English.

Paro-
moiosis.

the equality of the members *or clauses*, paromoiosis the similarity of the extremities, i.e. either the beginnings or the ends of the sentences. When it is at the beginning, *the similarity is* always one of *whole* words, when at the end, it is one of the final syllables, as of *different* inflexions of the same word or *a repetition of* the same word[1].

But the same sentence may combine all these points, being at once a case of antithesis, of balance of clauses (parisosis) and of similarity of terminations.

The beginnings of periods have been pretty fully enumerated in the [2]Theodectea.

There are not only true but false antitheses, as in [3]Epicharmus.

Chap. X.
Clever sayings (τὰ ἀστεῖα).

Having discussed and determined these points, we have next to consider the sources of clever and popular sayings. The invention of such sayings is the work of natural ability or of long practice; but

---

[1] Aristotle in the text cites the following instances : (1) of initial paromoiosis, ἄγρον γὰρ ἔλαβεν ἀργὸν παρ' αὐτοῦ and δωρητοί τ' ἐπέλοντο παράρρητοί τ' ἐπέεσσιν, (2) of final paromoiosis ᾠήθησαν αὐτὸν παιδίον τετοκέναι, ἀλλ' αὐτοῦ αἴτιον γεγονέναι, and ἐν πλείσταις δὲ φροντίσι καὶ ἐν ἐλαχίσταις ἐλπίσιν, (3) of varied inflexion ἄξιος δὲ σταθῆναι χαλκοῦς, οὐκ ἄξιος ὢν χαλκοῦ, (4) of repetition σὺ δ' αὐτὸν καὶ ζῶντα ἔλεγες κακῶς καὶ νῦν γράφεις κακῶς, (5) of syllabic parallelism τί ἂν ἔπαθες δεινόν, εἰ ἄνδρ' εἶδες ἀργόν;

[2] Upon the Aristotelian *Theodectea*, see Mr Cope's *Introduction*, pp. 55 sqq.

[3] The line quoted is

τόκα μὲν ἐν τήνων ἐγὼν ἦν, τόκα δὲ παρὰ τήνοις ἐγών,

where there is no true antithesis between τόκα μὲν and τόκα δὲ or between ἐν τήνων and παρὰ τήνοις.

the explanation of them belongs to the present treatise. Let us enter then upon a complete enumeration of them. We may start with the assumption that learning without trouble is naturally agreeable to everybody, and that, as names *or words* possess a certain significance, those which impart instruction to us are most agreeable. Now rare words are unintelligible to us, and the proper *or ordinary* names of things we know already. It is metaphor which is Metaphor and simile. in the highest degree instructive; for when e.g. [1]Homer calls old age "the sere, the yellow leaf," he imparts instruction and knowledge through the medium of the genus, as both old age and the sere leaf are withered. The similes of poetry again produce the same effect, and hence a simile, if it is well constructed, shows cleverness. For the simile, as has been already said, is a metaphor with a difference p. 239. only in the mode of statement. Hence it is less agreeable, being couched in longer terms; also it does not *directly* say that one thing is another, and, as this is not said, it is not looked for by the minds *of the audience, and accordingly there is no opportunity of instruction.* It follows in regard to Enthymemes. enthymemes as in regard to style that they are clever, if they convey to us rapid instruction. And hence it is that the enthymemes which are popular are not such as are superficial, i.e. such as are perspicuous to everybody and need no research, nor such as are unintelligible when stated, but those which are either

---

[1] *Odyssey*, XIV. 214. The "sere leaf" will perhaps represent Homer's καλάμη, although it is used in a somewhat different train of thought.

apprehended at the moment of delivery, even though
there was no previously existing knowledge of them,
or which are followed at little interval by the minds
of the audience. For what is virtually instruction,
whether immediate or subsequent, takes place in
these cases, but not otherwise. These being then
the species of enthymemes which are popular, if
considered relatively to the meaning they convey,
relatively to style they may be considered in respect
either of their structure or of the *single* words *employed in them.* Enthymemes are popular from their
structure, if it is antithetical, as e.g. *in* [1]*Isocrates*,
"considering the peace which all the world enjoyed
as a war against their own private interests," where
there is an antithesis between war and peace ; and
from their single words, if the words are such as
contain a metaphor, and this a metaphor which is
neither farfetched nor superficial (for in the former
case it is difficult to comprehend at a glance, and in
the latter it leaves no impression), or again, if they
vividly represent *the subject* to the eye, as it is desirable that the things should be seen in actual performance and not merely in intention. There are
then these three objects to be ever kept in view, viz.
metaphor, antithesis, and vividness of representation.

Metaphors.
p. 232.

[2]Metaphors are of four kinds, and of these the
proportional are the most popular. An instance of
a proportional metaphor is the [3]saying of Pericles,

[1] *Phil.* § 82.
[2] The four kinds of metaphor are enumerated in the definition
given in the *Poetic*, ch. 21, p. 172, §§ 22—25.
[3] Already quoted p. 27, l. 12.

that " the blotting out of the youth who had perished
in the war from the state was like the taking of the
spring out of the year." Another is the saying of Lep-
tines about the Lacedaemonians, that he "would not
have *the Athenians* look on quietly, when Greece had
lost one of her eyes." Again, Cephisodotus expressed
his indignation at the eagerness of Chares for the
audit of his accounts in the Olynthiac war, by saying
that he had [1] "driven the people into a choking fit by
trying to get his accounts audited." The same Cephisodotus in one of his exhortations to the Athenians
told them they ought to "march to Euboea [2] with
the decree of Miltiades for their commissariat." Again,
Iphicrates showed his indignation at the truce which
the Athenians had made with Epidaurus and the
maritime states by saying that they had "stripped
themselves of their journey-money for the war."
Pitholaus called the [3] Paralian trireme the "people's
bludgeon" and Sestos a [4] "corn-stall of the Piraeus."
Pericles exhorted the Athenians to sweep away

---

[1] Reading ἀγαγόντα.

[2] This difficult expression seems to mean that the Athenians
were to march without any regard to the commissariat, but
in the spirit of the resolution which Miltiades proposed at
the crisis of the first Persian War. It is the use of ἐπισιτίζεσθαι
in conjunction with such a word as ψήφισμα which is in Aristotle's
language "metaphorical."

[3] The Paralus or State galley, as being used in carrying
prisoners of state, might be called the people's bludgeon or
weapon against their enemies.

[4] It is clear that Sestos must have been an emporium of the
corn which was exported from the coasts of the Euxine Sea
to Greece.

Aegina, that "eyesore of the Piraeus." Moerocles said he was every whit as virtuous as a certain respectable citizen whom he named, as the respectable citizen "got 33 per cent. for his roguery and he himself got only 10 per cent." There is an instance too in the iambic line of Anaxandrides in pleading the cause of *somebody's* daughters who had been a very long time in getting married:

<blockquote>[1]"The ladies' marriage-day is overdue."</blockquote>

Similarly Polyeuctus made the remark about a certain paralytic person named Speusippus that he could not keep himself quiet, "although Fortune had set him fast in the pillory of disease." Cephisodotus again called the triremes [2]"painted millstones," and the Cynic *Diogenes* called the wine-shops the "Athenian [3]public messes." Aesion said that *the Athenians* had "drained their whole city into Sicily" (which is a metaphor and a metaphor of a vivid kind); and again "so that Greece cried aloud" (which is also in some sense a vivid metaphor). I may instance too the advice of Cephisodotus *to the Athenians* to beware of converting many of their [4]mob-*meetings*

[1] The point lies in the legal term ὑπερήμερος, which is strictly applicable to somebody who has failed to pay a fine imposed upon him within the time prescribed.

[2] It must have been the grinding exactions in which the triremes were employed against the subject States of Athens that gave this name its appropriateness.

[3] φιδίτια was the Spartan term for the συσσίτια which were so characteristic a feature of the Lycurgean legislation. See *Politics,* ii. ch. 9.

[4] The word συνδρομὰς is substituted for συγκλήτους (ἐκκλησίας) " extraordinary assemblies."

into assemblies ; or the address of [1] Isocrates to those "who flock together at the general festivals." Another example is the one in the [2] Funeral Oration, that "Greece might well have her hair cut off at the tomb of those who had perished at Salamis, as her liberty was buried in the tomb with their valour;" for had he only said that she "might well weep for the valour that lay buried with them," *his expression* would have been a metaphor and a vivid one, but the addition of the words "her liberty with their valour" contains a sort of antithesis. Similarly Iphicrates said, "The course of my argument runs through the heart of Chares's conduct;" this is a [3] proportional metaphor, and the phrase "through the heart" sets the thing vividly before our eyes. Again, the phrase "to invite dangers to the help of dangers" is a vivid metaphor. The same is true of the phrase used by [4] Lycoleon in behalf of Chabrias, "not awed even by that symbol of his supplication, the bronze image," which was a metaphor at the time when it was used, although not a permanent one, as it

[1] *Phil.* § 14. It is the strange use of συντρέχοντας, as of συνδρομὰς in the last example, that makes the "metaphor."

[2] The Funeral Oration, which seems to be here ascribed to Isocrates, is usually regarded as the composition of Lysias, although its genuineness has been much disputed.

[3] The "proportion" may perhaps be expressed thus:

A road : a country :: the speech : Chares's conduct.

[4] A statue of Chabrias with his shield resting on his knee and his spear advanced, had been erected in honour of his victory over Agesilaus B.C. 378. Twelve years later, when Chabrias himself was standing his trial, his advocate Lycoleon must have pointed to this statue.

is only in the hour of his peril that the statue can be said to supplicate, but a vivid metaphor, *arising from* [1] the supposed animation of the inanimate memorial of the services he had rendered to the State. Or again "practising in every way meanness of spirit" is a metaphor, as practising is a species of increasing. Or *the saying* that "God lit up the light of reason in the soul," both light and reason being means of illumination. Or again [2] "we are not putting an end to the wars but only putting them off," *which is a metaphor*, as postponement and such a peace as is described are both merely means of delay. Or again, if we say that [3] "the treaty is a very far finer trophy than those won in war; for that is commemorative of a trifling success and a single chance, whereas the treaty commemorates *the issue of* a whole war;" for both are signals of victory. Or *lastly if we say* that States [4] "pay a heavy reckoning in the censure of mankind;" for the *audit or reckoning* is a sort of legal damage.

CHAP. XI. It has been stated then that the sources of clever sayings are proportional metaphor and *vivid or*

[1] Reading τὸ ἄψυχον δέ.

[2] Isocrates *Paneg.* § 200. The "metaphor" is, I think, the use of ἀναβάλλεσθαι, as a peace would properly be said not to "postpone" but to "terminate" a war.

[3] *Ibid.* § 211.

[4] The word εὔθυνα, meaning properly the audit, to which officers of State were called to submit at the expiration of their term of office, is applied metaphorically to the audit which states or nations undergo at the bar of history.

A reference to the *Poetic*, ch. 21, is necessary for the understanding of the "metaphors" cited in the present chapter.

ocular representation of the facts; but we have still
to say what we understand by such representation
and what are the means of producing it.

I mean that expressions represent a thing to the Vividness.
eye, when they show it in a state of activity. For
instance; to describe a good man as [1]"square" is a
metaphor, as a good man and a square are both
perfect *of their kind*; but it does not signify a state
of activity. On the other hand such a phrase as
[2]"with his vigour all in bloom" or [3]"thee like as
sacred kine that roam at large" or in the [4]line

"Then the Greeks bounding forwards,"

the expression "bounding" is energetic as well as
metaphorical. It is the same in Homer's favourite
treatment of inanimate objects as animate by the
use of metaphor. But it is always by representing
things as in action that he wins applause, as e.g.

"[5]Down down again to the valley the shameless boulder came
    bounding,"

or

"[6]the arrow flew,"

or [7]the arrow

"yearning for its mark"

or [8]the spears

"stood fixed in earth all panting to taste blood,"

[1] Perhaps "an all-round man" would better give the idea
in English.

[2] Isocrates *Phil.* § 12.　　　　[3] *Ibid.* § 150.
[4] Euripides, *Iphig. in Aul.* 80.　　　[5] *Odyssey*, xi. 598.
[6] *Iliad*, xiii. 587.　　[7] *Ibid.* iv. 126.　　[8] *Ibid.* xi. 573.

or

> "[1]through the breast
> The point sped quivering,"

for in all these instances the living character of the expressions invests the objects with an appearance of activity, shamelessness, quivering eagerness and the like being so many forms of activity. These expressions Homer applied to the objects by means of proportional metaphor; for ²as the stone is to Sisyphus, so is a shameless person to the victim of his shamelessness. But in his most approved similes too he treats inanimate things in the same way, *e.g. in the line*

> "*Waves that are* arched, foam-crested, some foremost, others pursuing;"

for he represents them all as moving and living, and activity is a form of motion.

Sources of metaphor. p. 232. It is proper to derive metaphors, as has been said before, from objects which are closely related to *the thing itself* but which are not *immediately* obvious. Similarly in philosophy it is a mark of sagacity to discern resemblances even in things which are widely different, as when Archytas said that an arbitrator and an altar were identical; for both are refuges of the injured ; or if one should say that an anchor and a hook were identical; for they are both the same kind of thing, only they differ *in position,* ³one being

---

[1] *Ibid.* xv. 542.

² It is certainly noticeable that Aristotle understands Homer's ἀναιδής as an epithet of a stone to mean literally "shameless".

³ The meaning is that an anchor holds fast something which is above it, and a hook something which is below it.

above and the other below.   The [1]equalization of
states in regard to things very dissimilar, *as e. g.*
equality in area and in perogatives, would be another
case.

While metaphor is a very frequent instrument of Deception
clever sayings, another or an additional instrument is (παρὰ προσδοκίαν).
deception, as people are more clearly conscious of
having learnt something from their sense of surprise
at the way in which the sentence ends, and their soul
seems to say "Quite true, and I had missed the
point." Again, the characteristic of clever apophthegms is that the speaker means something more
than he says, as e.g. the [2]apophthegm of Stesichorus
that the cicalas will have to sing to themselves on the
ground. This too is the reason of the pleasure
afforded by clever riddles; they are instructive and
metaphorical in their expression. And the same is
true of what Theodorus calls "novel phrases", i.e.
phrases in which *the sequel* is unexpected and not, as
he expresses it, "according to previous expectation",
but such as comic writers use when they alter the
forms of words. The effect of jokes depending upon
changes of letters is the same; they deceive the expectation. *Nor are these jokes found only in prose,*
they occur also in verses, where *the conclusion is* not
such as the audience had expected, e.g.

> And as he walked, beneath his feet
> Were—chilblains,

---

[1] The cleverness or originality lies I think, in the comparison
of things so different as superficial area and political privilege
(or perhaps military strength).
[2] Cp. p. 92, l. 2.

whereas the audience expected *the writer* to say
"sandals". But *in all such cases* the point must be
clear at the moment of making the joke. A play
upon the letters of a word arises not from using it in
its direct meaning but from giving the meaning a new
turn[1].

Clever say-
ings as
ornaments
of style.

A proper enunciation is requisite in all such
sayings. Take e.g. the remark that Athens did not
find the [2]rule of the sea a rule of misery, as it was a
source of profit to her, or as [3]Isocrates put it, that
the rule of the sea was a rule of misery to the state.
For in both these cases there is something said which
one would not have expected to be said, and *yet* it is
recognized as true; for there is no cleverness in
calling the rule a rule *in the second example*, but the
word "rule" is employed in different senses, and *in
the first example* it is not "rule" in the sense in
which it has been used before, but "rule" in a
different sense which is contradicted. But in all
these cases the merit consists in the proper applica-

---

[1] Aristotle illustrates the "literal joke" by two expressions
which would be untranslateable, even if it were possible to be
sure of their meaning. The first of them (for the σε of l. 33
should be omitted) may apparently be pronounced either as
θράττει "it confounds you" or as Θρᾶττ᾽ εἶ "you are a Thracian
slave girl." "This is amusing (he says) when its point is understood, for if you do not know the person to be a Thracian, it will
seem silly." The second, βούλει αὐτὸν πέρσαι, has never been
explained. "Both (he adds) need a proper enunciation."

[2] ἀρχή has the meaning first of "empire" and then of "beginning" in this expression.

[3] The passage which Aristotle has in mind is apparently
either *Phil.* § 69, or *de Pace* § 125.

tion of the term employed, *i.e. in the appropriateness of it to the thing described*, whether it is employed in a *double-entendre* or in a metaphor. Such an expression e.g. as "Mr [1] Bearable unbearable" is a contradiction only of the *double-entendre*; but it is appropriate enough, if the person in question is a bore. So too the line

[2]"You should not be more stranger than a stranger,"

or in other words, not stranger than you are bound to be, which is the same thing. Or again, "A stranger must not always be a stranger"; for here too there is change of signification. The same is the case in the much lauded line of Anaxandrides

"'Tis well to die ere meriting the death;"

for this is equivalent to saying "'Tis a worthy thing to die unworthily" or [3]"to die not being worthy of death" or "doing nothing worthy of death". The species of style is the same in all these instances; but the more concisely and antithetically it is expressed, the more popular is the saying. The reason of this is that its instructiveness is enhanced by the antithesis and accelerated by the conciseness of its terms. But there should always be the additional element of some personal appositeness or propriety of expression, if what is said is to be true and not superficial. For

----

[1] Plainly ᾽Ανάσχετος is a proper name, which lends itself to a play upon its meaning.

[2] Vahlen's reading of the line

οὐκ ἂν γένοιο μᾶλλον ἢ ξένος ξένος,

gives the best sense and is supported by the context.

[3] The clause is probably spurious.

truth and depth are not always combined, as e.g. *in the phrases* "One should die void of offence" or "A worthy man should wed a worthy wife", where there is no point at all. It is only when you combine the two *that you make a pointed phrase*, e.g. "It is a worthy thing to die unworthily." But the greater the number of such elements in a sentence, the more cleverly pointed it appears, as e.g. if its words convey a metaphor, and a metaphor of a particular kind, *i.e. a proportional metaphor*, an antithesis, a *parisosis or* balance of clauses and a vividness of action.

Similes.
p. 240.
Successful similes too, as has been said above, are always in a certain sense popular metaphors, being invariably composed of two terms, like the proportional metaphor. For instance, the shield, as we say, is Ares's goblet, and a bow a stringless lyre. Such a form of expression is not a ¹simple one; but to call the bow a lyre or the shield a goblet is so.

A simile is formed e.g. by the comparison of a flute player to a monkey or of a ²shortsighted person to a lamp with water dripping upon it, as both ³keep shrinking. A successful simile is one which is *virtually* a metaphor. For we may compare the shield to "Ares's goblet" or the ruin to a "tatter of a house"; or we may describe ⁴Niceratus as a "Philoctetes stung

¹ It is "not simple" because e.g. the comparison is not merely between shield and goblet but between the shield and Ares on the one hand and Dionysus and the goblet on the other. Op. p. 118, l. 30.   ² Omitting εἰς.

³ The winking of the shortsighted person and the sputtering of the lamp are both describable by the verb συνάγεσθαι.

⁴ Niceratus seems to have engaged in a rhapsodical contest with Pratys.

by Pratys", using the simile of Thrasymachus when
he saw Niceratus after his defeat by Pratys in the
rhapsody with his hair still dishevelled and his face
unwashed. It is here that poets are most loudly condemned for failure and most warmly applauded for
success, when *they so form their simile that* the two
members of it correspond, as e.g.

> "Like parsley curled his legs he bears"

or

> "Just as [1] Philammon tilting at the quintain."

These expressions and all others like them are
similes; and that similes are metaphors is a truth
which has been already stated more than once.

Proverbs again are metaphors from one species to Proverbs.
another, e.g. when somebody has invited a person's
help in the hope of gaining by it and has afterwards
found it to be a source of injury, [2] "'Tis as the
Carpathian says of the hare"; for they are both the
victims of this fate.

The sources of clever sayings and the reasons of
their cleverness have now been pretty fully discussed.

All approved hyperboles are also metaphors, as Hyperboles.
when it is said of a man whose face is bruised, "You
might have taken him for a basket of mulberries".
For a bruise *like a mulberry* is something purple;
but it is the number of the bruises supposed which
makes the hyperbole. But there are other phrases
resembling those given above which are hyperboles

---

[1] Philammon was a celebrated athlete.

[2] It is supposed that some Carpathian had brought some hares
or rabbits into his island and that they had multiplied and
devoured all his crops.

with only a difference of expression, as if you change

> "Just as Philammon tilting at the quintain"

to "You would have thought he was Philammon fighting with the quintain" or

> "Like parsley curled his legs he bears"

to "You might have thought he had not legs but parsley; they were so curly".

There is a character of juvenility in hyperboles as showing vehemence. Hence people generally employ them in moments of passion, *as in the* [1]*lines*

> "Not tho' he gave me gifts
> As many as the sand-grains or the dust."
>
> . . . .
>
> "But Agamemnon's daughter wed I not,
> Tho' Aphrodite's beauty were her own
> And all Athene's art."

This is a favourite figure of the Attic orators. But, *as being juvenile*, it is unbecoming to elder people.

CHAP. XII. Propriety.

It must not be forgotten that every kind of Rhetoric has its own appropriate style. For there is a difference between the literary and controversial styles and *in the controversial style* between the political and forensic styles. But the orator should be familiar with both; for the one (the controversial style) implies a power of expressing oneself in pure and accurate Greek, and the other (the literary style) a deliverance from the necessity of holding one's tongue, if one has anything that he wishes to impart to the world, as is the case of those who have no skill in composition.

[1] *Iliad* ix. 385 sqq.

It is the literary style which is the most finished Literary and contro-versial styles.
and the controversial which is the best suited to
declamation. Controversial oratory again is of two
kinds, ethical and emotional. This is the reason why
actors are fond of such dramas and poets of such
dramatis personæ as lend themselves to the treatment of character or emotion. But it is poets who
write to be read whose works are in everybody's
hands, such as Chaeremon who is as finished as a
[1] professional speech-writer and Licymnius among the
dithyrambic poets. Also a comparison of the speeches
of literary men and those of rhetoricians shows that
the former are found in actual contests to be meagre,
and the latter, although highly commended, to be inartistic, when taken in the hands *and closely studied*.
The reason is that they are adapted to an actual contest; hence the speeches which are intended to be
declaimed, when the declamation is removed, appear
ridiculous, as failing to discharge their proper function. Thus the use of asyndeta and the frequent
repetition of the same word are rightly reprobated
in the literary style, but are actually sought by orators
in the controversial style for their dramatic effect.
[2] (But in such repetitions there must be some variety *of
expression*, which paves the way, if I may so speak,

---

[1] The term λογογράφος is fully discussed by Mr Cope in
his note on ii. ch. 11 § 7. It means here not so much one
who composed speeches to be delivered by others in a Court of
Law as one who wrote panegyrical or epideictic speeches, meaning
them not to be delivered at all but to be read and studied at
home.

[2] The sentences placed in brackets contain remarks which are
rather incidental than necessary to the subject of the chapter.

for declamation, *as e.g. in the words* " Here is he
who robbed you ; here is he who cheated you ; here
is he who at the last essayed to betray you." We
may instance too the [1]trick of the actor Philemon
in Anaxandrides's play *The Old Man's Dotage* at the
passage *beginning* "Rhadamanthys and Palamedes",
or his repetition of the personal pronoun in the prologue of the *Devotees*; for unless such passages are dramatically declaimed, the case is like that of [2]a man
who has swallowed a poker.   And the same is true of
asyndeta, e.g. "I came, I met, I implored"; it is
necessary to declaim the words dramatically and not
to utter them, as if they were all one thing, with the
same character and intonation.   There is this especial
property also in asyndeta, that they make it possible
to present an appearance of saying several things in
the time which would otherwise be required for
saying one.   For the effect of the connecting particle
is to convert several things into one ; hence, if the
connecting particle is taken away, the consequence
will clearly be the opposite effect of converting a
single thing into several.   The asyndeton is thus a
means of amplification. *Take for instance the words,*
"I came, I conversed, I entreated"; the audience
seems to survey several things, as many things in fact

---

[1]   The allusion is admittedly obscure ; but it seems most
probable that these were well-known passages in which the art of
the actor Philemon had emphasized slight varieties of expression,
where several similar clauses occurred together.

[2]   "The porter who carried the beam" was a typical Greek
instance of stiffness like "the man who has swallowed a poker"
in English.

as the speaker mentioned. And this is Homer's purpose *in the reiteration of the name Nireus in the
successive* [1]*lines*

> "Nireus of Syme,
> "Nireus Aglaia's son,
> "Nireus the fairest man,"

for as a person of whom several things are said will
necessarily be mentioned several times, it follows
that, if a person is mentioned several times, it seems
as if several things had been said of him. So that
Homer by a single mention of Nireus exaggerated
his importance through this fallacy and makes him
famous, although he never alludes to him again).

The style of political oratory is precisely similar to *Political rhetoric.*
scene-painting. For the greater the crowd, the more
distant is the view : hence it is that in both a finished
style appears superfluous and unsuccessful. The
forensic style on the other hand is more finished,
especially when addressed to a single judge ; for he is
least subject to rhetorical influences, as he can take a
more comprehensive view of what is germane to the
case or alien to it and, as there is no actual contest, is
not prejudiced in his judgment. Accordingly it is
not the same orators who succeed in all the different
styles of Rhetoric; but, where there is most opportunity for declamation, there is the least possibility of
finish. And this is the case where voice, and especially
where a loud voice, is required.

The epideictic style is best suited to literary pur- *Epideictic and forensic*
poses, as its proper function is to be read ; and next *Rhetoric.*
to it the forensic style. It is superfluous to add such

---

[1] *Iliad*, ii. 671—3.

distinctions as that the style should be pleasant and stately; we might as well say that it must be chastened and liberal and characterized by any other ethical virtue. For it is clear that the [1]qualities enumerated above will render it pleasant, if we have been right in our definition of virtue of style. What *other* reason is there why it should be clear and not commonplace but appropriate? For it will not be clear, if it is prolix or too concise. But it is evident that it is the intermediate style which is the appropriate one. Pleasantness will result from the elements above enumerated, if successfully combined, viz. familiar and foreign words, rhythm and the persuasiveness which is the outcome of propriety.

We have now concluded our remarks upon style whether as belonging equally to all kinds of Rhetoric or as peculiar to the several kinds; it remains to consider arrangement.

CHAP. XIII.
Parts of a speech.

A speech has two parts. It is necessary first to state the case and then to prove it. It is [2]impossible therefore to state your case without proceeding to prove it or to prove it without having first stated it; for a proof is *necessarily* a proof of something, and a preliminary statement is not made except in order to be proved.

There is then the exposition of the case on the one hand and the proof on the other, like a problem and its demonstration, according to the natural distinction

---

[1] Purity, propriety, vividness, rhythm and the like, as Mr Cope justly says. See p. 135. l. 2.

[2] The impossibility arises not from the nature of the case but from the necessary conditions of Rhetoric.

in Dialectic. The division which is current among modern writers upon Rhetoric is a ridiculous one; for a ¹narrative of the facts clearly belongs to forensic oratory alone, but where is the possibility in epi-deictic or political speeches of such a narrative as they describe or of a reply to an adversary or in demon-strative speeches of a ²peroration? Again, an exordium, a comparison of cases and a recapitulation occur in political speeches only when there is a controversy. *It might as well be said that accusation and defence are proper parts of political speeches;* for it is true that they often occur in them, but not ³so far as they are deliberative. ⁴Nor again is the peroration in all cases a part even of forensic speeches, as e.g. where the speech is a short one and the subject such as can be easily remembered, as something is then subtracted from the length of the speech.

It appears then that the only indispensable parts *of a speech* are the statement of the case and the proof.

These are the only proper *or characteristic* parts; but if more are added, they must not exceed four, viz. exordium, exposition, proof and peroration. For the reply to one's adversary falls under the head

¹ It would hardly be correct to say that "narrative" is con-fined to the forensic kind of Rhetoric, unless it were taken in a limited sense as meaning a set argumentative statement of a case.

² The peroration (ἐπίλογος) is the subject of ch. 19. It would be out of place (says Aristotle) in demonstrative or closely-reasoned speeches.

³ Reading ἀλλ' οὐχ ᾗ συμβουλή.

⁴ There should be no stop after ἐπίλογος.

of proof, and the comparison of cases, being an amplification of one's own case, is a branch of proof, as there is in some sense a process of proof in such a comparison, although not in the exordium or in the peroration which serves only to refresh the memory. If one adopts then such divisions as these, one will come to the inventions of Theodorus and his school, distinguishing narrative, post-narrative and pre-narrative, refutation and re-refutation. But a special name should not be used unless to express a species or *specific* distinction; otherwise it proves to be idle and frivolous, like the [1] terms invented by Licymnius in his handbook, "impetus" (ἐπούρασις), "digression" (ἀποπλάνησις) and "ramification" (ὄζοι).

CHAP. XIV.
Exordium.

The exordium is the beginning of a speech and corresponds to a prologue in poetry and a prelude in a musical performance, all the three being beginnings and, as it were, preparations for what follows. Now the musical prelude resembles the exordium in epideictic speeches; for as musicians, when they have anything that they can play well, open their performance with it and then unite it *with the subject* by the [2]introductory bars, so it is proper to adopt the same style in epideictic speeches, i.e. to say at the outset anything that one may wish to say and then insert the introductory or connecting sentences. This is in fact a universal practice, of which the exordium

[1] The reading is very doubtful, some editors giving ἐπόρουσις or ἐπέρωσις or ἐπέρρωσις; but assuming that ἐπούρωσις is right, I should connect it, as Mr Cope does, with οὖρος.

[2] The ἐνδόσιμον, as Spengel says, seems to be here "non ipsum exordium, sed id quod exordium cum oratione connectit."

of Isocrates's *Helen* is an example, as there is no connexion between the disputatious dialecticians and Helen. It may be added that such a flight of the orator into a new region has the pleasing effect of relieving the uniform character of the speech.

The exordia of epideictic speeches are derived from praise or censure. Thus Gorgias opens his [1]Olympic speech *with the words*, "It is from many lips that you obtain admiration, men of Hellas" praising those who first convened the great assemblies. But [2]Isocrates blames them for having rewarded physical excellences with presents and yet not having offered any reward to wisdom. Another source of such exordia is counsel. *It may be urged* e.g. that it is our duty to honour the good, and accordingly the orator praises Aristides, or to honour those who are not famous and yet not vicious but whose virtues are buried in obscurity, such people e.g. as Priam's son Alexander; for the use of such language is a species of counsel. Again, such exordia may be taken from the exordia of forensic speeches, i.e. from appeals to the audience, when the subject of the speech is paradoxical or difficult or very trite, in the hope of winning a favourable hearing from them, as in *the* [3]*lines of* Choerilus *beginning*

"But now when all is spent."

---

[1] A speech delivered at the Olympic games with the view of uniting the peoples of Greece against the Persians.

[2] The reference is to *Paneg. in init.*

[3] The lines of Choerilus as quoted by the Scholiast, form a lament that the field of poesy which was once so rich is all worked out, and that every theme is now hackneyed or unpoetical.

Such are then the sources of exordia in epideictic speeches, viz. eulogy, censure, exhortation, dissuasion and appeals to the audience. The introductory sentences of the speech should be either foreign or closely connected with the speech itself.

As to the exordia of forensic speeches, it must be understood that they are equivalent to the prologues of dramatic or the proems of epic poetry; for the proems of dithyrambs resemble epideictic exordia, as e.g.

> [1] "For thee and thy gifts or spoils."

In Rhetoric as in epic poetry *the exordium* is a sample of the subject, being intended to supply the audience with some previous knowledge of it and to prevent their minds from being kept in suspense. ·For indefiniteness is a cause of distraction; hence the speaker or writer who places the beginning as it were in their hands gives them *a clue* by which, if they hold it, they will be able to follow the course of the argument. This is the purport *of such exordia as*

> [2] "Sing Muse the wrath,"
> [3] "Tell me the man,"
> [4] "Teach me another strain, how Asia's soil,"

or

> [4] "To Europe came a mighty war."

So too the tragic poets explain the subjects of their dramas, if not at the opening, like Euripides, yet

[1] The source of the quotation is unknown.
[2] *Iliad*, i. 1.
[3] *Odyssey*, i. 1.
[4] The quotations are said to be lines of Choerilus.

somewhere or other in the [1]prologue, [2]as Sophocles himself *in the lines beginning*

"My sire was Polybus,"

and the same is true of comedy. The most essential function then or characteristic of the exordium is to explain the end or object of the speech; hence if the subject is itself clear and unimportant, there is no need of employing an exordium.

There are other kinds of exordia which are employed; but they are merely means of remedying defects[3] in the audience and are not distinctively exordia. They may be derived from the speaker himself or from the audience or from the subject or from the adversary. They refer to the speaker and his opponent, when their object is the removal or creation of a prejudice. But there is this difference, that in apology the prejudicing circumstances should be placed first and in accusation they should be reserved for the peroration. Nor is the ground of this difference hard to see; for the defendant, when about to introduce himself, will necessarily dissipate the force of such circumstances as stand in his way and will therefore begin by removing the prejudice conceived against him, but the accuser, whose object it is to excite prejudice, will be led to state the

---

[1] Aristotle himself defines the prologue of a tragedy as μέρος ὅλον τὸ πρὸ χοροῦ παρόδου (*Poetic*, ch. 12); but he must give it a still wider meaning here, if it strictly includes the passage quoted, which does not begin until v. 774 of the *Oedipus Tyrannus*.

[2] Omitting δηλοῖ.

[3] "defects, such as inattention, unfavourable disposition, and the like" (Cope).

prejudicing circumstances in the peroration, that they may be more easily remembered. An appeal to the audience consists in gaining their goodwill and exciting their indignation, sometimes too in arresting their attention or the contrary; for it is not always well to make them attentive, and this is the reason why so many speakers try to move them to laughter.

Means of exciting attention. There is not one *of the topics belonging to the exordium*, nor indeed the appearance of high character, which may not be employed, if one chooses, as a means of creating receptivity in the audience ; for it is character which most commands attention. The things to which an audience is most attentive are things which are important in themselves or specially interesting to them or wonderful or pleasant to hear ; hence it is proper for the speaker to produce the impression that the subjects with which his speech is concerned are of this kind. If on the other hand he wishes that they should be inattentive, he should try to convey the impression that his subject is trifling, irrelevant to the audience or disagreeable. It must not however be forgotten that all such things are extraneous to the speech, being addressed to the audience because it is corrupt and ready to listen to what is foreign to the subject ; for if this is not the character of the audience, there is no need of an exordium, except for the mere purpose of stating the case summarily, that it may not be, as it were, a body without a head. For the art of exciting attention is one that belongs equally to all the parts of a speech, if it is needed, *and perhaps especially to the other parts;* for people are apt to become inattentive at any other part rather than at the beginning. It is absurd then to speak of the beginning as its proper place, when every one is listening most attentively. Hence, whenever there is occasion, it is proper to employ such phrases as "Pray give me your attention. It concerns you every whit as much as myself" or

> "A strange thing, such as never you have heard,
>   I'll tell you,"

or "a thing so marvellous." This is like Prodicus's rule, whenever his audience was drowsy, "of slipping in a taste of the Fifty Drachm speech [1]."

It is evident however that *such tricks as I have described* are addressed to the audience not *qua* audience, *i.e. not as impartial and unemotional hearers of the facts;* for it is the universal practice of orators to use their exordia as means of creating a prejudice *against their adversaries* or of removing apprehensions *entertained in regard to themselves. Let me instance the prologue beginning*

> [2] "My lord I will not say how hastily,"

or *the interruption of Thoas*

> [3] "Why all this preluding?"

---

[1] The Fifty Drachm speech, which was apparently so called as being purchasable at the price of 50 δραχμαί, must have been one of Prodicus's favourite and most effective speeches. Cp. Plato, *Cratylus* p. 384 B.

[2] Sophocles, *Antigone* 223.

[3] Euripides, *Iphig. in Taur.* 1162. The first passage is an instance of a speaker apologizing for his own apparent fault ; the second one of a speaker who is trying to throw suspicion or blame on somebody else.

Again, exordia are the devices of those whose case is
or is supposed by them to be a bad one, as it is better
for them to dwell upon anything than upon the case
itself. This is the reason why servants, who are accused of something wrong, never give a direct answer
to the questions but beat about the bush and make
long prefaces *before they come to the point.*

The means of conciliating goodwill and of ex-
pp. 114 sqq. citing the various other emotions have been already
described. But as there is an appropriateness in the
lines

> [1] "Oh! let me drift to the Phaeacian land
> Beloved and pitied,"

it follows that *love and pity* are the two objects at
which we ought to aim.

In the exordia of epideictic speeches the hearers
should be led to fancy themselves participators in the
eulogy, whether personally or in respect of their
families or pursuits or somehow or other ; for it is a
true [2]remark of Socrates in his funeral oration that
there is no difficulty in lauding the Athenians at
Athens, the difficulty is to laud them at Sparta.

The exordia of political oratory are taken from
the same sources as those of forensic oratory, but are
naturally very rare, as the subject is one which is
familiar to the audience, and there is no occasion for
an exordium, except—if at all—for the sake of recommending the speaker himself or meeting his adversaries, or if the estimate which the audience en-
tertains of the importance of the case is either greater

[1] *Odyssey*, vii. 327.
[2] Plato, *Menexenus*, p. 235 D.

or less than you think right. Hence the necessity of
either creating or removing prejudice and of either
exaggerating or depreciating the importance of a
subject. It is for this purpose that an exordium is
necessary, or for ornament, as without it a speech has
an extemporaneous air. The encomium pronounced
by Gorgias on the men of Elis is a case in point; he
uses no preliminary sparring or flourishing, but begins
abruptly *with the words* "Elis, blessed city."

As to [1]calumny *or prejudice and the means of*
combating it, there is one topic which consists in
using all the possible means of getting rid of un-
pleasant suspicion; for as it makes no difference
whether the suspicion has been expressed or not, the
rule is one of universal application. Another topic[2]
consists in meeting the points at issue either by
denying the fact alleged or by asserting that it is not
injurious or not injurious to the particular person
who complains of it or that its magnitude has been
exaggerated or that it is not criminal or that it is not
serious or not disgraceful or not of much importance.
For these are the points upon which the issue of a
case turns, as in the speech of Iphicrates in reply to
Nausicrates, when he admitted the action alleged
and its injuriousness but denied its criminality.
Another topic is, while one admits the criminality, to
allege some compensating circumstance, as that it was
injurious but at the same time honourable, or painful
but at the same time beneficial, and so on. Another

---

[1] The meaning of διαβολή hovers between "calumny" and
"prejudice" which is the natural result of calumnious malice.

[2] Reading τόπος with Spengel, and so *infra*.

is to plead that *the crime* was a mistake or a misfortune or that it was committed under compulsion, as when [1]Sophocles said that his trembling was not assumed, as his calumniator alleged, for the sake of presenting an appearance of old age, but arose from necessity, as it was no fault of his that he was eighty years old. Or again, to urge the motive of the act as a compensating circumstance, saying that it was not your intention to inflict an injury but something else, not what was calumniously alleged against you, and that the injury was only an accidental consequence. "I should deserve to be hated," *you may add*, "if I had had this intention in so acting." Another topic arises, if your calumniator has been involved *in a similar charge*, whether now or on some previous occasion and whether personally or in the persons of his relations or friends. Another, if others are involved in the calumny, who are admitted to be innocent; thus if *it is argued* that a [2]person is an adulterer because he is a dandy, *it may be replied that* then Mr So-and-So must be an adulterer. A third, if your accuser has ever alleged the same calumny against others or if somebody else has ever alleged it against yourself or if without a directly calumnious accusation others, who have been proved to be innocent, were ever exposed to the same suspicion as you are now. A fourth is the topic of recrimination, where you urge that it is monstrous

---

[1] If the Sophocles, of whom this story is told, was the poet, the "calumniator" can hardly have been his son Iophon, as it was Iophon's object to prove him to be in his dotage.

[2] Reading εἰ ὅτι καθάριος, μοιχός.

that a man's allegations should be trusted, when he is wholly untrustworthy himself. Another is the appeal to a previous decision, as in the reply of Euripides to Hygiaenon, who in the action for an exchange of properties accused him of impiety for the line he wrote in recommendation of perjury

[1] " The tongue hath sworn, the mind is still unsworn,"

when he replied that Hygiaenon had no right to transfer cases from the Dionysiac contests to the Courts of Law, as he had already given an account of his language there or was ready to give it, if Hygiaenon chose to accuse him. Another topic consists in inveighing against calumny, showing its enormity and how it raises points which are foreign to the issue and places no reliance on the strength of the case. A topic which belongs equally to the prosecutor and the defendant is the use of signs or *probabilities*, as when Odysseus in the *Teucer* of Sophocles argues that *Teucer is friendly to the enemy* because of his relationship to Priam, his mother Hesione having been Priam's sister, and Teucer answers that *this is impossible, because* his father Telamon was Priam's enemy and he did not betray the spies to Priam. There is another topic which a calumniator may use with advantage, viz. to eulogize some trifle at great length and then introduce some serious censure in a few words, or to begin by mentioning a number of good points and then to mention one point only which is censurable but that a point which has a

---

[1] *Hippolytus*, 612.

direct bearing on the case. It is topics like these which are the most artful and unfair, as people who use them try to convert what are *really* good points into means of injury by intermingling with them such as are bad. Lastly, there is another topic of which both the prosecutor and the defendant may avail themselves, viz. to utilize the various possible motives of the same action and, if your object is to excite prejudice, to depreciate an action by putting a bad construction upon it, and, if it is to remove it, *to extol the same action* by interpreting it in the most favourable sense, e.g. by urging that [1] Diomedes preferred Odysseus as his companion either on the one hand because he thought him the bravest of the Greeks or on the other because Odysseus was such a craven fellow as to be the one man of whose rivalry he was not afraid.

CHAP. XVI. So much then it may suffice to say in regard to calumny.

Narrative (1) in epideictic speeches, Narrative in epideictic speeches is not continuous but fragmentary. *Still it is an indispensable part of such speeches*, as the facts which form the subjects of an epideictic speech must be related. For in the composition of the speech there are two elements, one which is inartistic *or which does not admit of artistic treatment*, as the orator does not invent his own facts, the other artistic, i.e. the proof that the fact is true, if it is incredible, or that it is of a particular quality or magnitude or all three. Accordingly it sometimes happens that it is not proper to relate all the facts

[1] The reference is to the episode known as the Δολώνεια, *Iliad*, x. See especially vv. 242—247.

seriatim, as such a proof would be difficult to remember. Thus there are certain facts which tend to
prove that a person is brave, certain other facts which
prove that he is wise or just; *and these should not be
confused.* Also there is a greater simplicity in the
speech, if so divided, whereas in the other case it is
involved and deficient in smoothness. If the facts are
notorious, it is proper merely to recall them to the
memory of the audience. Hence in such cases
ordinary people do not need a narrative, e.g. if it is
your wish to eulogize Achilles; for everybody knows
his exploits, and you have only to comment upon
them. But if it is Critias *whom you wish to eulogize,
a narrative* is necessary, as his actions are not
generally known....¹The popular doctrine that the (2) in
narrative should be rapid is an absurd one. Surely forensic
the case is like that of the man kneading dough who speeches,
asked if he should knead it hard or soft and received
the answer "Why? is it impossible to knead it well?"
The narrative should not be prolix any more than the
exordium or the statement of proofs; for in them as
well as in the narrative it is not rapidity or conciseness which constitutes excellence but the due
observation of the mean i.e. the using just so many
words as will explain the facts of the case or will produce in the minds of the audience the impression
that they have occurred or have been injurious or
criminal or of such importance as you wish them to

¹ There is clearly a lacuna in the text before this sentence.
For not only is the remark about rapidity introduced abruptly;
but the sentences which follow are found to relate to forensic
oratory, which has not yet been mentioned in the chapter.

be considered; or an opposite impression, if you are taking the opposite side.

You may properly slip into your narrative anything that tends to show your own virtue, i.e. *such a remark as* "I was for ever admonishing him, urging the injustice of leaving his children in the lurch", or anything that tends to show the wickedness of your adversary, e.g. "But he said in reply that, wherever he himself was, he would find other children"—the answer of the revolted Egyptians according to [1]Herodotus *to the king who besought them to return*. You may slip in also anything that gratifies the jury.

On the side of the defence the narrative part of the speech may be briefer, as the issues raised are the contentions that *the circumstance which is alleged* has not occurred or is not injurious or not criminal or not so serious as has been supposed. Hence there is no need to waste time in proving facts already admitted, unless they bear upon the issue which has been raised, as e.g. when the fact is allowed but the criminality of it is denied. Again, it is proper to speak of events as already past, except when the actual representation of them excites either compassion or indignation. An example of this is the [2]story of Alcinous *in the Odyssey*; for it is told to

---

[1] Herodotus, ii. ch. 30.

[2] The four books, *Odyssey*, ix—xii, in which Odysseus recites to the Phaeacian king Alcinous the story of his wanderings, seem to have formed a single "rhapsody" under the title Ἀλκίνου ἀπόλογος. This long story is condensed into 60, or more exactly 55 lines, when Odysseus repeats it to Penelope as a mere narrative of past events (*ibid.* xxiii. 264—284, 310—343).

Penelope in only sixty lines. Other examples are
Phayllus's *summary of* the Epic Cycle and Euripides's
prologue in the *Œneus.*

But the narrative should be ethical; and in order
that it may be thus, we must know what it is that
imparts an ethical character. The first thing is the
indication of a moral purpose. It is upon the quality
of this purpose that the quality of the character imparted will depend, and the quality of the purpose
will be determined by its end. Hence there is no
moral character in mathematical treatises, as they
have no moral purpose; for they have no moral *or
practical* end in view. But the [1]Socratic dialogues
are ethical, as dealing with ethical subjects. There is
another source of ethical effect in such characteristic
marks as are the concomitants of particular characters;
e.g. "*So-and-so* kept walking as he talked", for this
is a sign of audacity and boorishness of character.
Another is to seem to speak not from policy, like the
speakers of the present day, but from the heart, as
e.g. "That was my wish; it was my purpose; true, I
gained nothing by it; but still it was best." Here
you have the difference between prudence and virtue,
prudence consisting in the pursuit of self-interest and
virtue in the pursuit of nobleness. If *a trait of
character* is incredible, then it is proper to add the
explanation of it, as in the example that Sophocles
supplies in his [2]*Antigone,* where she says that she
cared more for her brother than for husband or

---

[1] For the "Socratic dialogues" (Σωκρατικοὶ λόγοι, Socratici
Sermones) see Grote's *Plato* vol. III. pp. 469—473.

[2] The passage quoted is *Antigone* 911—2. It illustrates

children; "for husband and children, if they were
lost, might be replaced,

"But they being dead, my father and my mother,
I never could have brother born anew."

If you have no explanation to give, you must at any
rate say that "you know you will not induce anybody
to believe you, but it is your nature to be disinterested; for the world does not believe in any
motive of action except self-interest".

Again, topics may be derived from emotional signs
by describing the usual accompaniments and familiar
features of emotion and the special characteristics of
your opponent or yourself, as e.g. "He departed with
a scowl at me"[1] or "hissing and shaking his fists" as
Aeschines says of Cratylus; for there is a certain
persuasiveness in such language, because the facts
which are familiar to the audience are treated as
signs of facts with which they are not familiar. There
are a great number of such instances in Homer, e.g.

"[2] He spake, and in her hands she clasped her brow",

for people when beginning to weep are apt to clasp
their eyes.

Present yourself to the audience from the outset
in a certain moral light, that they may form a proper
view of yourself and of your adversary ; only do not
betray your design. That it is easy to do this is
evident in the case of messengers ; for without know-

Aristotle's rule, as the sentiment, which seems so strange, is
justified by the reasoning which follows.
    [1] Changing the full stop after ὑποβλέψας to a comma.
    [2] *Odyssey* xix. 361.

ing anything of the message we *often* conceive an idea of it *from the aspect of the messenger.*

The narrative should be distributed over the speech, and should sometimes not occur *in its natural place*, at the beginning.

It is in political oratory that there is least room for narration, as no one ever narrates what lies in the future. Narrative, if it occurs at all, must refer to the past, that with the facts of the past in their recollection the audience may be better fitted to deliberate on the future. Or it may be employed in disparagement or in eulogy, but in that case the speaker is not really discharging the function of a counsellor. ¹If there is anything incredible in the narrative, *it is proper* to promise that you will add an explanation of it immediately and to set it forth to the satisfaction of the audience, as the Jocasta of Carcinus in his *Œdipus* perpetually promises in answer to the man who is looking for her son, or as the Hæmon of Sophocles. *(3) in political speeches.*

The proofs should be demonstrative in their nature. But as there are four points on which the issue may possibly turn, the one to which the proof should be directed is the particular point at issue in the case. Thus if it is the question of fact which is at issue, it is the proof of this especially that should be urged in the trial ; but if it is the question of injury, then the proof of this, and *similarly* if it is *Chap. XVII. Proofs.*

¹ The sentence is hardly intelligible, as it stands, especially as the instances cited are unknown. But it must, I think, express some rule for recommending to the audience a statement which in itself is incredible or improbable.

a question of magnitude or of criminality, *the process of proof being essentially* the same as if the question at issue were one of the fact. But it must not be forgotten that the issue of fact is the only one in which one or other of the two parties must be a rogue ; for it is impossible here to plead ignorance, as it might be pleaded, if the question were the justice of the action. Accordingly it is in such cases, but in such only, that it is right to dwell upon *this particular topic.* In epideictic speeches it will be generally amplification that is used to prove the moral or utilitarian nature of the facts ; the facts themselves must be taken on trust, as it seldom happens that epideictic orators adduce proofs of them, *and only* when they are themselves incredible or [1]somebody else has got the credit of them. In political speeches it may be contended that the policy *of one's adversary* is impossible or that it is possible but unjust or inexpedient or that it will not have the important results which he anticipates. But at the same time the orator must be on the look out for any fallacy outside the actual issue, as such a fallacy *in the statement of extraneous matters* is taken for a proof of fallacy in the statement of the case itself.

Examples. Examples are especially appropriate to political, and enthymemes on the other hand to forensic oratory. For the former, being occupied with the future demands examples drawn from the history of the past ; the latter turns upon matters of fact, which admit to a larger extent of demonstrative and necessary con-

---

[1] Reading ἄλλος.

clusions, as there is a sort of necessity in the past, *i.e. the past is irrevocable.*

The enthymemes should not be stated in an un- Enthy-
broken series, but should be intermingled *with* memes.
various other topics; else one enthymeme destroys
the effect of another. For there is a limit of quantity
in such things, as Homer shows in the [1]*line*

> "Dear friend, thy words are many as a man
>   May speak, being prudent."

"*as many words," be it observed,* not "such words",
in reference not to their quality but to their quantity.

Nor is it proper to search for enthymemes on all subjects ; otherwise you will be acting like some professing philosophers, whose conclusions are more familiar and more credible than the premisses from which they deduce them. And further, avoid the use of an enthymeme in exciting emotion ; for the enthymeme will either expel the emotion, or, if not, will have been constructed in vain, as simultaneous motions are mutually exclusive, and the one obliterates or else enfeebles the other. Nor again should you resort to an enthymeme at a time when you are seeking to invest your speech with an ethical character ; for there is nothing of character or moral purpose in demonstrative argument.

Maxims on the other hand in virtue of their Maxims.
ethical character should be used both in narrative
and in proof. *The ethical force of a maxim is evident,
if you say e.g.,* "I have given it, and that though I

---

[1] *Odyssey* IV. 204. It is Menelaus who is addressing Pisi-
stratus the son of Nestor.

know it is folly to trust anybody". *If you wish however to work upon the emotions of your audience, you may put it thus* "And I do not regret it, although I have been injured; for if my enemy has the advantage in profit, it is I who have the advantage in justice."

Comparison of political and forensic Rhetoric.

Political oratory is more difficult than forensic, for the sufficient reason that it relates to the future, whereas forensic oratory relates to the past, which, as Epimenides the Cretan said, may be known even to diviners; for he himself was not in the habit of divining the future but only the obscurities of the past. (Besides this, the law itself forms a subject in forensic speeches; and when you have a starting-point, it is not difficult to find a proof.)[1] Nor does *political oratory* allow of many diversions such as attacks upon your opponent and apologies for yourself, or again of appeals to the emotions. There is less room for them in political than in any other kind of oratory, unless the orator departs from his proper subject. Accordingly the orator, when at a loss for something to say, should follow the example of the rhetoricians at Athens and of Isocrates who in a deliberative speech introduces an accusation, as e.g. of the [2]Lacedæmonians in his *Panegyric* and of

---

[1] This remark upon the law as a rhetorical subject is parenthetical.

[2] The Panegyrical speech of Isocrates is properly a λόγος συμβουλευτικός, its object being to unite the forces of Athens and Sparta against the Persians; but there are certain passages, §§ 140—147, which reflect in bitter terms upon the policy of Sparta.

¹Chares in his speech on the Alliance, *i.e. he should import alien subjects.*

In epideictic speeches it is proper to introduce eulogies by way of episodes, as is the practice of Isocrates, who is always bringing in somebody. It is this that Gorgias meant when he declared that he was never at a loss for something to say, for in speaking e.g. of Achilles, he eulogizes Peleus, then Æacus, then the God, *i.e. Zeus the father of Æacus,* and similarly valour, and so on. This is just what I have been describing. _{Epideictic Rhetoric.}

If you have proofs to adduce, your language should be both ethical and demonstrative, but if you have no enthymemes, it should be exclusively ethical; in fact to a person of good character it is more appropriate that his virtue should display itself *in his speech* than that his speech should be accurately reasoned.

Among enthymemes the refutative are more popular than the demonstrative, as a refutation brings out the syllogistic conclusion more clearly, the opposites being more easily recognizable by juxtaposition. _{Demonstrative and refutative enthymemes.}

The reply to an adversary is not a separate branch of the speech; it is rather a part of the proofs to refute his arguments either by objection or by counter-syllogism. In deliberative and in forensic speaking alike it is right, if you are the first speaker, to begin with a statement of your own proofs and _{Arrangement of a speech.}

---

¹ The συμμαχικὸς λόγος must be the speech known as *de Pace,* where an indirect attack is made upon Chares the Athenian general for his conduct in the Social War.

then to meet the arguments on the other side by *directly* refuting them and by pulling them to pieces in anticipation. But if the opposition is of a varied character, it is right *to deal* first *with* the opposing arguments, as Callistratus did in the Messenian Assembly, when he first disposed of the arguments which would be urged by his adversaries and then made his own statement of the case. If you speak last, you should begin with the answer to your adversary's arguments, by refutation and counter-syllogism, especially if they have been well received. For as the mind does not give a favourable reception to a person against whom it has conceived a prejudice, so neither does it receive a speech favourably, if the speech on the other side is considered to have been successful. You have to make room then in the minds of the audience for the speech you are about to deliver, and the way to do this is to dispose of your adversary's speech. Accordingly you must first contend against all or the most important or the most popular or the most easily refuted of his arguments and then proceed to establish the credi-bility of your own case. *This is what Euripides has done in the [1] lines*

> "First will I prove the goddesses' ally,
> Methinks not Hera;"

here he begins by touching on the weakest argument. So much then for the consideration of proofs. As to character, since there are some things which, if

Ethical effect.

---

[1] The lines quoted are 969 and 971 of the *Troades*, from the beginning of Hecuba's reply to a long preceding speech of Helen.

you say them of yourself, are either invidious or tedious or highly disputable and which, if you say them of others, imply either calumny or coarseness, it is as well to put them into the mouth of a third person, as in the example of Isocrates in his ¹*Philip* and in his ²Speech on the Exchange of Properties and as in the lampoons of Archilochus, who represents the ⁸father as using the line about his daughter,

"Nought is improbable, nought can never be"

or Charon the carpenter uttering the line beginning

"Not mine the wealth of Gyges."

Similarly ⁴Sophocles makes Hæmon plead with his father for Antigone in language quoted from the lips of others.

Again, you should occasionally change the form of your enthymemes and express them as maxims. Thus *the maxim* "Sensible men should patch up their quarrels in the hour of prosperity, as they will then be likely to get the best terms" may be expressed enthymematically in the form "If it is right to patch up one's quarrels, when it is possible to get most beneficial and advantageous terms, you should do so in the hour of prosperity."

Enthymemes and maxims.

¹ Probably Spengel is right in thinking that the passage referred to is §§ 4—7.
² §§ 149 sqq.
³ Archilochus, it is meant, in attacking the lady who had rejected him put his lampoon into the mouth of her own father. Similarly in inveighing against the vanity of riches he ascribes his own sentiments to the contented carpenter, Charon.
⁴ *Antigone* 688—700.

CHAP.
XVIII.
Interroga-
tion.

We come now to the interrogation *of one's adversary.* It is a device which may be most opportunely used, when your adversary has already said the opposite, and when therefore an absurdity results from a single additional question. Thus Pericles interrogated *the soothsayer* Lampon as to the sacrificial ritual of the [1]Saving Goddess and, when he answered that it could not be told to one who had not been initiated, inquired if it was known to Lampon himself; Lampon said "Yes," and then he rejoined, "How can it be, when you have not been initiated?" *It may be used* secondly, when there are two points of which one is self-evident and the other will clearly be admitted as soon as the question is put. For in such a case, when you have obtained one of your premisses in reply to your question, you should not proceed to put what is self-evident in the form of a question but should state the conclusion *immediately.* Thus [2]Socrates, when accused by Meletus of denying the existence of gods asked if there was anything which he (Socrates) called divine; when Meletus admitted this, he inquired if divine things were not either children of the gods or something divine, and on his answering "Yes" said, "Is there anyone then who believes in the existence of children of the gods

[1] Tho saving goddess is Demeter; cp. Aristophanes, *Ranae* 378.

[2] The passage of Plato *Apology*, p. 27 does not exactly correspond with the text. Apparently the point is that, instead of obtaining a minor premiss by putting a second question, the speaker should abruptly present the conclusion itself in the form of a question.

but denies the existence of the gods themselves?"
Thirdly, interrogation may be used, when it is your
intention to display your adversary in a self-contra-
diction or a paradox. Or fourthly, when it is impossible for him to meet the question without giving
a sophistical answer ; for if he replies that a thing
"is so and yet is not so," or "is partly so and partly
not," or "so in one sense but not in another," the
audience shows its perplexity by loud disapprobation.
These are the only conditions in which interrogation
should be attempted ; for if your adversary interposes
an objection, you are thought to have been defeated,
as it is impossible to put a series of questions owing
to the *intellectual* weakness of the audience. Hence
your enthymemes should be condensed as far as possible.

In replying to questions, if they are of an am- Reply.
biguous kind, you should proceed by *distinction or
definition*, and should not express yourself too concisely. Where on the other hand the questions are
such as seem to land you in a contradiction, you
should give your explanation at the outset of your
answer before your adversary puts his next question
or draws his conclusion ; for it is not hard to see
what is the point of his argument. But a reference
to the [1] *Topics* will explain this as well as the means
of refutation.

In drawing a conclusion, if your adversary puts
the conclusion in the form of a question, you should
state *at once* the explanation *of your conduct*. For

---

[1] Τοπικά, Bk. VIII.

instance, ¹Sophocles being asked by Pisander if he
had agreed with the other members of the Council
in recommending the appointment of the Four Hundred said, "Yes." "Why? did not you think it
wrong?" was the reply. "Yes," he said. "So you
committed this wrong action." "Yes," he rejoined,
"for it was the best thing possible." Similarly the
Lacedæmonian, being called to account for his ad-
ministration of the ephoral office, in answer to the
question whether he thought that the other ephors
had deserved to be executed, said "Yes." "Well,
did not you act in concert with them?" was the
reply, and he assented. "Well then, do not you
equally deserve to be executed?" "No," he said,
"for they acted so for a bribe, and I on the contrary from conviction." It is a mistake then to put
a further question after the conclusion, or to express
the conclusion itself in the form of a question, unless
the truth is superabundantly clear.

We come now to the subject of jokes. As it
appears that they have a certain value in controversy
and Gorgias laid it down rightly enough as a sound
maxim to confound the seriousness of one's adversary
by jocularity and his jocularity by seriousness, the
various kinds of jokes have been stated in the
²treatise on *Poetry*. Some of these are suited to
gentlemen, but not all. You must be careful then to

---

¹ Not the poet, but the politician who was one of the πρόβου-
λοι appointed at Athens after the Sicilian disaster in 413 B.C.
(See Thucydides VIII. ch. 1). It was by them that the oligarchy
of the Four Hundred was set up.

² Cp. *Rhet.* i. ch. 11. *ad fin.* and the note there given.

make use of none but such as are appropriate to your character. Irony, it may be observed, is more gentlemanly than buffoonery, as the former is used simply for its own sake and the latter for some ulterior object.

There are four elements *or objects* of the peroration, viz. to inspire the audience with a favourable opinion of yourself and an unfavourable one of your adversary, to amplify or depreciate the subject, to excite the emotions of the audience and to recall the facts to their memory. For it is the natural order first to prove the truth of your own case and the falsity of your adversary's and, when this is done, to introduce the eulogy or censure and to elaborate *these topics*. In all this you should aim at one of two objects, viz. to prove either your own virtue or the wickedness of your adversary either absolutely or in relation to the audience. The topics which you may properly employ in representing yourself as virtuous or your adversary as vicious have been already enumerated. The next step in the natural order is to amplify or depreciate what has been already proved *by yourself or your adversary;* for facts must be admitted, if one is to discuss the question of degree, just as the growth of a body implies that it already exists. The topics of amplification and depreciation have been exhibited in an earlier part of this treatise. When this has been done and the quality and magnitude of the facts are clearly seen, the next thing is to work upon the emotions of the audience, such as compassion, indignation, anger, hatred, envy, jealousy and contentiousness. The topics suited to this purpose have also

CHAP.
XIX.
Peroration.

pp. 60 sqq.

pp. 46 sqq.
63 sqq.

pp. 115 sqq.

been described. There remains then the recapitulation of the statements already made in the speech.
And here it is appropriate to do what has been sometimes urged, wrongly enough, as proper to be done in
the exordia i.e. to repeat your points several times
for the sake of intelligibility. In the exordium you
should simply state the subject, so as to elucidate the
matter at issue, but in the peroration you should
summarily mention the steps by which your case has
been proved. And in so doing the first thing is *to
show* that you have performed all that you promised;
hence you must state the points you have made and
your reason for making them. One species of recapitulation consists in a comparison of one's own
case with one's adversary's. We may either put side
by side all that he said and that you said on the same
subject e.g. "My opponent said this, and I that, on the
subject, and this was my reason"; or you may
proceed indirectly. Or again you may use irony, e.g.
"My opponent said that, and I this. I wonder what
he would have done, if he had proved this instead of
that." Or interrogation e.g. "What have I failed to
prove?" or "What has my adversary proved?" You
may proceed thus or by comparison or in the natural
order, as was said, stating your own points and then,
if you like, your adversary's points separately.

An asyndeton forms an appropriate conclusion, to
make it a true peroration and not an oration, e.g. "I
have spoken, you have heard me; the case is in your
hands, pronounce your judgment".

INDEX.

CAMBRIDGE: PRINTED BY C. J. CLAY, M.A. AND SONS, AT THE UNIVERSITY PRESS.

CLASSICAL PUBLICATIONS.

Æschylus.—SEPTEM CONTRA THEBAS. Edited, with Introduction and Notes, by A. W. VERRALL, M.A., Fellow of Trinity College, Cambridge. 8vo. [*In the Press.*

Aristotle.—THE POLITICS. Edited, after SUSEMIHL, by R. D. HICKS, M.A., Fellow of Trinity College, Cambridge. 8vo. [*In the press.*

THE POLITICS. Translated by Rev. J. E. C. WELLDON, M.A., Fellow of King's College, Cambridge, and Head Master of Harrow School. Crown 8vo. 10s. 6d.

AN INTRODUCTION TO ARISTOTLE'S RHETORIC. With Analysis, Notes, and Appendices. By E. M. COPE, M.A., late Fellow and Tutor of Trinity College, Cambridge. 8vo. 14s.

Attic Orators.—FROM ANTIPHON TO ISAEOS. By R. C. JEBB, M.A., LL.D., Professor of Greek in the University of Glasgow. 2 vols. 8vo. 25s.

SELECTIONS FROM ANTIPHON, ANDOKIDES, LYSIAS, ISOKRATES, AND ISAEOS. Edited, with Notes, by Professor JEBB. Being a companion volume to the preceding work. 8vo. 12s. 6d.

Babrius.—Edited, with Introductory Dissertations, Critical Notes, Commentary and Lexicon. By Rev. W. GUNION RUTH-ERFORD, M.A., LL.D., Head Master of Westminster School. 8vo. 12s. 6d.

Cicero.—THE ACADEMICA. The Text revised and explained by J. S. REID, M.L., Litt.D., Fellow and Tutor of Caius College, Cambridge. 8vo. 15s.

THE ACADEMICS. Translated by J. S. REID, Litt.D. 8vo. 5s. 6d.

Euripides.—MEDEA. Edited, with Introduction and Notes, by A. W. VERRALL, M.A., Fellow and Lecturer of Trinity College, Cambridge. 8vo. 7s. 6d.

Herodotus.—BOOKS I.—III. THE ANCIENT EMPIRES OF THE EAST. Edited, with Notes, Introductions, and Appendices, by A. H. SAYCE, Deputy Professor of Comparative Philology, Oxford; Honorary LL.D., Dublin. Demy 8vo. 16s.

Homer.—THE ILIAD. Edited, with Introduction and Notes, by WALTER LEAF, M.A., late Fellow of Trinity College, Cambridge. 8vo. Vol. I. Books I.—XII. 14s.

THE ILIAD. Translated into English Prose. By ANDREW LANG, M.A., WALTER LEAF, M.A., and ERNEST MYERS, M.A. Crown 8vo. 12s. 6d.

Homer.—THE ODYSSEY. Done into English by S. H. BUTCHER, M.A., Professor of Greek in the University of Edinburgh, and ANDREW LANG, M.A., late Fellow of Merton College, Oxford. Fifth Edition, revised and corrected. Crown 8vo. 10*s.* 6*d.*

Horace.—STUDIES, LITERARY AND HISTORICAL, IN THE ODES OF HORACE. By A. W. VERRALL, M.A., Fellow of Trinity College, Cambridge. Demy 8vo. 8*s.* 6*d.*

Juvenal.—THIRTEEN SATIRES OF JUVENAL. With a Commentary. By JOHN E. B. MAYOR, M.A., Professor of Latin in the University of Cambridge. Crown 8vo. Vol. I. New Edition, 10*s.* 6*d.* Vol. II. 10*s.* 6*d.*

Livy.—BOOKS XXI.—XXV. Translated by ALFRED JOHN CHURCH, M.A., of Lincoln College, Oxford, Professor of Latin, University College, London, and WILLIAM JACKSON BRODRIBB, M.A., late Fellow of St John's College, Cambridge. Cr. 8vo. 7*s.* 6*d.*

Phrynichus.—THE NEW PHRYNICHUS; being a Revised Text of the Ecloga of the Grammarian Phrynichus. With Introduction and Commentary by Rev. W. GUNION RUTHERFORD, M.A., LL.D., Head Master of Westminster School. 8vo. 18*s.*

Pindar.—THE EXTANT ODES OF PINDAR. Translated into English with an Introduction and short Notes, by ERNEST MYERS, M.A., late Fellow of Wadham College, Oxford. Second Edition. Crown 8vo. 5*s.*

THE OLYMPIAN AND PYTHIAN ODES. Edited, with an Introductory Essay, Notes, and Indexes, by BASIL GILDERSLEEVE, Professor of Greek in the Johns Hopkins University, Baltimore. Crown 8vo. 7*s.* 6*d.*

Plato.—PHÆDO. Edited, with Introduction, Notes, and Appendices, by R. D. ARCHER-HIND, M.A., Fellow of Trinity College, Cambridge. 8vo. 8*s.* 6*d.*

TIMÆUS. Edited, with Introduction and Notes, by the same Editor. 8vo. [*In the Press.*

THE REPUBLIC OF PLATO. Translated into English, with an Analysis and Notes, by J. LL. DAVIES, M.A., and D. J. VAUGHAN, M.A. 18mo. 4*s.* 6*d.*

EUTHYPHRO, APOLOGY, CRITO, AND PHÆDO. Translated by F. J. CHURCH, M.A. 18mo. 4*s.* 6*d.*

Theocritus, Bion, and Moschus.—Rendered into English Prose with Introductory Essay by A. LANG, M.A. Crown 8vo. 6*s.*

Virgil.—THE ÆNEID. Translated by J. W. MACKAIL, M.A., Fellow of Balliol College, Oxford. Crown 8vo. 7*s.* 6*d.*

MACMILLAN AND CO., LONDON.